Oregon's Seacoast Lighthouses

Frontispiece: Piercing beam from Yaquina Head Lighthouse on a foggy night.

Coquille River Lighthouse

Exciting Books

→Availability and prices subject to change. This is a _partial_ list←

Panic! At Fort Stevens Japanese Shell Ft. Stevens, Ore. in World War-II. - _Documentary._ Bert Webber. Only 6 months after Pearl Harbor, Japanese Navy shells Fort Stevens, Oregon at mouth of Columbia River. Here's facts of this attack and U. S. failure to shoot back. 146 pictures/maps. $ 9.95

*_Silent Siege-III: Japanese Attacks on North America in World War II; Ships Sunk, Air Raids, Bombs Dropped, Civilians Killed._ Documentary Bert Webber. Hundreds of Japanese attacks on 28 U.S. states – kids killed – and Canada never reported in papers by agreement between gov't and press not to cause public panic. 304 pg, 462 photos, maps. BIG BOOK ! 8½x11 $28.95

Shipwrecks and Rescues on the Northwest Coast. Bert and Margie Webber. Amazing true episodes of disasters includes separate chapter on every ship attacked or sunk by Japanese in WW-II along the U. S. west coast. 262 pages, 155 photos, maps $14.95

Top Secret: Details of the Planned WW-II Invasion of Japan and How the Japanese Would Have Met It. (_The Japanese Atomic Bomb_) _Documentary._ James M. Davis and Bert Webber. Japan tested its A-bomb day after Nagasaki, planned its use during November invasion of Japan. Invasion beaches, American troop units identified. Japanese A-bomb defense strategy. 88 pages, 84 rare photos. Invasion maps. Index. $ 9.95

Aleutian Headache, Deadly World War-II Battles on American Soil – _Documentary._ Bert Webber. Japanese seize islands. Battle of Attu; Japanese secretly abandon Kiska, the U.S. didn't know it – mounted major offensive against empty island! Tells exactly how the Japanese did it. Book loaded with rare stuff not found elsewhere. 225 pages, 228 photos, 11 maps. Index. $14.95

Battleship Oregon: Bulldog of the Navy. Documentary. Bert Webber. Most amazing battleship ever, won the navy side of the Spanish-American war for the U.S.A. while other U.S. ships still trying to get up steam. Only U.S. battleship to be in Spanish-American, First World War, WW-II. $12.95

Camp White Oregon 91st (Fir Tree) Infantry Division. Documentary. Chris Hald w/Bert Webber. Action-packed narrative. Rigors of training, faux-pas, of Camp White, preparing for deadly battles in Italy. 128 pages, 90 rare and contemporary photos. Surprise on every page! Maps. Index. $ 9.95

MUSTANG: Fury Over Europe. 8th Air Force Fighter Command, WW-II. F. Franklin Craig. Story of teen-age boy suddenly thrust into the stress of a fighting man's world who became Ace P-51 fighter pilot in the skies of Europe. Engrossing adventures and bloody mis-adventures. 104 pages. Photos. Aircraft silhouettes / maps. Index. $9.95

We offer many books other than military. See our full display on the Internet or send stamped, self-addressed envelope to speed copy of latest catalog to you. See full color catalog on the Internet www.pnorthwestbooks.com

---

WEBB RESEARCH GROUP, PUBLISHERS

P. O. Box 314 Medford, OR 97501 USA

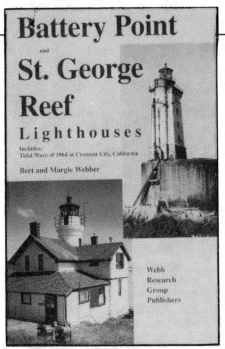

Battery Point
and
St. George Reef
Lighthouses

L i g h t h o u s e s

Includes:
Tidal Wave of 1964 at Crescent City, California

Bert and Margie Webber

Webb
Research
Group
Publishers

THE TWO MOST NORTHERN California lighthouses, Battery Point lighthouse, at the Crescent City Harbor entrance (41° 45' N), and St. George Reef lighthouse (41° 50' N.), perched on a rocky reef about six miles at sea nearly on the Oregon-California line (42° N. Lat.), were the line extended into the ocean, are so close to Oregon and isolated from the rest of California lighthouses they are often considered part of the Northwest lighthouse scene.

AT CRESCENT CITY, one can walk across the bottom of the ocean at low tide and visit inside Battery Point lighthouse. This is one of the few 19th century lighthouses still operating with a resident keeper-of-the-light. The present visitor schedule is from April through September. Of note in the book is Chapter 5 "Lighthouse Ghost Stories – Things That Go BUMP in the Night."

ST. GEORGE REEF LIGHTHOUSE is inaccessible but those with a suitable boat can cruise to and around it. Some charter boats journey to the lighthouse from the port of Brooking-Harbor, Oregon. The giant granite lighthouse shaft is impressive with its lantern room 146 feet above high water. Men used to live in the lighthouse for months at a time!

ALSO A PART OF THIS BOOK is the story, with pictures, of the giant tsunami that swept away much of the downtown portion of Crescent City in 1964 leaving death and destruction. Here is an eye-witness account of the tidal waves – 5 of them one after the other as they pounded the city– as viewed by the keeper from Battery Point lighthouse.

88 Photographs Map Bibliography Appendix Index

ISBN 0-963738-92-8 (Year 2000 edition) $12.95 + $2.50 mailing in USA. Cover pictures by Bert Webber
As with all of our books, prices and availability may change

Oregon's Seacoast Lighthouses

An Oregon Documentary by
James A. Gibbs
(With Bert Webber)

Includes
Nearby
Shipwrecks

→Expanded Edition←

WEBB RESEARCH GROUP

Printed in Oregon, USA

Published by:
WEBB RESEARCH GROUP PUBLISHERS
P. O. Box 314
Medford, OR 97501

Library of Congress Cataloging in Publication Data

Gibbs, Jim, 1922-
    Oregon's seacoast lighthouses : an Oregon Documentary / James A.
Gibbs ; Bert Webber, editor
        p.   cm.
    Includes bibliographical references and index
    ISBN 0-936738-57-X
    1. Lighthouses—Oregon—History. 2. Oregon—History, Local.
    I. Webber, Bert. II. Title
VK1024.07G53 1992   92-3682
387.1'55—dc20   CIP
_____Published in 2000_____

Contents

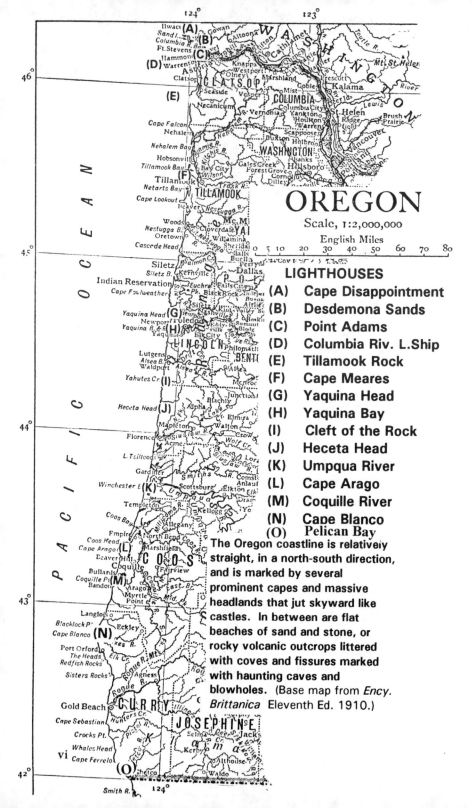

OREGON

Scale, 1:2,000,000

English Miles
0 5 10   20   30   40   50   60   70   80

LIGHTHOUSES

(A) Cape Disappointment
(B) Desdemona Sands
(C) Point Adams
(D) Columbia Riv. L.Ship
(E) Tillamook Rock
(F) Cape Meares
(G) Yaquina Head
(H) Yaquina Bay
(I) Cleft of the Rock
(J) Heceta Head
(K) Umpqua River
(L) Cape Arago
(M) Coquille River
(N) Cape Blanco
(O) Pelican Bay

The Oregon coastline is relatively straight, in a north-south direction, and is marked by several prominent capes and massive headlands that jut skyward like castles. In between are flat beaches of sand and stone, or rocky volcanic outcrops littered with coves and fissures marked with haunting caves and blowholes. (Base map from *Ency. Brittanica* Eleventh Ed. 1910.)

vi

Introduction

When one stands on the shore at a maritime crossroads and hears the dissonant clang of a bell buoy, it almost seems that the clanging bell is relating the dramatic story of aids to navigation as the story has unfolded down through the decades. From the tethered buoy to the lonely lighthouse there is a history unlike any other. Such outer guardians of our shores and waterways have been a part of Americana from its inception. Their importance has never been fully understood by the general public, but to the mariner these aids have often spelled the difference between safe haven or tragedy—a ship reaching its destination safely or gutting itself on hidden rocks and vomiting its cargo into the sea.

It would be hard to estimate the vast number of vessels saved by a skipper's sighting of a powerful marine beacon, or the guttural moaning of a foghorn. Such aids were indispensable before the advent of high-tech electronic navigational apparatus capable of seeing through the thickest weather. Many of the traditional lighthouses have been eliminated and others reduced to a secondary role. But those that have weathered the test of time, in our changing world, are finally being appreciated by all who pass by. Lighthouses have gained respect similar to a celebrated statesman who may also have become gray with years of service but still function.

What does the reader think of when the word "lighthouse" is mentioned? Sentinels of solitude are endowed with multiple personalities and have different meanings to different people. The navigator looks upon them as the protector of the sealanes; the photographer and artist as a premier subject for a camera or canvas; the clergy likens them to a spiritual monument; travelers see them as a roadside attraction. Writers and poets view lighthouses as subjects to appear in print. Nothing is quite so thought-provoking as the sight of a tapering lighthouse tower reaching skyward with a shining jewel in its crown.

Oregon's scenic ocean coastline, with its many attractions, does not have as many lighthouses as some other states with long ocean frontage. But the ones it has are unique, each vastly different from the other. An even dozen lighthouses and one lightship have graced the Oregon seacoast at one time or another since it became a state. Some are currently active. Others are now only historic attractions.

Some are gone. Whether active or inactive, all have won their way into the hearts of Oregonians, for each has become a vital part of the maritime history of the state. Their importance reached an apex during the decades of intense coastwise and inter-coastal commercial shipping when ocean-going ships hugged the coast, depending heavily on the lights and fog signals. In early times, sailing vessels and steamers provided cargo for all the bar ports along the Pacific Northwestern coast. And nearly all carried lumber on return trips to San Francisco and as far south as San Diego. Southbound manifests showed items such as dimension lumber, shingles, railroad ties and tan bark. Northbound cargo included everything from foodstuffs to pianos and from mill supplies to farm machinery. Hundreds of sailing vessels were engaged, manned by salty characters and know-ledgeable skippers who had no fear of the terrors that haunted every "doghole" where they dared to go. Once steam power was added to the sailing schooner, a fleet of well over 200 vessels arrived on the scene carrying lumber products from Puget Sound, the coastal ports of Washington and Oregon, and redwood from northern California. Even with lighthouses and buoy systems, shipwreck was unfortunately common and the loss in property and lives was legion.

During the years of the tall square-rigger, thousands of tons of golden grain from eastern Oregon and Washington were shipped from northwest ports on the long haul around Cape Horn to the United Kingdom and Europe. Several of the graceful carriers were victims of disaster along Oregon's shores. These founderings were often due to storm, fog, and faltering winds. The evolution of ships into larger steam freighters and specialized carriers paralleled the evolution of modern aids to navigation. Radio beacons allowed shipping to remain well offshore until nearing the port of entry. So revolutionary are the latest innovations in navigational aids, that shipwrecks have become almost incidental. The only exception appears to be the commercial fishing fleet which often must work in waters near shore where greater dangers exist. Despite their radar and sonar gear, those who man the fishboats still appreciate the friendly glow of the lighthouse or the sound of a fog signal.

For more than two centuries, hardy men and a few women were keepers of the lights. With the evolution in electronics came the age of automation, thus the need for people as lighthouse keepers was all but eliminated. That special breed of folks have become a part of our history yet they should never be forgotten. Seldom were they highly educated, few having gone beyond the common schools. Records

Yaquina Bay Lighthouse, abandoned for over a Century, now restored, is feature of a state park in city of Newport. Modern Coast Guard observation tower is in its back yard in this 1991 view.

reveal that their spelling was often faulty and their grammar incorrect. They were, however, faithful and noble in their task yet certainly not without occasional outbreaks of misbehavior which sometimes demanded transfer or even dismissal from the Lighthouse Service. Most were versatile and ingenious as they were often times isolated, no help available, therefore having to make the best of unfortunate situations depending on nothing but their own resourcefulness. Whatever they may have lacked in education, most were fully aware of their responsibility for keeping their lights glowing.

One could usually find a modicum of pride and gallantry among the light keepers. They were aware that despite their isolation and separation from the world at large, their role contributed to the welfare of those who sailed the sea.

In several lighthouses, the keepers were allowed to have their families live on the premises, and in most cases the offspring enjoyed their surroundings and became well-rounded in personality and ability to cope with the outside world. Lighthouse wives were frequently as faithful to their husbands as their husbands were to the lighthouses they manned.

Where once Oregon lighthouse reservations encompassed large

9

pieces of acreage, the Coast Guard today is only concerned with the navigational aid and the immediate surroundings. Most of the large properties have been turned over to state and federal agencies for use as public parks and recreational areas. Abandoned lighthouses are often operated by preservation groups and may be open at prescribed times.

Active lighthouses, for the main part, are closed to the public except on special occasions, but all are visible and most have easy access to interested parties with but few exceptions.

For several years following the advent of automation, slowly, almost imperceptibly, scores of lighthouses on America's seacoasts began to suffer. Some were abandoned, burned, demolished, vandalized, disfigured and neglected. Now the process has been reversed and every standing sentinel, especially in Oregon, has become a treasure. Federal and private funds are keeping them alive and kicking, whether active or inactive.

> Far in the bosom of the deep
> O'er these wild shelves my watch I keep
> A ruddy gem of changeful light,
> Bound on the dusky brow of night.
>
> —Sir Walter Scott

Long renowned for its rugged beauty, the Oregon Coast draws an estimated 29 million visitors annually for pastimes ranging from sightseeing and beachcombing to ocean fishing. It is a certainty that many of those visitors gaze on Oregon's lighthouses with great fascination. The State of Oregon maintains more than 50 parks on the coast for both day use and overnight camping. Some of the parks are maintained adjacent to Oregon lighthouses, near bar entrances and/or at locations where the government has erected jetties at river entrances.

The coastal areas of Oregon embrace two distinct marine environments. These include the vast offshore waters of the Pacific Ocean, and the estuaries of the coastal rivers.

The coast rivers of Oregon include 217 square miles of estuaries that provide a priceless ecological asset. Much of the same arena contains important commercial harbors and recreational areas. Though Oregon's lighthouses aren't as essential to navigation as they once were, they are of even greater importance to passersby, many of whom pay tribute to the historic old sentinels that add so much charm to the Oregon ocean seascape.

In the early 1800's navigation from the ocean into the coastal rivers was extremely dangerous and often impossible. The very nature of rivers includes the continual accumulation of large quantities of sand and sediment at their mouths, building up shallow areas referred to as bars. Main river channels constantly shift, making it both hazardous and difficult to find deep enough water under the ship when negotiating the entrance. Every major river entrance on the Oregon coast that catered to commercial shipping claimed a host of unfortunate vessels that found the entrance to Davy Jones' Locker while seeking out the main channel. Such occurrences were an impediment to the growth of waterborne commerce along the Northwest coast. The effort to eliminate shipwrecks was the principal reason for lighthouses, buoy systems, jetties and dredging, especially before the advent of the electronic revolution in navigational aids.

Why are lighthouses and ghosts so closely linked?

This universal question has been pondered in the maritime world for centuries. Perhaps it is because the masonry walls are slapped by salt spray and the whining storm winds create weird noises. Then again maybe it's the iron grates of the spiral staircases which echo eerily with each step. Still, maybe it is the haunting tales of nearby shipwrecks and sailors that went down with their ships. Or perhaps it was a keeper who died while on duty—or a wife, or child of an attendant claimed by a disease or a regrettable accident whose wraiths come back to haunt their former abode. Whatever the reason, every lighthouse has traditionally had it's ghost in one spectral form or another.

Severe isolation in some cases has caused lighthouse keepers to become mentally unbalanced and be driven to do things that no normal person would do.

Shafts of light from revolving lenses not only confuse birds in flight but have also been known to form the appearance of strange apparitions. Foghorns with their dismal drones cannot only jangle the nerves when operated for long periods, but their very cadence is a reminder of abnormal, out-of-this-world thoughts.

Yes, it is all this, and perhaps other events that lead to the intelligence regarding the affinity between lighthouses and the world of spectral beings.

As a former lighthouse attendant, the author must confess that he has been asked more about ghosts than any other facet of pharology when questioned by an interested party. Indeed, each of Oregon's lighthouses had it's own peculiar ghost, some of which will be mentioned in this writing.

As this book went to press, a move was being implemented whereby five of Oregon's major working government lighthouses would be turned over to the Bureau of Land Management to designate to one of its branches for upkeep and maintenance. The classic Fresnel optics would no longer be the aids to navigation but would remain in place as historic attractions. Rangers, or hosts, would be in place to conduct tours of the historic towers for the public. Regrettably the Coast Guard has been unable to provide this service for many years. In turn, auxiliary lights, mostly of the 250mm variety, would provide the navigational aid, either from the lighthouse gallery (balcony) or from utilitarian standards on the grounds.

In one way, it's unfortunate that great French and British manufactured lenses, long the jewel in the crown of these great lighthouses, must be forever eclipsed. But we live in a fast-changing world where the steamer lanes are for the most part beyond the reach of the old Fresnels which no longer have the importance for navigation they once did. Coastal craft, and the larger ships entering coast ports, note the lights, but every vessel of any size is equipped with a great variety of gadgets with electronic eyes that can penetrate any kind of adverse weather.

Consider the fact that lighthouses have been in existence for nearly 2,500 years. The first marked the ancient Mediterranean portals, while the first in the United States was in 1716. They have come through the centuries with a variety of lighting technologies. It is unfortunate that in the present age that our sentinels have lost their importance, but mere light and sound never could penetrate very far through fog. The grand old keepers of the lights of the past have mostly been laid to rest but the aging lighthouses remain. Automation brought on by the revolution in electronics sounded the death knell, and a colorful part of Americana—the keeping of old oil lamps trimmed and lit, and maintaining steam powered fog signals—is gone.

*   *   *

A writer meets and converses with many wonderful people while working on a manuscript. Some encounters are quite casual while others are more detailed and friendships develop. In the present work I have made a number of friends who substantially helped with this project. I wish to thank them here.

Jerry Hebert, a Coast Guard electrician, spent several months servicing lighthouses along the Oregon Coast and more recently he and his wife center at the Mukilteo Lighthouse on Puget Sound. Jerry, who loves lighthouses, has shared his experiences with me and provided valuable data.

A special thankyou to Bob Schwemmer who is with Warner Brothers Studio in Hollywood, for his willingness to assist me.

Thanks also to others including Dorothy Wall and her husband Les; George Moorhead and the entire volunteer team of hosts who perform as the Friends of the Yaquina Bay Lighthouse.

I am pleased to have the long-time acquaintance of Bob DeRoy, Vallejo, California, who grew up at Heceta Head and Warrior Rock Lighthouses where his father was one of the last of the breed of lighthouse keepers who served under the old U. S. Lighthouse Service; Ken Black. curator, Shore Village Museum, Rockland, Maine who has knowledge of many lighthouses and publications about them; Larry Barber, writer and former marine editor, Portland, Oregon; Sam Foster, Seaside and Portland, historian and retired press photographer and TVNEWS cameraman; Mimi Morissette, CCMI, Portland and Los Angeles, principal in the Eternity at Sea Columbarium, present owners of Tillamook Rock.

There is also Vic West, author-historian, North Bend, Oregon; Nadine and Jerry Tugal, once curators of the lighthouse museum and keepers-of-the-light at Battery Point Lighthouse at Crescent City, California; Pam Brown, Victoria, B.C., long associated in aids to navigation with the Canadian Coast Guard.

Many of the personnel associated with the 13th Coast Guard District in Seattle, and personnel of the various stations along the Oregon coast and at Yaquina Bay, Florence, North Bend, Charleston and Winchester Bay units were very helpful. Also a thank you to the custodians of the Heceta Head House.

M. Wayne Jensen, Jr., Director of Tillamook Pioneer Museum, was of assistance, for which I thank him, with unique historical data and photographs of the Cape Meares Lighthouse.

I am thankful to Bert Webber, Editor and Publisher, for his interest in my manuscript and for his efforts in bringing forth a book from it.

And to my late wife Cherie who is in my dreams and was always my favorite "light housekeeper."

Should readers have additional information that seems pertinent, or constructive criticism, I can be reached through my publisher.

James A. "Jim" Gibbs
Cleft of the Rock Lighthouse
Cape Perpetua

Cape Blanco Lighthouse

Chapter 1
Let The Lights Shine

Salt sprays deluge it, wild waves buffet it,
        hurricanes rave;
Summer and winter the depths of the ocean girdle it
        round;
In leaden dawns, in golden noontide, in silvery
        moonlights
Never it ceases to hear the old seas' mystical sound.
        Surges vex it evermore, by grey cave and
Sounding shore.

                                        -Lewis Morris

When one considers the prodigious number of seagoing vessels afloat in the past as well as presently, and the frequency of gales and fogs, it is not so much a matter of surprise that shipwreck should sometimes occur but that it hasn't occurred more often.

There is an old saying that light shines the brightest in the darkest places. That statement has never been challenged, either from an earthly or a spiritual standpoint. When a mariner saw a bright light piercing the abysmal black of night, it was like a glimpse of heaven, especially under adverse weather and sea conditions. It was blessed assurance for a shipmaster to be able to get his bearings from a beacon along the shore or from a light clearly marking a sea-girt obstruction, for there are no more horrifying sounds to any mariner than those of the unexpected roar of breakers in the inky blackness of night and then the grinding, scraping screams of a ship being ripped open by an immovable encrusted reef.

In former times, shipwrecks were common occurrences and even today command television and front page news coverage. Shipwreck and drama go hand in hand. Human life is always involved. Though modern electronic innovations have lessened the role of the lighthouse, it remains a symbol of hope to those who reap their living from the sea. In former times, their importance was unrivaled, for the lion's share of shipwrecks did not occur on the high seas but on approach to shore. Consider this account of how it was for a navigator a century ago.

Lookouts peered through the scud that whipped off a churning sea in the din of early morning where neither stars nor moon could penetrate the heavy curtain of cloud that hung from horizon to horizon. It was the remnants of a three day storm through which the square-rigger had come. Reduced, patched canvas faltered in the ephemeral light airs like ghostly fleece.

The master of the vessel, weary after his long vigil, stood at the rail following a lengthy, eastbound crossing of the Pacific from the land of the rising sun. Light in ballast, the ship rode high, dipping and rolling and wallowing in a sickening, almost submissive manner in the face of an angry ocean. The shipmaster was anxiously awaiting word from the watch that the Columbia River lightship had been sighted. The destination was Portland, Oregon, one hundred miles up the Columbia River from Astoria, to pick up a cargo of grain.

It was early December 1899. The vessel neared what the skipper hoped was the dreaded entrance of the Columbia River. Littered with hazards, there was nary a master who wasn't apprehensive about that infamous bar. As testimony to the hidden danger that lurked at its mouth, scores of ships had come to grief there.

Shifting his weight from one foot to the other, the nervous captain hoped his present course was correct for picking up the lightship. He checked the compass and uttered the words of confidence helmsman crave at such moments: "Steady as she goes, son."

With possible dangers at every quarter, all hands were alert for any clue to their actual position. Their ears were tuned for the faint moan of a far away fog horn. Their eyes probed the inky darkness for the glimmer of a distant lighthouse. The wind was picking up again, its incessant howl in the rigging sounded like the tones of a pipe organ in a haunted house.

Little did the shipmaster know that only a short time earlier the lightship had been carried from her station and driven up on the beach where she was held a prisoner, and that Point Adams Lighthouse had been discontinued. He would have to make a landfall with either Cape Disappointment or the new North Head lighthouse. There was the chance his ship had strayed southward and it may be dangerously near Tillamook Rock. On the other hand the dead reckoning may be northward and he would have to look for Willapa or Grays Harbor lights.

Suddenly the lookout on the fo'c's'le head shouted, "Light off the port bow!"

"Where away!" cried out the bucko mate squinting through the murk.

"Two points off the port bow!" the watch sounded.

The skipper's eyes lit up with hope that his calculations were correct. There were fixed lights at Cape Disappointment and on the lightship but where was the red glow from Point Adams light and how close was he to shore?

His out-of-date charts and the thickness of the weather made him wonder if he was seeing the dim shape of another ship, or was it a lighthouse with the light blown out by the storm? Suddenly that old fear returned. Would he soon hear the sound of breakers? Would he tremble at the sound of his ship striking an outcrop that would rip the guts out of his floating domain?

Danger lurked as the helmsman fought the kick of the wheel against the angry billows. A pale dawn approached. Fog was thickening and the wind cut like a knife. It seemed as if the whole world had closed down on the ship and there was little distinction between sea and sky. The faint outline of the bulwarks rose sluggishly, reluctantly out of the foam-crested gray-green sea and then disappeared.

"Right full rudder!" came a sudden and strident command from the captain. His sixth sense told him he may be heading into trouble. The crew scurried aloft and, on the orders of the mate, shortened sail to the maximum. The wheel was put hard over, the ship seemingly caught in a vortex of confused water. Pumps were manned constantly, powered by the straining muscles of sailors working the handles. The only alternative was to remain well off-shore until the terrible fog evaporated. The ship's hand fog-horn was blaring for fear other vessels might be lurking near by, but when no return sounds were heard, the captain continued to sail with the wind at his back, impatiently waiting for a change in the weather.

The traditional signal flags had been hoisted in the hope that somewhere out in the maw a pilot boat was tacking about looking for a fee. But what good would a pilot be in pea soup fog even if one could be found let alone the difficulty of putting a pilot aboard in mountainous seas?

*   *   *

Thus one can understand the difficulties often faced by vessels of sail encountering such waters before the advent of mechanical propulsion and of strategically placed aids to navigation.

For two centuries ships from the nations of the world have been guided into American ports by navigational signposts and thousands of mariners have appreciated their presence. As earlier mentioned, it has rarely been the open seas that have struck fear in the hearts of navigators, but rather the approach to land. It goes without saying that the abundance of shipwrecks have been where the sea meets the shore, especially around bar entrances where opposing currents clash in a mishmash of random, venomous motion.

Ever since men turned to the sea to earn their daily bread, many salt-encrusted occupational hazards have also been reluctantly accepted as a necessary part of life. For millennia, seafarers the world over have challenged the elements, in fragile craft, guided by omens, superstitions and a smattering of the most elementary astronomy. In time, man developed the cross-staff and astrolabe, crude instruments that enabled navigators to determine their position by measuring the angle of the sun. Accuracy improved dramatically with the development of reliable quadrants, sextants, chronometers and compasses. Still, with all these, when a mariner approached his landfall, it was the lighthouse for which he searched. He longed for the powerful beam generated by the warm glow of the oil lamps illuminating prismatic lenses, or the mournful cry of the foghorn in sour weather. Though such aids to navigation were the principal guides until modern times, the scene radically changed with the electronic revolution.

The effectiveness of the traditional lighthouse and foghorn paled by comparison with radio beacons, radio direction finders, radar, depth finders, racons, LORAN and Omega systems.

Ship-to-shore radio units have greatly altered the helplessness experienced by captains of old when they could not send out an effective distress call beyond the few thousand yards afforded by flags or flares. Not being able to tell anyone of distress compounded the long list of vessels that went missing with all hands.

The latest navigational aids compared to the traditional lighthouse and foghorn is like comparing jet plane travel with crossing the country with horse and wagon. Many have asked, if something is good, why change it? In this case, simply because new inventions better safeguard those who travel and work on the sea. Lighthouses are not just for symmetrical beauty. They were symbols of hope kept by those entrusted with lighting the path of life and safe passage along the shore for the good of all seafarers. Automation has cast out the faithful old keepers, and though some of their former charges keep on shining, it is the invisible hands of electronic systems that now reach out eliminating the human touch. What has been lost is a piece of Americana that can never be replaced; the personal touch.

Oregon's seacoast lighthouses have a unique history. Though the

A great aid to navigation is the building of jetties and maintaining channel depth by the Corps of Engineers. Hopper dredge in mid-Yaquina Bay channel. Yaquina Bay lighthouse marked X.

coastline is relatively straight, in a north-south direction, it is marked by several prominent capes and massive headlands that jut skyward like castles. In between are flat beaches of sand and stone, or rocky volcanic outcrops littered with coves and fissures marked with haunting caves and blowholes. Well over 300 miles, as the seagull flies, Oregon's coast stands as a prominent barrier against the constant pounding of the relentless Pacific rollers, currents and tidal actions. Along the coastal expanse are several river bar entrances, only a few of which still cater to cargo ships, although in the early times the transport by sea was totally necessary to the survival of pioneer communities. Virtually every bar entrance that had any depth of water was utilized by cargo and/or passenger vessels, both steam and sail.

Inside bar entrances, commercial and sports fishing fleets find haven in growing numbers today. With the cessation of most coastwise shipping due to vast highway connections and large trucking fleets, mainly tugs and barges continue to cross the bars usually with lumber products or petroleum, only the Columbia River, Coos Bay and Yaquina Bay cater to deep sea shipping.

Some Oregon bar entrances, never accorded jetties, have virtually silted in channels once negotiated regularly by coastal trading vessels. One can visualize the necessity of lighthouses and foghorns in the old times when the ocean was the principal highway for commerce. Cargo and passenger vessels hugged coastal sealanes and when the fog rolled in, or rain and sleet were driven in on the wings of a storm, the

19

lights and foghorns were indispensable. When the wind died while a sailing vessel was crossing a bar, it was a certainty that the chances of running aground were great. Although early aids to navigation had their limitations, without them the toll in lives and property would have been far greater than history has recorded.

Very active on the waterways of the Oregon coast, the U.S. Army Corps of Engineers has played a dominant role. It was in 1866 that Congress initiated a series of River and Harbor Acts that made the Corps responsible for developing and maintaining all officially designated federal waterways. This included Oregon's ten major coastal rivers.

Early Corps works included fortifications as well as public works. Fort Stevens was constructed by the Corps on the Columbia's south shore in 1863. The fort was shelled by a Japanese submarine in World War II* and was the only United States continental fort fired on since the War of 1812.

The Corps of Engineers was also responsible for the construction of most of Oregon's early lighthouses. Also to the agency's credit are 22 jetties on the ten major rivers, plus accompanying navigation channels on nine of them. There are 30 miles of jetty, the longest of which is the Columbia River south jetty at six and a half miles. Some 30 million tons of rock and cement compose these projects.

One jetty (south jetty, Coquille River), contains the hull of a wrecked freighter (the 307-foot long *Oliver Olson*), to help stabilize the heavy rock. Some $200 million is the current value of the projects, which must be continually repaired and maintained and sometimes extended. Further, breakwaters and entrance channels have been constructed for a dozen small boat basins in various coastal harbors including a breakwater at exposed Port Orford. The maintenance of the harbor entrance and boat basin at the nation's smallest harbor, Depoe Bay, on the central Oregon coast is also a Corps project.

Bar entrances, jetties and allied projects under the Engineers are found at the Columbia River, Nehalem Bay, Tillamook Bay, Depoe Bay, Yaquina Bay, Siuslaw River, Umpqua River, Coos Bay, Coquille River, Port Orford, Rogue River and Chetco River.

Until recent decades, it was the traditional lighthouses that played the prime role in the safeguarding of Oregon's coastal commerce, backed by the U. S. Lifesaving Service which was amalgamated into

*See: SILENT SIEGE-II: Japanese Attacks on North America in World War II, Ships Sunk, Air Raids, Bombs Dropped, People Killed. See: Bibliography.

20

the U. S. Coast Guard in 1915.

The Pacific Northwest was not among the early recipients of lighthouses. Though Native Americans inhabited its seashore for thousands of years, their only aids to navigation were big bonfires.

America's first official lighthouse was located on Little Brewster Island in Boston Harbor in 1716. The Spanish had some minor oil lamps in the mission ports of what is present day southern California, in the early 1800's. Russia had an official light atop the government building in Sitka (New Archangel), sometimes referred to erroneously as Baranof's Castle, in 1837, and the Hawaiian Kingdom lighted its first official beacon in the early 1840's. The first United States government light on the Pacific Coast was not commissioned until 1854. This was, of all places, on Alcatraz Island, in San Francisco Bay. In those early years it did not have a prison but only a small contingent of soldiers. All 16 of the original lighthouses for the Pacific Coast suggested by the pioneer surveyors were built by 1860.

Initial concern for a lighthouse on the West Coast was for the notorious entrance to the Columbia River, to be located at Cape Disappointment. "Cape D" might well have been the first commissioned had it not been that the bark *Oriole,* carrying supplies for that lighthouse and others, was totally wrecked just below the mighty monolith where the beacon was to have been erected.

When land was first secured for a light at Cape Disappointment, the long running boundary dispute between the United States and England had just been settled by the 1846 Treaty of Ghent. This made the Columbia gateway an American exclusive. It became a part of Oregon Territory. Before the lighthouse was operative, Cape Disappointment found itself in Washington Territory until 1889, when Washington became a state.

Though the Columbia was seen as the maritime gateway to the Pacific Northwest, some of the early settlers were visualizing the Umpqua River as the Golden Gate of the Northwest. And some people looked farther northward to the wide, deep Strait of Juan de Fuca which led to promising lumber ports in both Puget Sound and British Columbia.

It was obvious that all of those waterways urgently needed aids to navigation if tragedy was to be averted. The locations for lighthouses in Uncle Sam's earliest recommendations included not only Cape Disappointment and the Umpqua River, but also Cape Shoalwater (Willapa Bay), Cape Flattery, New Dungeness and Smith Island. However, talk was cheap without the allotted funds. Some of the proposed projects faced delays. In truth, it was the discovery of gold in California in 1848-1849 that gave the impetus for lighthouses in the wake of the huge armada of ships converging on San Francisco Bay.

Talk about "red tape" in the nation's capitol today? Rest assured it wasn't too much different in the 1850's. Prior to the American Revolution, early colonies were totally responsible for the construction and maintenance of American lighthouses. On August 7, 1789, following the establishment of the Federal Government, Congress flexed its neophyte muscle and Uncle Sam accepted his responsibility for aids to navigation. Accordingly, the colonies, between 1789 and 1795, gladly turned over their sentinels, lock, stock and barrel. The "Potentate-In-Charge" until 1820 was the Commissioner of Revenue and the Secretary of the Treasury. As of 1820, the Fifth Auditor of the Treasury Department took over the reins, but it was obvious that the entire operation rated a poor "three" on a scale of ten. And that rating kept going down with accusations of graft and insufficient leadership.

With commerce growing rapidly and shipwrecks increasing dramatically off the coasts of America, a fire was lit under the Congress, and that body finally acted with authority in 1851. Experts were appointed to make a serious study of a badly neglected sector of the American maritime. Among the recommendations was that a lighthouse board be appointed and given full charge with overhauling the system of aids to navigation. Action was immediate. In 1852, a nine-member board was in place with the Secretary of the Treasury acting as president. Admiral William B. Shubrick was chairman. The new Lighthouse Board set up 12 districts, the twelfth included the entire Pacific Coast—the far away west—and little known to members of Congress and generally unfamiliar to those on the nine-member Lighthouse Board. Most solons considered the west coast as only the home of California gold and savage Indians.

Remoteness made supply difficult. Getting things accomplished "out west" was often a major undertaking. An inspector was appointed to each district and was charged with supervision of construction, supply and maintenance of the navigational aids in his district. In addition he had the responsibility for appointing keepers for each lighthouse. Over the inspector was the Collector of Customs who, in essence, became Supervisor of District Lighthouses.

Who would have guessed that Spain's former dominance in California would have generated so little interest in the field of pharology when they actually controlled the Pacific sealanes for more than two centuries? When the United States annexed California from Mexico, things began to look brighter on the maritime horizons because west coast shippers prodded the solons in Washington D.C. to the concern for safety along the coast. Although the California gold rush created a navigational aid urgency, it was General Persifor F. Smith who was instrumental in creating action. This was even before the gold rush came to fruition. Congress had authorized the building of lighthouses on the west coast in 1848, including sites in Oregon Territory, but because of the meager funds allotted, it would seem the buildings would be more of the size of outhouses than lighthouses. It required another two years before a genuine effort was made to get construction underway. The United States Coast Survey had staked out several isolated sites for beacons along the Pacific Coast, but what good were strategic locations that remained unlighted? It was on September 28, 1850 that Congress finally authorized the construction of lighthouses. Six would be in California on the searoad to the Golden Gate, and in the bay where ships arrived in amazing numbers filled with eager gold-seekers.

Alcatraz Island, Fort Point, Farallon Islands, Point Pinos, Point Conception and Point Loma were California's pioneer beacons.

Only three were originally designated for the Pacific Northwest. These were Cape Disappointment, Cape Flattery and New Dungeness.

When Oregon became a state in 1859, there was only one oceanfront lighthouse along its extensive shoreline discounting of course, Cape Disappointment, which suddenly found itself in Washington Territory. The one on Oregon real estate was at the entrance to the Umpqua River and ironically, it was to see only a couple years of service before being undermined and toppled by coastal erosion. It was not reestablished for more than three decades.

Initial contractors for West Coast lighthouses was a firm headed by partners, Francis A. Gibbons and Francis X. Kelly of Baltimore, Md. Almost immediately they found themselves with quite a challenge concerning supply and almost impossible access to some of the locations for their projects.

For each of the California lighthouses completed, Gibbons and Kelly were to receive $15,000. For the most difficult Cape Disappointment project, $31,000. Their pay for eight lighthouses would be $136,000. All were to be completed by November 1853. Regrettably not one was finished by that date, but the contractor, seeing the impossibility of his task, asked for and received an extension to May 1, 1854.

The partners purchased the bark *Oriole,* a wooden-hulled sailing vessel of 1,223 tons burden (a large craft for her day), in which to carry both building materials and construction workers to the sites. It

> The Contracting firm of Francis A. Gibbons and Francis X. Kelly, Baltimore, Maryland, built the first light houses along the U. S. West Coast. These were located at:
> Fort Point
> (Now near South Pier of Golden Gate Bridge)
> Alcatraz Island
> (In San Francisco Bay)
> S.E. Farallon Island
> (About 30 miles into the ocean off San Francisco)
> Humboldt Harbor
> (Humboldt Bay—Eureka)
> Point Conception
> (West of Gaviota)
> Point Pinos
> (South side, Monterey Bay)
> Cape Disappointment
> (North side, at mouth of Columbia River)

would be a rugged, uncomfortable voyage around the Horn from the East Coast.

In addition to the ship's crew, there were two stone masons, 14 mechanics, two brick layers, two carpenters, one painter, a blacksmith, a plasterer and five laborers. Among the passengers was W. H. Hemmick, clerk and distributing agent; Roger Mahon, superintendent over the building of all eight lighthouses and Wm. J. Timanus, bookkeeper and purchaser.

The *Oriole's* cargo included all building materials except brick and lime. Departure from Baltimore was August 12, 1852. The sea-weary crew and passengers cheered when the vessel finally entered the Golden Gate on January 29, 1853. Terra firma never felt so good.

By the time the *Oriole* arrived in San Francisco, an additional party arrived via the overland route in covered wagons and had already begun the forms for the foundations at Fort Point and on Alcatraz Island. As the two teams became one, progress accelerated. Within a few months, both lighthouse towers were completed. By rights, Fort Point should have been operating first but it had been measured wrong for the lighting apparatus, thus taking extra time for partial reconstruction. Alcatraz, therefore, has the honor of being the first United States Pacific Coast light to display its illuminated Fresnel. In the interim, work was underway at the rugged Farallon site. This was a craggy, ancient upheaval of rock well off the Golden Gate. Work had also started on Point Pinos near Monterey. The *Oriole* had come northward with the building materials and construction crews. It was at this point, when the ship was at the Columbia River entrance, just below the prominent cape, that it was lost. It went to the bottom with not only the building materials for Cape Disappointment, but for four other lighthouses as well.

The ship's company narrowly escaped with their lives and were unable to save anything. What a setback. Good old Yankee ingenuity prevailed however, and the crew put the loose ends back together. They gathered more materials and with occasional delays set about to complete the contract.

To speed the operations, Roger Mahon was named construction boss for Cape Disappointment and Humboldt Harbor lights. William Timanus was placed in charge of Point Conception and Point Loma. Eventually, the original eight lighthouses became functional as official navigational aids between 1854 and 1856.

Fortunately, the early west coast lighthouses were recipients of the state-of-the-art lighting systems. France had taken the primary leadership in manufacturing techniques of sophisticated lighthouse optics by capitalizing on the genius of Augustin Fresnel. He was a scientist who developed what came to be known as the Fresnel lens. His lens refracted and reflected light through hand-ground and polished prismatic glass set in cages of brass or bronze. The system was a giant breakthrough in the field of pharology and made former optics virtually obsolete.

Lt. Washington A. Bartlett, USN, was dispatched by the Secretary of the Treasury to Paris to contract for the manufacture of lenses and allied lighting apparatus for the new sentinels. He signed with Sautter & Co., Paris, to produce two third order lights for Fort Point and Alcatraz, as well as a first order and second or third order for the other projects, with further purchases pending. Cost of such brilliant creations of glass and metal in those early years ran from $3,810 to $11,150. The price included lenses, lamps, frame, lantern and appendages, but not freight.

It was in April of 1853 that the first two lenses arrived in New York for transshipment to San Francisco. Twelve months passed before the others arrived which left some of the completed towers unlit during the interim.

25

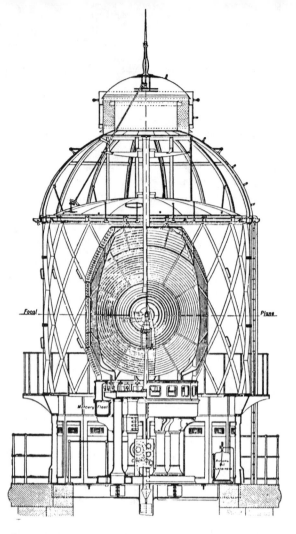

Focal   Plane

Classic Fresnel-design dioptric lens and operating mechanism atop
tower. Lantern house surrounded a central bulls-eye lens with a
series of concentric glass prismatic rings. By adding triangular prism
sections above and below the main lens, it steepened the angle of
incidence at which rays shining up and down (lost light) could be collected and made to emerge horizontally. All the collected light
emerged through the bulls-eye as a narrow, horizontal pencil-like
beam. This is known as the full *Fresnel catadioptric system.* Spire on
top of tower is lightning rod. Light source was incandescent oil vapor
burner. Diagram is a First Order Light. Fresnel designed different size
apparatus to meet requirements for various lighthouses. These were
designated First, Second, through Sixth Order and varied in size from
7 ft. l0 inches high (First Order) to l ft. 5 inches (Sixth Order) inside
diameter.

The other lighting apparatus didn't arrive until the spring of 1855. Due to the delicate nature of the materials, the government decided on separate contractors to install the lighting apparatus. Captain Henry W. Halleck, lighthouse inspector for the west coast lights, was obviously concerned that no damage occur to the expensive cargo which was much more valuable than the former Argand lamps and reflector systems used in many lighthouses in earlier years. Another personality who was instrumental in dispersing lighting systems to the early Pacific Coast lights was Major Hartman Bache. He was sent from the east coast to put his talents to work following a successful career in aids to navigation along that coast. Thus the Pacific Coast was the late comer in receiving primary lighthouses. Only Alaska would be longer neglected.

Actually, there were a dozen lighthouses in existence when the first United States Congress met in 1789. Recognizing the importance of lighthouses to a young nation's marine commerce, the ninth law passed by the first Congress created the "Light-House Establishment" as a unit of the Federal Government. Congress delegated to the Secretary of the Treasury the authority and responsibility for:

> necessary support, maintenance and repair of all lighthouses, beacons, buoys and public piers, erected, placed or sunk before the passing of this act, at the entrance of, or within any bay, inlet, harbor or port of the United States, for rendering the navigation thereof easy and safe....

Among the 16 original west coast lighthouses suggested by the early authorities, only eight were on the original contracts. However, between 1856 and 1866 several others were contracted for and placed in operation. Among sentinels in the Pacific Northwest* were:

Name	Location		Year Built /Rebuilt	Elev. Above High Water	Miles Seen	Colors of Beam
Umpqua River	43°39'8"	124°11'9"	1857	165ft	21W 20R	Red/White
Cape Arago	43°20'5"	124°22'5"	1866/1934	100ft	16	White
Willapa Bay** [Cape Shoalwater]	46°44'	124°4'4"	1858/1941	80ft	13	White
Cape Flattery	48°23'5"	124°41'1"	1857	165ft	24W 20R	Red/White
New Dungeness	48°10'9"	123°6'6"	1857/1927	67ft	14	White
Smith Island	48°19'1"	122°5'6"	1858/1957	97ft	16	White

* Although the "Pacific Northwest" is generally defined as the states of Idaho, Oregon and Washington, the editors take only minor license and include mention of Battery

The decade of the 1870's saw several more splendid lighthouses constructed on the Pacific Coast. At last, coastal and offshore commerce, so often plagued by shipwreck on the jagged outcrops of the Pacific rim, were receiving government attention. Although aids to navigation were slow in coming, this was a new, pristine frontier ripe with promise for the future in a nation growing rapidly and extremely dependent on waterborne commerce.

The cry had gone out, "Go West, young man" (Horace Greely - 1855), and to the West they came. Many came by covered wagon over the Oregon and California trails. Many others came by ship directly to San Francisco Bay. Now, men began to answer the call of the new timber industry in the Pacific Northwest.

Point Lighthouse at Crescent City, California. This homey-atmosphere installation is very close to Oregon and draws thousands of visitors now that it is both a part of the Del Norte County Museum as well as being a fully-operating, attended, lighthouse. Battery Point Lighthouse opened in 1856 as Crescent City Lighthouse being in the second round of orders for construction. It is the only "Cape Cod" type construction north of San Francisco. For the revealing story of this lighthouse, see *Battery Point Light and the Tidal Wave of 1964 (Includes St. George Reef Light). See:* Bibliography.
** Cape Shoalwater failed to withstand coastal erosion and is now totally gone. It is third, after Umpqua River and Smith Island, of west coast lighthouses to fall into the water. Others have been moved "hop-scotching around the property" to keep out of the way of the water. Corps of Engineers declared there is "nothing cost-effective" that can be done to save the area. Present light is "portable," can be moved on short notice. For exciting reading about Cape Shoalwater and other erosion losses, see *Bayocean: The Oregon Town That Fell Into the Sea. See* Bibliography.

Chapter 2
Cape Blanco Lighthouse

The lengthy seacoast of Oregon was somewhat overlooked in the early years of the establishment of lighthouses. In fact, the oldest lighthouse within the boundaries of Oregon state is Cape Blanco light. It was first activated in 1870 and continues to serve to the present day.

```
CAPE BLANCO LIGHTHOUSE
Location:
42°50'N  124°34'W
Nearest town: Sixes
Built: 1870
Type: White conical tower
Height above water: 245ft
Height above ground: 59ft
Light source: Electric
        incandescent bulb
Beam: White
Optics: 1st Order
Power: 80,000cp
Seen: 22 miles


NOTE Classic data is from Light List 1960.
U.S. Treasury Dept., Coast Guard, and reflects
details then in effect.
```

A splendid masonry tower, it has stood the test of time and the howling weather. Not only is it the oldest in the state, it is the most westerly. (Cape Flattery lighthouse on Tatoosh Island, Washington is the farthest west in the contiguous states—124°44'6"W.)

There's a small cemetery on Cape Blanco where virtually every tombstone bears the name Hughes. In truth, the Hughes acreage was about the only spread on the west end of the cape aside from the lighthouse reservation in early years.

Patrick Hughes, a true pioneer, left his native Ireland in the wake of the potato famine. Landing in New York by ship, he eventually met an Irish girl in Boston and with good Irish fashion they were married. The call to go west beckoned them to scout out the new frontier. He traveled across the country with an ox team. She, Jane,

The changing scene at Cape Blanco Lighthouse Reservation. *Top:* When under U.S. Lighthouse Service. Photo shows oil storage house at left; tower and its workroom; keeper's dwelling; assistant keeper's house; water tank. *Lower, clockwise from left corner:* Two-story officers' duplex and garage; road to Highway 101 (6 miles); old officer's quarters—enlisted men's family quarters; barracks; utility shops; enlisted men's garage; garage for C.G. vehicles; water tank; lighthouse tower. Long building in center was offices; mess hall and recreation room. LORAN towers (not shown) are right of photo. All this community of buildings is now gone.

decided that the lesser of two evils was to go around the Horn by ship. The two were reunited in San Francisco. When they didn't find the spread of land in California that satisfied them, the couple ventured northward to the Pacific Northwest. They settled near the town of Langlois in Oregon. The land reminded them of their native Ireland. Though Patrick's original plan was to search for California gold, he now found himself laboring for landowner A. H. Thrift in order to trade labor for an 80 acre parcel of land. This plot was near the shore between the mouth of the Sixes River and the north slope of Cape Blanco. He also purchased a black sand operation on the south side of the cape called Sullivan's Mine. There he pursued his dream of finding gold. Regrettably, he met with only limited results. His many trips between his ranch home and the beach caused him to turn an old Indian trail into a road.

While working at mining in the 1860's, he was able to start a dairy. Thus he entered the dairying business. In a short time, this became much more lucrative than his mine. Meanwhile, the Hughes family was growing in number and formed the total population for miles around—that is until Uncle Sam purchased the tract at the far end of Cape Blanco. It was not long before Hughes saw new activity in his little corner of the world.

At the time, he had no way of knowing that one day his second son, James, would become a light keeper at Cape Blanco. James built a ranch on the north side of the Sixes River but he later sold this then moved back to the cape where he spent two decades as a lighthouse keeper.

Many referred to the cape as the Hughes' dynasty, as the senior member of the family built his dairy farm to more than 100 milk cows on 1,000 acres of land. San Francisco was a demanding market and the Hughes family sought their part of it. They built their own barrels to get their cheese and butter products shipped. The first haul was by wagon to Port Orford, a half day away. It was a rugged trek to dockside but always rewarding. Coastal vessels waited his arrival to promptly get the dairy products to San Francisco.

With all their responsibilities, one would wonder how Patrick and his wife, Jane, had time for each other. Obviously they did for their family numbered five boys and two girls. All of them first saw the light of day in the cape ranch house.

After 38 years, it was time to celebrate by building a new Queen Anne style classic residence on the north slope of the cape. It was not far from the lighthouse. It overlooked the lush green acreage, with the Sixes River and the ocean as a gorgeous backdrop. Without doubt, it was the showplace of the entire area when it was completed in 1898. Built of durable Port Orford cedar, it encompassed some 3,500 square feet at a cost of a dollar a foot. Little was spared in making it a first class home. It included a small chapel with a painted sky ceiling. Visiting Catholic clergy often said mass there.

Adding another dimension to the Hughes dynasty, the eldest son Edward, educated at the St. Andrews Academy in Vancouver, returned home and built a one-room schoolhouse. He became teacher of all the children in the community.

School District No. 15 became affectionately known as "Cape Blanco University." The family even erected a church on the cape.

Patrick died at age 71 in an accident on the cape beach. Jane lived to a ripe 90 years, succumbing in 1923. The ranch gradually changed from cattle to sheep and in later years the church, school and barns fell into disrepair. In 1971, Mary Farrier, Patrick and Jane's great grand-daughter, sold the ranch house and 1800 acres to the State of Oregon. The classic ranch house was placed on the *National Register of Historic Places* and has become a frequently visited tourist attraction.

Simultaneous with the colorful history of the Hughes family, Cape Blanco lighthouse also had an outstanding personality who was not a part of the Hughes clan. This was James Langlois, who gained fame for his long tenure of duty at the lighthouse.

Langlois was one of those unusual persons who not only had a love affair with the sentinel, but was very content in his isolated surroundings. He was completely dedicated to his profession and spent the better part of his life as principal keeper of the light, with a tenure of duty there spanning 42 years.

He had been assigned as an assistant keeper in 1875 under Captain S. P. Pierce. In a few years he was promoted to full command. Born at Silverton, Oregon in 1848, Langlois came to the Oregon coast where he settled near Floras Lake, in Curry County, with his parents, William and Mary in 1854. Elizabeth Rudolph, who became his wife in 1873, bore him five children–two sons, Murton and Oscar and three daughters, Mary, Idella and Audrey. All were reared on the lighthouse reservation and were well indoctrinated into lighthouse life. The children attended the little nearby school where the Hughes kids were educated. The two families were closely knit.

Oscar Langlois followed in the steps of his father and, in 1905, became an assistant lighthouse keeper at Cape Arago. He served under Captain Frederick Amundsen and Captain William Denning. Later he was assigned to Coquille River lighthouse at Bandon, under Captain Wiren. Still later, he was appointed head keeper at Coquille River and remained in that post until that facility was abandoned as an aid to navigation in 1939.

The senior Langlois became a legend in his own time. Though Cape Blanco was well off the beaten track, many visitors in olden times managed a visit during the summer months in order to see the lighthouse and the superb natural surroundings. This was tantamount to a green Valhalla.

The Langlois' were known for their friendly acceptance of visitors who ventured over the rough wagon road and its washboard contour in order to gain their destination. From 1896 until 1916, the lighthouse journal recorded 4,050 visitors. (By contrast, the lighthouse with the fewest visitors was Tillamook Rock which listed only a few dozen during its entire life.) Most camped overnight and frolicked in the delightful surroundings. Beachcombing on the beaches north and south of the cape brought much pleasure. Each visitor was offered a full tour of the lighthouse by one of the keepers, always dapper in their neatly pressed blue uniforms with brass buttons.

Keeper Langlois' wife, Elizabeth, worked as hard as the keepers with her household duties, bringing up her children as well as acting as hostess to the many visitors.

A different chapter at Cape Blanco occurred at the turn of the century when a woman was assigned as an assistant keeper at the lighthouse. She was one of the only women ever assigned to an ocean front, first-order lighthouse on the Pacific Coast and, she was probably the very first in Oregon. Her name was Mabel E. Bretherton. The appointment raised many eyebrows among the grizzled male keepers of the day who insisted that a woman's place was in the home, keeping house and raising children.

Be that as it may, she was assigned as second assistant keeper for the usual probationary period of six months. Time proved her worth. She signed on March 30, 1903, and a few years later was transferred to North Head lighthouse where she retired from the service in October 1907 still holding the rank of Second Assistant Keeper.

Another woman keeper was also attached to Cape Blanco for a brief period, a Mrs. Alexander.

James Langlois, who continued his vigil through thick and thin held another distinction. It is said that during his more than four decades of service, he never stepped foot inside of any lighthouse with the exception of his beloved Blanco.

Cape Blanco was sighted by Spanish sea Captain Martin de Aguilar on January 19, 1603. Due to its chalky appearance, he named it *Cape Blanco de Aguilar*. For many years, following the pioneer American surveys, it was called Cape Orford. When the lighthouse was built (1868-1870), it was referred to as "Cape Orford lighthouse." The old Spanish title was later restored (but the *de Aguilar* was dropped as cumbersome) as historians agreed the name Blanco rightfully belonged to this promontory.

Before the lighthouse was constructed, there were several tall trees on the outer cape. Many were felled by the strong, gusty winds so frequent in the area thus, those remaining were cut down as they were considered a hazard to the station buildings. The tree-denuded cape offered excellent grazing grounds for the livestock which roamed the area.

Cape Blanco and its Lighthouse.
Aerial camera faces slightly southeast.
Photographed autumn 1990.

Typical summer foggy day at Cape Blanco.

Though Blanco is the most westerly cape in Oregon, another cape is the most westerly in the continental United States. This is Cape Alava (48°10' 124°44'), 13 miles south of Cape Flattery in Washington state. Cape Alava was never crowned with a lighthouse.

The seaward face of Cape Blanco is a steep cliff, 200 feet high. It has many different contours where the pounding breakers have beaten relentlessly against its furrowed brow through the centuries. On each of the nearby beaches, coastal vegetation has been eroded and at times, the beaches strewn with driftwood, flotsam and jetsam, and some glass fishnet floats, collected over vast areas of the Pacific Ocean.

The variety of weather changes the mood of the cape. Sometimes the sky is clear and blue. A summer fog will obliterate the sky and limit visibility to a few feet. And it rains and it blows! Cape Blanco, what a multi-faced personality!

As seen broadly from seaward, the cape is a somewhat inconspicuous object, not because it is not outstanding in character but because of the higher lands behind it. At ten miles seaward, it appears a mere change of color in the long line of mesa land bordering the sea, especially if the cliffs are not showing brightly in the sun. It is however, easily recognized by those familiar with it. Its lighthouse is a welcome signal to craft of all sizes.

At its inception, Cape Orford (Blanco) lighthouse was designed as a primary seacoast light. The 59 foot tower is situated on the highest part of the cape about 200 yards from the western pitch. Prominent in its coat of white-painted masonry, the tower is the frustum of a cone, surmounted by an iron lantern house.

The original two-story brick keeper's dwelling, painted white with green window blinds, was 35 yards southwest of the tower. Several years ago it was razed, and with the advent of automation in the 1960's, many of the older outbuildings were dismantled.

The Coast Guard built units on the reservation to house the electronics crew that once handled the radio beacon and maintained the light.

During World War II, there was considerable action on the cape as a Coast Guard Beach Patrol Detachment was headquartered there in addition to the lighthouse personnel. Due to the belief there was considerable risk of Japanese invasion along the Northwest Coast, every foot of the beach, in all coastal states, was patrolled 24-hours a day, seven days a week.*

With the total conversion of the light and radio apparatus at Cape Blanco to automation, the personnel were transferred and the station was put in caretaker status. Shortly after that, all of the community of buildings—offices, crew quarters, shops, mess deck and galley, separate officers and family quarters and small visitor's center were dismantled. Today, except for the original conical tower and a workroom, Cape Blanco's grounds are open to visitors (of which it gets many being on the adjoining property to Cape Blanco State Park). The sun still shines. The fog is just as thick. And the wind doth blow, and blow, and blow.

The lighting apparatus originally installed at Cape Blanco was a fixed white light of the first order of the system of Fresnel. It was

*For a superior account of Beach Patrol operations, *see:* Chapter 10, "The Coast Guard at Floras Lake in World War II" in *Lakeport Ghost Town of the South Oregon Coast. See:* Bibliography. The Coast Guard Detachment at Floras lake was one of the largest, 85 men with war-dogs and horses, as that section of the beach was considered "most vulnerable" for invasion by the Japanese. *See also:* the Beach Patrol chapter in *Silent Siege. See:* Bibliography.

Aerial view of Cape Blanco light station in 1970's. Note one of two loran towers. View looks north toward Sixes River. Excellent beachcombing on high tides here in winter.

initially exhibited December 20, 1870 and displayed from sunset to sunrise. The arc of visibility over the water was 240 degrees. The height of the focal plane (center lens) above the base of the tower was 59 feet, and above the mean level of the sea, 256 feet. The light was visible 21 miles at sea on a clear night. It is the highest elevated lighthouse in the state. As in all lighthouses, before automation, the lens was covered by a curtain, during the daylight hours, to protect the delicate prisms from the glare of the sun's rays. The sun tended to discolor the glass.

Numerous reefs, sea stacks and rock outcrops surround the cape and mariners have traditionally given the place a wide berth. Winds

37

howl over the cape with fury during the winter months, sometimes exceeding 100 miles an hour, and storm damage has been frequent through the years. Some mariners liken Cape Blanco to California's Point Conception.

Cape Blanco has prominent streams on either side—the Sixes River to the north and the Elk River to the south. Both are of great benefit to farmers.

At the mouth of the Elk River, a beachcomber discovered a bottle, on May 18, 1860, which contained a message. It had been tossed overboard from the coastal paddle wheel steamer *Brother Jonathan* on March 23rd of the same year. The bottle was thrown into the sea at a latitude of 42 degrees N. Lat. and 124 degrees W. Long. The bottle was carried an estimated 50 miles from the steamer before washing ashore. In virtually the same location, five years later, the *Brother Jonathan* struck a rock and foundered carrying nearly 200 souls to a watery grave. This proved to be one of the most tragic sea disasters on the Pacific Coast. A direct result of this wreck brought about the building and operation of St. George Reef lighthouse off Crescent City. (Only 17 persons survived this shipwreck, escaping in a lifeboat. Colonel George Wright, who led a punitive expedition against Indians near Spokane some years earlier, was one of the passengers who drowned.)

Cape Blanco lighthouse is perched on a headland described as being close to the "crimson bars of evening." Building supplies were landed on the beach at the base of the cape by the pioneer lighthouse tender *Shubrick* in the late 1860's. The lens, lantern parts and clockwork, transported in crates, were valued at $20,000. After the light was installed and the oil lamp fitted, the illuminated beacon produced 45,765 candlepower. At a much later unrecorded date, the big first order lens was replaced by a second order revolving lens. With electrification, a powerful incandescent bulb increased the candlepower to 320,000. That second order lens is still in use at this writing.

(Left page)
Conical tower lighthouse and workroom is backdrop for Dale Webber who holds a "standby oil lamp" (not an original). When Fresnel designed his lenses the light source was a simple oil lamp and wicks. About 1900, when oil "vapor" lamps were developed, these were made in specific sizes thus a First Order lens was equipped with a First Order lamp. *Inset:* Automation at Cape Blanco lighthouse with modern 1000 watt projection lamps. One lamp was spare, automatically went into position when first lamp burned out. Lamps have "rated life," so attendant visits to replace burned out bulbs and to polish glass on a schedule.   39

Though fog sometimes masks the cape, Cape Blanco was never blessed, or should one say cursed, with a fog signal. That fact was much favored by those who tended the station because keepers much preferred fog signal-free posts. Fog "sirens," as they were called in the early years, were steam driven. Such stations had boilers that had to be fired up before the horn could blast, sometimes long hours at a time. Later, generators and compressors cut down the physical effort.

Most striking view of the lighthouse is from along the curving beach near the mouth of the Elk River. It was there that Joaquin Miller, Oregon's poet-laureate, courted Minnie Myrtle. That courtship was before the construction of the lighthouse or undoubtedly, there would exist a memorable poem mentioning the light, for both were great writers. The same year the lighthouse was commissioned, the two divorced. Eleven years after their separation, she went back to her former husband who was then in New York.

"I have come to you to die," she said, still expressing love to her sorrowing and repentant ex-spouse.

*   *   *

Another pioneer, who had a closeness to the rugged seascape in the Port Orford-Cape Blanco area was Louis Knapp. He was proprietor of the vintage Knapp Hotel in Port Orford. His concern for tempest-tossed mariners voyaging the rugged coastline prompted him to keep an oil lamp burning every night in the seaward window of his establishment. Right up until the lighthouse was built, that feeble lamp undoubtedly was a blessing to many mariners.

Knapp, who had come west from Baltimore was to become one of the most prominent citizens of Curry County. His hotel catered to many dignitaries, as well as common travelers along the way, over a period of almost 75 years.

Knapp's concern for seafarers was more than justified. Many heart-rending tragedies occurred in the general area in former times when ships depended heavily on lighthouse beacons and foghorns while skirting the perilous shores.

Probably the shipwreck most closely associated with Cape Blanco lighthouse was that of the oil tanker *J. A. Chanslor*. The ship was driven into the rocky outcrops between the lighthouse and the Sixes River. En route from Goleta, California to Northwest ports, the Associated Oil tanker was navigating in rough seas with thick fog when she drove ashore near Tower Rock on that fateful day of December 18, 1919.

It was a maritime nightmare that followed. Crashing seas broke over the wreck, snapping her steel hull in two. Captain A. A. Sawyer and two crewmen somehow struggled into an open lifeboat in the mishmash of confused seas, covered with oil and wreckage. The lighthouse was less than a quarter mile away but thick weather blotted out the scene of the disaster. For 34 hours the open craft drifted, pummeled like a cork. In trying to gain the beach, its occupants were thrown into the seething breakers and miraculously swept up on the sand. The men were blue from the cold, as well as bruised and battered. Rescuers found and revived them.

The remaining 36 crew members never had a chance. All were drowned in the watery onslaught that inundated the wreck. Most of the bodies were never recovered. In the vessel's tanks were 30,000 barrels of oil that gushed out with the breaking of the ship. The beaches were polluted, killing hundreds of seabirds and fish. The fore section of the wreck remained visible for several weeks, protruding from the outer surf a few hundred feet off the beach. It was a grim tombstone for those who lay asleep in the deep.

Several years earlier, less than a decade and a half after the commissioning of the lighthouse, a terrible drama was enacted off Cape Blanco. It involved the coastal passenger steamer *Alaskan,* commanded by Captain R. E. Howes, a Massachusetts native who had been going to sea since age 12. Extracts from the ship's log kept by Howes survived to tell the story of that unfortunate voyage.

The steamer had left Portland, Friday, May 10, 1889, at midnight arriving at Astoria the next day at 8 A.M. She departed the Oregon Railway and Navigation Company dock at 11:30 A.M. and crossed over the Columbia bar, southbound. Twelve hours later in the dark, Cape Foulweather (Yaquina Head) light was sighted and the course altered amid rain showers and rising seas. On Sunday, while nearing the vicinity of Cape Blanco, the *Alaskan* was 18 miles offshore. The wind increased, as it so often does in that latitude, and the seas grew angry. Laboring heavily, the ship began to leak and Captain Howes broke off from a nine knot gait to dead slow. Rolling and pitching, a trysail was set at 3 P.M. to keep the ship's head to the wind. An hour later, the port guard began to break up and the after house began to pull loose. Seas swept the deck. The crew tried to stop the leaks below with bedding. At 6 P.M., the guard just forward of the wheelhouse carried away and the covering board burst one of the upper plates. Pumps were already working to capacity but it appeared a losing battle as the wind continued to increase. The steamer's upper works soon went to pieces thus water poured in unchecked. The bilge was full and soon the oozy liquid was rising up to the red hot boilers. Fortunately, the vessel was not carrying many passengers or cargo en route to San Francisco for drydocking and repairs. She and her sistership *Olympian* had come to the west coast from Wilmington, Delaware, five years earlier. They had been built for the Oregon Railway and Navigation Company. Both were iron-hulled, sidewheel steamers, beautifully appointed but extremely expensive to operate because their hungry boilers commanded tons of coal to generate steam. At times these ships were cast in the role of white elephants.

By 11 P.M. the following night, the vessel was being brutally treated by the voluminous seas and was settling in the water. The exhausted crew was standing by the four lifeboats awaiting the command to abandon ship. Suddenly, steam hissed up from below, the fires went out and the paddles stopped. Rockets were sent skyward and torches were burned in the hope that if there were vessels nearby they might come to their aid. But that last hope faded. With great difficulty the boats were lowered. Only the captain and nine crewmen elected to stay behind just in case the distress signals had been sighted. The 280-foot vessel remained afloat until Monday at 2 P.M., then went down stern first, breaking in two as she slipped beneath the tempest. Captain Howes leaped away from the ship just in time to keep from being sucked down in the resulting whirlpool. As he and the others struggled desperately in the ugly sea, their plight appeared hopeless. Captain Howes found a piece of wreckage and hung on for dear life, and though the saltwater stung his eyes, he could see Chief Engineer Swain also clinging to wreckage. Suddenly the pilot house floated by with three others hanging on to it.

Hours later, the tug *Vigilant,* towing a Bowers dredge, sighted the *Alaskan's* pilot house and rescued the desperate trio. Further search located the lifeboat containing First Officer G. W. Wood and other seamen, plus a few more on a liferaft. For 33 hours the master of the ill-fated steamer drifted on his piece of wreckage, frozen to the marrow, but at long last the *Vigilant* found him. He revived and recovered.

Some of the survivors were injured badly and others died from exposure. An estimated 31 persons perished in that tragedy, the toll perhaps being higher as it was known there were stowaways aboard.

One of the lifeboats, after a lengthy, exhausting drift at the mercy of the southerly winds, came ashore near the entrance to the Siuslaw River. Its occupants were still alive.

Of the numerous wrecks that have occurred around Cape Blanco, perhaps none was closer to the lighthouse than that of the *SS South Portland*. It was on October 19, 1903 that the vessel, en route from Portland to San Francisco, slammed into Blanco Reef in thick weather. In command was Captain J. B. McIntyre, who was part owner. The steamer carried 14 passengers, a crew of 25 and a full cargo of grain. Startling was the impact, because the vessel struck bow-on at a speed of seven knots. The shock threw all on board to the deck. Immediately water poured into the wrenched hull and the skipper was quick with his command to abandon ship. All this confusion came so quickly. Two of the boats, including the captain's, capsized and the occupants had to struggle in the sea for their lives.

Chief Mate Charles Bruce stayed aboard the wreck and with what steam remained in the boilers, he managed to back the steamer off the reef and run her toward the base of the cape. He got in as close as possible and left her to the elements which were hasty to do their dastardly deeds.

Of the 39 persons aboard the *South Portland,* 18 perished, including an assistant engineer who died of exposure while being removed from a liferaft as it was pulled up on the beach.

The unusual circumstances of the incident prompted the justice of the peace and acting coroner of Curry County to impanel a jury to look into the cause of the tragedy and the loss of life.

The jury's verdict found, "that Captain J. B. McIntyre was criminally negligent in abandoning the wrecked steamer before seeing to the safety of passengers and crew." It was claimed that he had left his ship in the first lifeboat, totally against the tradition of the sea where a captain is the last to leave a sinking ship. In the captain's favor was a strange remark at the hearing made by Chief Mate Charles Bruce, that "it was at his request that McIntyre take charge of the first lifeboat cleared away." His testimony however, did not halt the revoking of the captain's license.

Another weird twist to the story, told of the *South Portland* coming out to the Pacific Coast from the Atlantic in 1898 under the newly formed Boston & Alaska Steamship Company. The vessel was the former SS *Dawn* of British registry, and was purchased by the American firm to cash in on the lucrative Alaska trade. But the big push of the Alaska gold stampede had somewhat subsided and the newly formed company went into bankruptcy a short time after regular service began. She was purchased by J. Jerome who had earlier lost three steamers (colliers) with all hands, off Cape Flattery. These were the *Matteawan, Montserrat* and *Keweenaw*. All were lost between 1894 and 1901. The *South Portland* in 1902, was sold to

The Old and the New. Oregon's oldest lighthouse, Cape Blanco, is visited by a modern Coast Guard Search and Rescue jet helicopter (1980).

Pacific Alaska Transportation and Coal Company, then just two months before she was wrecked at Cape Blanco, passed to ownership of W. S. Scammell of San Francisco and the convicted Captain McIntyre. Some ships, like people, live jinxed lives, and of such was the *South Portland*.

Several other wrecks in the area included the U.S. transport bark *Anita* in 1852; schooner *Bunkalation* in 1870; steamer *Fulton* in 1904; schooner *Harriet Rose* in 1876; steamer *Victoria* in 1883; *T.W. Lucas* in 1894; steam schooner *South Coast* in 1930 (with all hands); steam schooner *Susan Olson* in 1942; the fishing vessel *Alice H.* in 1950.

One of the more interesting wrecks was that of the British ship *Melanope*, an iron-hulled sailing vessel, in December of 1906. The tall ship went over on her beam ends after her ballast shifted. Seas boarded and the rigging was in disarray, the deck a shambles. There appeared little hope for the survival of ship or crew. All hands were forced into the lower rigging to keep from being swept overboard by the boarding seas which were voluminous off Cape Blanco. Among those clinging to the shrouds were Captain N. K. Wills, his wife and two daughters, and to say the least it was a nightmarish experience through the darkness. The next morning a valiant attempt was made to get a boat over the side, and all on board managed to enter its confines and to fend off the "floating coffin," which appeared ready to go to Davy Jones' locker.

The survivors were eventually rescued by a passing vessel, but the derelict just drifted aimlessly, refusing to sink. Several days later the steam schooner *Northland* crossed paths with the troubled ship, and the captain and crew, licking their chops over salvage possibilities, managed to get a hawser aboard and tow her to the Columbia River. With a neat piece of navigation they got the derelict across the bar and into Astoria. Salvage money was collected after which the ship was pumped out and sold to J. J. Moore of San Francisco who cut her down to a barge. She was afloat until 1946 when sold to become part of a breakwater at Royston, B. C.

Many changes have taken place at Cape Blanco lighthouse since automation. The Coast Guard now monitors its operation from the Coos Bay headquarters. But the staunch old tower remains as a monument to the glorious past. The second order Fresnel lens in its crown was manufactured by Henry LaPaute of Paris and includes eight flash panels. It is five feet in diameter and seven feet in height. The lens cage rotates on ball bearings sealed in a bath of oil which makes it rather unique. As of this writing the cage is rotated by a small 120 volt, 75 rpm electric motor and gear assembly that has seen several years of usage. Characteristic of the light is one white flash every 20 seconds of 320,000 candlepower.

Probably the radio beacon presently connected with the lighthouse is of greater importance than the light in aiding modern navigation requirements.

One wonders what thoughts must have gone through the minds of the early Spanish seamen when they first eyed Cape Blanco. Some two and a half centuries would pass before the great cape would be blessed with a lighthouse, but to the Spanish goes the credit for its discovery.

The colorful Coquille River Lighthouse is often just called
"Bandon Lighthouse." *Right:* The "blaster" fog horn pro-
trudes authoritatively out of the wall toward the sea. This
was a reed Daboll trumpet emitting a characteristic blast of
5 seconds during every 25 seconds "...all blessed night and
sometimes days at a time" quipped a Bandon old-timer.
Left: Lonely and battered by driftwood after a winter storm
in the 1970's.

Chapter 3
Coquille River Lighthouse

Bandon-by-the-sea is a colorful coastal town on the southern upper section of the Oregon coast that has adopted as its landmark the abandoned Coquille River lighthouse. It sits at the north entrance of the Coquille River.

```
COQUILLE RIVER LIGHTHOUSE
Location:43°7'  124°25'W
Nearest town: Bandon
Built: 1896  Discontinued 1939
Type:  White conical tower
Height above water:  47ft
Height above ground:  40ft
Light source:  Oil in regular
        service lamp
Beam:  White
Optics:  4th Order
Power:  2500cp
Seen:  12¼ miles
Horn:  Daboll trumpet

NOTE Classic data is from Light List 1906.
U.S. Dept. of Commerce, Lighthouse Service
and reflects details then in effect.
```

For years it has been affectionately referred to as "Bandon lighthouse" no local citizen ever calling it by its proper name, Coquille River lighthouse. It was abandoned in 1939 as a working lighthouse by the government, the same year the Coast Guard took over aids to navigation from the former Lighthouse Service.

After years of neglect and vandalism, the U.S. Army Corps of Engineers restored it as a tourist attraction and amalgamated it with Bullard's Beach State Park. (Access is through the state park north of Bandon). The old lighthouse, which has become the target of photographers and artists is poised on the river's edge in a position that challenges one's artistic imagination.

When first constructed, the sentinel rose on a small, rocky islet just a hop, skip and jump from the mainland. A footbridge led to the structure. The keeper's dwelling, barn and cistern were on the

Coquille River Lighthouse during construction, 1895. It was abandoned in 1939.

mainland side. A few years later, when the north jetty was built, it connected the islet with the mainland. The base of the lighthouse virtually became the land end of the jetty.

The masonry tower, fog signal house and oil house as well as the other station buildings were built in 1895-96. On completion it was described in the *Pacific Coast Light List* as:

> White conical tower with black lantern, attached to easterly side of a white fog signal building with black roof; white one-and-a-half story double dwelling, 150 feet eastward from the tower, and faces south.

The lighthouse displayed a fourth order lens and lighting apparatus 47 feet above mean high water. The lens characteristic was a fixed white light 28 seconds, eclipse two seconds. The French manufactured optic was visible about 12¼ miles in clear weather, with an oil lamp as the light source.

In the noise making category, the fog signal was a third class Daboll trumpet, blasting for five seconds with a silent interval of 25 seconds. A demand for more efficient fog warning equipment prompted the installation of a first class siren in 1910, much to the satisfaction of fog-bound mariners but to the dismay of near neighbors.

The town of Bandon is rich in maritime history. Attracted by gold, lumber and fishing, the first settlers arrived in 1853. A post office was established in 1877, and the town incorporated in 1891. This was five years before the lighthouse displayed its light. In truth, the earliest known white men in the lower Coquille River region were Hudson's Bay Company trappers who arrived as early as 1826. Although the area was a happy fishing and hunting grounds for the Indian for centuries, the white man was thorough in his conquest. The original name of Bandon was "Averhill" and for many years the surrounding country was rather cut off from the outside world due to poor roads. Nearly all traffic moved via ocean and river transport.

As late as 1886, there wasn't so much as a wagon road or a railroad between the Coquille River and Coos Bay, though they were only about 30 miles apart.

After the government constructed the two jetties at the mouth of the Coquille River in the late 1890's creating a reliable bar entrance, an established shipping line commenced regular service to the river port. It connected Bandon with both Portland and San Francisco. Between 1905 and 1910, the town gained prominence. It boasted five sawmills and two shipyards along its river banks. There was also a woolen mill. Such industries pushed the population to 1,800 by 1910, triple that of the 1905 count. As the mills prospered, the shipyards began turning out splendid wooden-hulled ships. The waterfront boomed, lined with steamers and sailing vessels. Tourists also came to enjoy the outstanding seascape, beaches and mild climate. The term Bandon-by-the-Sea became a household phrase.

Fire, unfortunately, became the bane of the Bandon vicinity. Two of the major saw mills burned in the early part of the century. Then, on June 11, 1914, a devastating fire swept Bandon's business district causing more than $200,000 damage. That fire, however, didn't compare with the tragic conflagration that swept the town on September 26, 1936. It began as a forest fire, but fed by acres of Scotch Broom and Gorse *(Irish Furze)*, first brought to the area by Europeans. The fire crept into the settlement like a crawling torch leveling virtually everything in its path. Amid blackened and charred ruins, only 16 of 500 buildings were left standing. Hundreds of people were left homeless. The fire bankrupt the town. The state offered immediate assistance but it was a slow and painful rebuilding that followed.

Fortunately, the lighthouse on the opposite side of the river escaped devastation, except for the thick smoke and ashes that rained

In Bandon's harbor in early 1900's (left to right), bar tug
Klihyam, three-masted commercial coastwise schooners
Oakland, Advance, Ruby, Oregon. Skippers of these and
other vessels putting in to Bandon were glad that they had a
lighthouse in their front yard.

down like black snow. The keepers had their hands full keeping the
equipment in working order. The lighthouse was a grandstand
location to watch the fingers of orange flame and billowing smoke
lifting skyward. There were some locals who sought refuge at the
lighthouse station.

The Lighthouse Service tender *Rose* happened to be in the area;
thus it played a major roll during the conflagration. With all
telephone communications knocked out, the ship's radio became the
voice of the devastated community. By keeping open contact with
13th District Headquarters, outside assistance was quick to come.
The coastal freighter *Alvarado,* in port at the time, also assisted.

Bandonites were not quitters and although they gradually rebuilt
their town, much of the old spark was missing. It didn't add to their
efforts when coastal shipping began to decline, or after the lighthouse
was discontinued as an active aid to navigation in 1939. The services
of the lighthouse were taken over by a minor unmanned light on the
jetty, thus the colorful facility became one of the first in the country
to be eliminated with the switch of government agencies.

The years that followed almost spelled the destruction of the
picturesque edifice. Eventually, the keeper's dwelling and
outbuildings were vandalized and ransacked. The lighthouse lost its
windows and doors and the metal parts turned a dirty red with rust. It

was like watching a once beautiful lady die a slow, tormenting death in her senior years. Kids and hippies painted graffiti on the masonry walls inside and out and bricks were separated from the mortar. It appeared the neglected tower was doomed.

Finally, in more recent years, the historic value of the structure was appreciated and though all the outbuildings had been razed, the tower with its near three-foot thick base walls still had some life. The Army Corps of Engineers was allotted funds to restore the tower to the minimum requirements. Though the lantern house remained dark, windows, doors and iron parts were restored and the place was made into a type of tourist attraction with a minor interpretive center in the attached former foghorn house. Visitors are permitted on a locally determined schedule.

Bandon folk began to appreciate their lighthouse with new enthusiasm. Though it was not a working facility it brought tourists. The town has been quick to publicize it in its new role in every possible way. A small section of the town not burned in the 1936 fire is designated "old town." It's interesting streets are narrow and most of its merchants are historically oriented.

Perhaps the former publisher of Bandon's *Western World* newspaper best extolled the pride of Bandon in his poem:

Where breakers roar,
Where white gulls soar,
Where ships pass out to sea;
Where driftwood logs
Mid seafoam bogs
Splash on so merrily;

Where mist and rain
Off bounding main
Sweep hills of rolling green
And shifting sands
Spread fairy lands
Upon a glittering screen.

Coquille River lighthouse was designated for dual purposes. It served both as a river entrance and seacoast light. The Coquille River is well known for its dangerous bar entrance, which is narrow and subject to voluminous bar swells and currents. The light was vitally essential to navigation following its completion in 1896. Toll in lives and property through the years has been high.

51

Top: Coquille River Lighthouse perched on its rocky islet with keeper's quarters across bridge at right. This is before completion of either north or south jetty. *Lower:* View in early 1970's, decades after jetties were completed and keeper's dwelling was dismantled.

Before the advent of the jetties, the bar entrance was unpredictable as the shoals were moved around by the whiplash action of the river meeting the ocean. Stabilization has assisted remarkably, due to the jetties, but dredging remains a necessity. The Corps of Engineers keeps an eagle eye on the condition of the bar.

No longer do coastal cargo or passenger vessels enter the river, with the possible exception of an occasional tug and barge, but a commercial and sport fishing fleet are housed at a town moorage as well as at spots along the river.

Many locals and tourists climb on the jetties with fishing poles. Their luck varies. Seals, sea lions and pelicans often put on a show amid the bar swells. Danger always lurks when the green seas leap over the jetty rocks—a single wave is able to strike with the force of 20 tons.

Coquille River lighthouse has witnessed considerable tragedy at the river entrance since its inception. The heyday of maritime commerce on the river occurred a few years after the lighthouse became a permanent fixture. Around the turn of the century the U.S. Lifesaving Service, from their local station, worked laboriously assisting tempest-tossed mariners. In fact, during the early years of the century, when coastwise shipping was booming, shipwreck was more common at the Coquille than the other Oregon bar portals. Even the completion of the north jetty, in 1904-05, did not eradicate shipwreck. Constant lookout was maintained from the station's cupola, atop the butte, at the south side of the river's mouth. During the period, 1894-1910, the heroic lifesaving crew assisted vessels with a total value of $363,000 with the positive result of 239 persons saved and only two lost. The surfmen acted as firemen whenever needed.

The strandings most associated with the lighthouse are of considerable interest.

The three-masted schooner, *C. A. Klose,* stranded November 12, 1904 within a stone's throw of the tower. She was hove to off the entrance at 10 A.M. Picking up a slight wind, she endeavored to cross the heaving bar, but the southerly breeze was insufficient to keep her from drifting and the canvas grew limp. There was no room to come about. Watched from the lifesaving station, the dilemma for the life-savers was whether to stay home and be needed later—too late—or to put to the boat (always some risk) and not be needed. The commander decided to get into the water with full gear just in case.

By the time the crew reached the ship, the *Klose* was already hard aground. Pulling up to her side, a hawser was passed over then

Coastwise lumber schooner *C. A. Klose* is hard aground on November 12, 1904 just a stone's throw from Coquille River Lighthouse. She was salvaged.

rowed out to the bar tug *Triumph,* that was on the scene, ready to try to muscle the schooner off her perch.

The lighthouse keepers were surprised, in looking out a window, to see the tall ship immobile and virtually at the base of the fog signal house. Keeper Frederick Amundsen noted that the masts of the *Klose* rose higher in the air than did the dome of his lighthouse. With the line secure and her boiler furnace red hot, the tug, puffing steam, exerted her total horsepower in an effort to free the stuck schooner. The vessel did not budge. More muscle was needed. The schooner's donkey engine was started up, but there was not enough line of sufficient strength to use for such a task. While the *Triumph* pulled for all its worth, the surfboat crew raced back to Bandon to get another hawser. Securing it to the south jetty gave the donkey engine the extra purchase it needed to do the trick. With both the *Triumph* and the donkey engine straining mightily, the *Klose* was gradually pulled free. Underwater obstructions, however, took their toll and the hull was badly damaged as the vessel scraped clear of the clutches of the bar. Without the tenacious efforts of Captain Robert Johnson and his surfmen, the *C. A. Klose* would have become another of the many casualties that occurred at the Coquille gateway. (Several months later, the repaired schooner almost went to Davy Jones locker in a storm off the Columbia River. Beaching herself like a dying whale, the *C. A. Klose* was later declared a total loss).

North jetty, Coquille River and abandoned but reconditioned lighthouse. Note that King Neptune has scoured all the driftwood off the beach.

Another vessel that appeared attracted to the Coquille lighthouse was the schooner *Advance*. A frequent visitor to the river, she often encountered trouble on the bar. It was only 11 days before the stranding of the *Klose* that the *Advance* ran aground (November 1, 1904) at the north side of the river. Captain Johnson and his crew were on hand then to perform a similar act as was done for the *Klose*. On that occasion the first effort of the bar tug to pull the *Advance* free was successful.

Then on December 29, 1905, seeming to have a will of its own, the *Advance* decided to get chummier with the lighthouse. Inbound with a cargo of hay, general cargo and explosives, the vessel ran out of wind on the bar and once again took up residence near the north jetty. This time it was 12:40 in the afternoon. There was an even greater urgency now, on the part of the lifesavers and the bar tug, for the wave action could cause the explosives to ignite.

When the towline was made fast between the *Advance* and the *Triumph*, the strain caused it to snap. The surfboat made the now customary mad dash to obtain a replacement tow line. This time the tug managed to pull the *Advance* into the channel only to have the

Wreck of tug *Elizabeth Olson* on north jetty Coquille River on November 30, 1960. Tug *Rebel (left)*, Captain Petersen, is in process of rescuing the 10-man crew. *Rebel* was wrecked in same location just four months later (March 27, 1961) and Captain Petersen was drowned.

second hawser part under the strain. The runaway schooner waltzed her way to the sandy beach close to the lighthouse.

The beacon was not due to go on until sunset, but if turned on early, its shaft would give aid and comfort to the tired crew of the immobile schooner. All the while, with little relief, the surfmen kept a close eye on the wreck for fear the hull would split, demanding immediate rescue efforts. Steel hawsers were run to the beach, set up and hauled taut to await high tide. Meanwhile, cargo was jettisoned to lighten the burden on the beached hull. The explosives were handled with the gentlest of care.

It was touch and go for several hours. When hope began to fade for salvaging the wreck, good fortune blossomed. Over a week had passed. On January 8—ten days later—there was an exceptionally high tide. The venerable tug, *Triumph,* was on the scene with the surfmen standing by. As the crest of the tide approached, the *Triumph* started pulling. To the cheers of the occupants of all three vessels, the schooner finally began to slide off the beach. The tug quickly towed her charge all the way across the bar. Of all the ships that stranded on the bar, none were able to get as close to the lighthouse as the *Advance* and the *C. A. Klose.* Both were pulled to safety.

Numerous other ships weren't as fortunate. Such fine old sailing schooners as the *Onward,* stranded just south of the Coquille, February 25, 1905 and left her bones to bleach in the surf. The schooner *Western Home* broke up on the beach opposite the lifesaving station after stranding on November 13, 1904.

Then there was the *SS Bawnmore,* a tramp freighter that missed its footing in fog and became a total loss on the beach 16 miles south of the Coquille River lighthouse on August 28, 1895.

The *Bawnmore,* Captain Alexander Woodside, a 279-foot steamer of British Registry, was almost new having been launched in 1889. Of 1,430 tons displacement she had 30 persons aboard including passengers.

The ship went hard aground in a dense fog when her compass faltered and the exact position could not be determined. The ship grounded about 700 feet offshore from Floras Lake, Curry County, at the site of the then-in-planning city of Lakeport.

The stranded steamer was first spotted from the shore when a surveyor, for the developer, was startled to see the wreck leering through the fog, when he went to the beach to make readings from his tide gauge. With a pocket telescope, the surveyor saw that an anchor had been dropped, the ship unable to withdraw herself from the surf.

The *Bawnmore* was out of ports on Vancouver Island and carried a general cargo (everything from canned ginger snap cookies to a deck herd of bulls and electric trolley cars, also many dozens of cans of yellow paint) bound for Peru. The surveyor chose a large, flat piece of driftwood that was white with age, then with a piece of partially burned driftwood—charcoal—he lettered a crude sign merely stating

WILL SEND HELP

in large letters. He had been spotted from the ship so when his sign was read by a crewman with a spyglass, the shrill whistle tooted a short blast answering that the message was understood.

The witness raced back to his camp, took a horse, galloped to the village of Denmark where he told the postmaster. He then rode to Bandon's Lifesaving Station to get help.

In summary, the crew was saved and a lot of cargo salvaged. After most of the cargo was off and stacked along the beach, the ship caught fire, broke in half and sank. All this over a period of several

At the Coquille River's edge next to the sea.

weeks that brought great excitement to the area. Three uniquenesses developed.

1. Some of the bulls, once landed, got loose with evidence of a lot of new calves being born during the following year .seems to indicate the bulls had a field day among the dairy cows. These offspring were dubbed "the *Bawnmore* breed."

2. Some of the trolley cars were landed—the only railroad cars in Curry County where there were no railroads—to be used as "out" buildings by farmers.

3. Those cans of yellow paint were purchased by farmers at a huge "beach sale" sponsored by the salvagers, thus dozens of farm buildings in the area were painted yellow, the color lasting many years.

For a full encounter with the drama of discovery and salvage efforts of the *Bawnmore,* see the book, *LAKEPORT: Ghost Town of the South Oregon Coast. (See:* Bibliography)

Pride of the Coquille River wooden shipbuilding era, the splendid steam schooner *Elizabeth,* almost met her demise on the middle grounds of the river entrance, October 6, 1905. Only the valiant work of the lifesaving crew and the tug *Triumph* saved the vessel.

Where the *C. A. Klose* and *Advance* had a close affinity with the lighthouse, the steam schooner *Fifield* became a permanent fixture against the rocks of the south jetty of the Coquille. En Route to

Bandon from San Francisco with a light cargo, the steamer arrived off the river, February 28, 1916, with a southerly gale brewing and resulting heavy seas. Captain Carl Bakman was concerned and awaited morning to try to cross. The steam schooner *Brooklyn* was also lying off the raging bar. The latter vessel crossed with difficulty the following morning, and the *Fifield* followed in her wake 15 minutes later. The shipmaster tried to compensate for the strong currents but the helmsman had trouble holding the course. The *Fifield* veered and struck the rocks on her port side, damaging her propeller. Uncontrollable, she came up on a swell and was slammed down hard, breaking steam pipes in the engine room. Without power, and with broken hull planks, she was a pawn of the elements, grinding along the jetty boulders like a saw being sharpened on a grindstone. The crew made the wreck fast by running lines to the jetty, then rigged a lifeline that helped bring the crew of 22 and four passengers safely ashore.

The Lifesaving crew left their station for the scene but most of the survivors were already ashore when they arrived. As for the vessel, salvage attempts were made by using empty oil drums. A salvage ship that tried to free the *Fifield* was able to move the cracked hulk about 100 feet but as a storm was blowing up the tow lines had to be dropped. The *Fifield* had come home to die. When she was being built in the local Price Shipyard nine years earlier, a fire broke out and she had to be towed to Coos Bay for finishing. This time, she did not sail again.

It was the keepers at Coquille lighthouse who first got word to the Coast Guard that the steam schooner *Acme* was in trouble in the fall of 1924. She was inbound from San Francisco with steel rails for the Moore Mill camp but had to wait off the river entrance until the seas moderated. Captain Miller decided to retire leaving his ship in command of First Mate Hoffman. Mr. Hoffman allowed the vessel to drift into the breakers four miles north of the bar. Captain Miller was then aroused from his slumber and seeing the perilous condition of his command, ordered full speed for the beach. The Coast Guard arrived just in time, as five men had tried to leave the ship by lifeboat, which promptly capsized. But the wet men struggled up on the beach to make a line fast to a log trying to save their shipmates. The Guardsmen finally set up their breeches buoy gear and managed to bring the others ashore safely.

Though the *Acme* eventually sat high and dry at low tide, and the cargo was off-loaded, salvage efforts over land and into the river, or back into the surf proved futile. The vessel was stripped of virtually

When King Neptune snorts up a storm, he sometimes totally obliterates Bullards Beach at the north jetty with driftwood. Only days before this picture was made, the State Park manager closed the road to the beach's parking area near the lighthouse.

everything but her main engine and was finally purposely set afire after the underwriters ruled that further efforts to save the 23 year old steam schooner would not be cost-effective.

A pert little cargo carrier, *Acme* was affectionately referred to as the "Flying Dutchman," because of her excellent sea qualities and ability to always deliver her capacity loads of 425,000 board feet of lumber on time.

The *SS Oliver Olson*, a 300 foot vessel, Captain Carl Hubner, ran aground at the end of the south jetty on November 3, 1953, near the place where her running mate, the *SS Cynthia Olson,*[*] had grounded

*The *Cynthia Olson* referred to in this incident, is a different ship than the *Cynthia Olson* of World War II. That ship, laden with lumber, was the first American merchant ship sunk by the Japanese after Pearl Harbor–being only five minutes after the start of the bombing. *Cynthia Olson* was about mid-way between Seattle and Honolulu when she was spotted, attacked and sunk by Imperial submarine *I-26,* Commander Minori Yokota. *I-26* was on station looking for any aircraft carriers that might have escaped the bombings and headed for the mainland, plausibly, the Japanese believed would be Bremerton Navy Yard. We know more now there were no U.S. aircraft carriers in Pearl Harbor during the raid thus Cdr. Yokota's mission would have been without victory had he not spotted *Cynthia Olson*. His chief gunner, Saburo Hayashi, photographed *Cynthia Olsen* when the ship was on fire before it sank. The complete story, with Mr. Hayashi's photograph, is in *SILENT SIEGE: Japanese Attacks on North America in World War II*. See Bibliography.

The *SS Oliver Olson* ran into the end of the south jetty on November 3, 1953. After various methods to pull her off failed, the ship was left where it rested and the hull was filled with rock to form a part of the jetty. Today, on a quiet, non-stormy day, one might risk a hike to see part of the ship protruding from its rocky grave.

61

the previous year. The *Cynthia* was eventually pulled free, but the *Oliver Olson* was not as fortunate. The Coast Guard aided in the rescue of the crew of 29, but the vessel was impaled on the jetty. In an effort to refloat her by lightening the load, most of the ship's upperworks and fittings were taken off, but the hull remained fast. Because the ship rested on a jetty, and there was some concern for damage to the jetty the remains of the ship were abandoned where it lay. In a novel undertaking, the empty steel hull, dating from 1918, was filled with rock and became part of the jetty.

One would have wondered in the pioneer years before the advent of the jetties and the lighthouse how the Coquille could ever have been considered an entrance for seagoing ships. But no matter what the dangers, if there was an honest buck to be made, there were those who trusted their sixth senses. At low tide, only a few feet of water covered the bar and the shoals were constantly changing, often putting the channel in direct line with menacing rocks that awaited their victims.

Federal funds were slow in coming in those pre-century years and it was obvious, if the entrance was to be of any real commercial use, jetties were essential. Feeble efforts were begun on a south jetty in the 1880's. In 1887, the jetty running from the south point was out 130 yards from the high water mark to get ten feet of depth at the extremity. But shoaling had taken place and there was then only a depth of five feet. Then in December of that year, a heavy southeast gale carried away 100 feet of rock near the middle of the jetty.

The undependable nature of the bar was of little encouragement to the lumber towns up the river. Bandon was a small town of 20 houses and had one small sawmill producing 8,000 board feet of lumber a day. Randolph, five miles upriver, had fewer than ten houses. Parkersburg, seven miles up the Coquille River had a sawmill that turned out 30,000 board feet a day. Coquille City, 23 miles up river, was the population center with 500 inhabitants.

As far back as 1851, the steamer* *Sea Gull,* of Port Orford and

---

* *Sea Gull* carried the initial landing party to Port Orford in 1851 for the purpose of founding the town. Fearing an attack by Indians who did not like the white's coming ashore from the ship, the men coaxed the ship's captain to let them have the small cannon on the ship's deck for protection. Indeed, the attack occurred while the men were atop a small on-beach island (which was surrounded by water at high tide), trying to keep some distance between themselves and the Indians. When the attackers were only a few yards away, the cannon was fired that "caused vacancy in the crowd." For the complete account, see the book *Battle Rock, The Hero's Story; How A Small Canon Done Its Work—A Desperate Encounter Of Nine White Men With Three Hundred Indians At Port Orford. See:* Bibliography.

"Battle Rock" fame, made several futile efforts to cross the Coquille River bar, but with a mere three feet depth of water at the entrance, the ship's master was forced to make his landing off the beach amid the rocks by dropping her anchors fore and aft. It was not until 1880 that government engineers developed a plan to stabilize the river channel to a depth of ten feet. The improvements led to regular marine traffic between 1883-85. Two years later the depth, due to the single jetty was ten to 12 feet at high tide, but eventually shoaling would prompt the construction of the second jetty. Some 66 coasting vessels braved the bar during the three year period, one of the ships with a capacity of 150,000 board feet of lumber.

Despite cries for a lighthouse, it was yet another decade before it became a reality and even longer before the completion of the second jetty.

There was a celebration when the bright glow of the lighthouse first cast its beam over the river entrance in 1896. A new era had begun.

The Indian name for the Coquille was *Koh-Kel*. LaPerouse, the French navigator and explorer, passed by the river at sea in 1796. He didn't mention a river but he named the nearest cape, Toledo. Little did he know that settlers would one day claim this land as a vital part of Oregon Territory.

Perhaps the best known light keepers of the Coquille River lighthouse were Captain Wiren and Oscar Langlois, the latter being the keeper in charge at the closure of the facility in 1939, after which he retired from the Lighthouse Service. He finished two generations of lighthouse keeping, along with his father, James Langlois, the latter having been a long-time principal keeper at Cape Blanco.

The Coquille lighthouse made good use of its foghorn. In fiscal 1929, it blasted a total of 1,086 hours. The foggy season was often a deterrent to bar traffic.

In recent years, public minded citizens of Bandon outline the historic lighthouse in a myriad of colored Christmas lights annually and have further, in cooperation with government agencies, placed a solar light in the old lantern house.

"Arago #2—built in 1909. This was a picturesque lighthouse from every angle and was loved by artists and early day photographers.

Vintage picture of Cape Arago Lighthouse and keeper's dwelling made in early 1900's, shows foot bridge between mainland and erosion-prone islet. On short beach below lighthouse is U.S. Lifesaving Station. Arrow points to original 1866 lighthouse in background. It was altered in 1896 but had to be abandoned due to threat of falling into the sea. It was finally demolished in 1937.

Chapter 4
Cape Arago Lighthouse

On July 2, 1864, when the United States was embroiled in the infamous Civil War, an appropriation of $15,000 was made for a lighthouse to be established at what was then known as Cape Gregory. This was south of Coos Bay. The site was on a tiny islet just off the mainland and a little north of the cape. Due to the exhausted federal funds from war expenditures, and the fact that Congress was unfamiliar with Oregon's so-labeled "Indian Country," the monies provided only for a second class lighthouse.

```
CAPE ARAGO LIGHTHOUSE
Location:
43°20'5"N  124°22'5"W
Nearest town:  Charleston
Built: 1866, 1909, 1934
Type: White conical tower
Height above water: 100ft
Height above ground: 44ft
Light source: 1 electric
              incandescent lamp
Beam: White
Optics: 4th Order
Power: 270,000cp
Seen: 16 miles
Horn: Chime diaphram, air

NOTE: Classic data is from Light List 1934.
U.S. Dept. of Commerce, Lighthouse Service
and reflects details then in effect.
```

Erected under government contract, the modest lighthouse built at the very western exposed tip of the islet was a truncated skeleton iron tower only 25 feet above the ground, which put it 100 feet above sea level and open to the full fury of the elements. Its light was first exhibited on November 1, 1866. Seemingly insignificant in stature, it was a welcome sight to mariners who had long demanded a guiding beacon near the south entrance of Coos Bay. The sentinel was painted white and had a black, iron lantern house.

The islet on which it stood became affectionately known as "Lighthouse Island," an oddly shaped hunk of terra firma about 100 yards from the mainland. Though the light stood at the end of a narrow finger, the larger bulk of the islet was nearest the mainland

65

and was partially tree-covered. Composition of the soil was sandstone and clay which made it susceptible to erosion.

It was a treacherous area in high winds. One could easily be swept off his feet when walking on the narrow finger of land leading to the lighthouse. From the inception, there was always concern that erosion from high seas might some day cut the island in half. Hammered and battered by the elements, the lighthouse was 2.5 miles north of the cape for which it was named. It was 31 nautical miles north-northeast of Cape Blanco.

Serving a dual purpose, the lighthouse was not only to be a guiding light for ships approaching Coos Bay, but also for offshore marine traffic. Further, it was a tongue-in-cheek replacement for the defunct Umpqua River lighthouse built in 1857 but destroyed by erosion in 1861. That beacon was the first major aid to navigation in what is now the state of Oregon. The placement of a light just south of Coos Bay tended to attract shipping away from the Umpqua River.

In 1867, when Cape Arago Light was still known as Cape Gregory Light, the station tramway was partially washed away by heavy seas. In 1875, a November storm caused considerable damage to the outbuildings. The storm season was so prolonged that repairs had to be postponed until a tender could deliver building materials the following June.

The keepers had to reach the island in a small boat until 1876, when a footbridge was built to the mainland. This bridge greatly eased the movement of personnel and supplies. At the same time, the battered keeper's dwelling underwent overhaul. A concrete floor was laid in the cellar and the kitchen floor renewed. The whole building was repainted and reshingled. A new plank walk was laid from the dwelling to the tower and a new cistern was installed. In June of that year, a double-wick Funck lamp replaced the former Franklin lamp that lighted the lantern's fourth order lens.

More repairs were necessary the following year including an overhaul of the optic's revolving machinery. The station buildings were again repainted and the footbridge repaired from storm damage. but all of that was to little avail because in 1878, high seas generated in a November gale carried away the footbridge, the boat house and a portion of the tramway used for hoisting supplies from the beach to the lighthouse.

It was obvious that maintenance costs were excessive, but still the keepers took it all in stride and with the improving weather the station was put back in proper condition.

From the time it was first conceived, the footbridge was a

headache. The keepers referred to it as the "Bridge of Sighs." In 1879, during inclement December weather, huge masses of kelp collected around the footings and aided by the punishing seas and its sheer weight, five of the iron brace rods were broken. The dwelling roof had to be repaired again and the cistern recemented. The following January, a severe storm, logged by the head keeper as a "tornado," ripped into the station causing considerable damage. In June of the same year, Hains mineral oil lamps replaced the lard oil Funck lamp, affording a cleaner burning material for the beacon.

In 1883, about an acre of lighthouse real estate was cleared of timber and sown with seed grass for a pasture. An old shed used as a storehouse was replaced by a new 10 x 20 foot building. A 400 foot whitewashed picket fence was built. At the boat landing, davits and a winch were fitted for hoisting the station boat from the water.

In 1885, the boathouse was rebuilt at a higher elevation and much of the island plateau seeded with grass. The proverbial ailing footbridge, broken earlier, was temporarily rebuilt across the lowest part of the abyss allowing keepers to use it at stages below half tide, where before the station boat had to be utilized for all crossings. The tramway also, once again, had to be reconstructed.

Following the annual lighthouse reservation inspection in the 1890's, the district inspector concluded:

> The light-keepers dwelling at this station, erected in 1866, was poorly built and ill-adapted to accommodate the two keepers and their families; it is old and decayed and on the verge of collapse. If a fog signal is erected here, still another keeper will be added and his family will need quarters. It is estimated that a double set of quarters similar to those erected at Turn Point and Patos Island light stations can be built here for not exceeding $10,000.

By an act approved March 3, 1891, $50,000 was appropriated for the establishment of a light and fog signal at the mouth of the Coquille River, according to the inspector, and he was of the opinion that this estimate was excessive and could be done for less. He therefore recommended that the Light-House Board be authorized to expend not exceeding $15,500 from the appropriation for establishing a light and a fog signal at the mouth of the Coquille River, as well as erecting light keepers' dwellings and fog signal at Cape Arago lighthouse.

The resulting report of the Light-House Board read:

> The commerce of these waters would be greatly benefited
> by placing a first-class fog signal on the point of the
> island on which the lighthouse is located. It is estimated
> that this fog signal can be established for not exceeding
> $5,500. The light keepers dwelling at this station was
> erected in 1866. It was poorly built and ill-adapted to
> accommodate the two keepers, with their families. It is
> therefore recommended that the Light-House Board be
> authorized to expend not exceeding $15,500 from the
> appropriation for establishing a light and fog signal at the
> mouth of the Coquille River, Oregon, be used in the
> erection of light-keepers dwellings and a fog signal at
> Cape Arago Light Station.

Authority was granted by an Act approved August 18, 1894.
And so it was, Cape Arago station got a genuine face-lift. Even with
all this, some of the problems were not solved as part of the trouble
was on the mainland. The old boathouse built originally on a
sandspit, at the mouth of the South Slough, for the use of the keepers
in transit, had been undermined and destroyed by heavy swells and
currents. As work on the Coos Bay north jetty progressed, the wave
action on the spit ceased and the slough appeared stabilized. The
wagon road leading from South Slough, an arm of Coos Bay, was
repaired, grades and ditches were attended to, two bridges built plus
224 feet of corduroy road, and 600 feet of new road, was constructed
leading to the mainland-side opposite Lighthouse Island. Further, a
survey was made to build a new footbridge to connect with the
station.

Despite the big expenditure to accomplish all this, the District
Lighthouse Inspector, in the interim, came to the conclusion that the
light and fog signal were in great danger of being carried away by the
constant pounding of the seas that were undermining the extreme tip
of the island peninsula. He proclaimed:

> The encroachment of the sea had removed materials
> overlying the rock to such an extent as to endanger the
> foundations of the lighthouse.

Adding to the crisis, the Light-House Board had received
complaints from masters of merchant vessels that Arago's light and
fog signal were antiquated and inefficient. Most insisted that the lack

of a proper light and fog signal delayed ships and rendered the
navigation of those waters both difficult and dangerous. The
dissidents demanded a better light and fog signal.

The Board in turn insisted the existing navigation aids were
satisfactory, but openly admitted that they might not be too practical
at long distances. Some consideration was given to raising the height
of the squat tower but it never came to fruition. Navigators further
claimed the Daboll fog signal was practically useless saying it could
only be heard when a vessel was dangerously near the shore.

It was estimated that a new lighthouse and fog signal could be
built for $20,000.

In 1896, continued improvements were made at the station but
most in the form of maintenance. The 1896 *Pacific Coast Light List*
described the Cape Arago station:

> Skeleton tower, truncated, pyramid of eight sides, painted
> white, dome and lantern black, white dwelling, 1050 feet
> S.E. from tower.

With the addition of the innovations, the *Light List* the
following year described the station:

If it was standing today, unique Keeper's duplex at Cape Arago Lighthouse would probably be nominated for *National Register of Historic Places*. It was spacious and provided comfortable living.

> White, octagonal, pyramidal tower; dome and lantern black; attached to the rear of a white one-story fog signal building with black roof. White one-and-one-half story building double dwelling, with lead colored trimmings and brown roof, stands 1,050 feet from the tower and faces south.

It appeared that the major changes of renovating the lighthouse, dwelling, fog signal and appendages would have sufficed. But it was a fact that the little lighthouse was still only 25 feet above the ground and with all the monies expended in maintaining the facilities the problems refused to go away. Though attempts had been made to stabilize the end of the islet, the fear of erosion and collapse of the lighthouse was ever present. Still, the same fourth order light continued to shine each night, a fixed white light varied by a white flash every two minutes, and the Daboll trumpet blasted for five seconds, alternate silent intervals of eight and 42 seconds, when the fog rolled in.

This August 1968 aerial view demonstrates smallness of island. Fence made this place look good but was really a safety measure. Rectangular scar on ground near top is site of earlier keeper's dwelling.

Neither the Light-House Board nor merchant mariners were satisfied with what appeared to many to be a jinxed station.

After the turn of the century, a drive began for an entirely new lighthouse and fog signal. The elements were, to say the least, harsh on the station buildings. The dirge of the constant winds seemed to whisper, "tear that old lighthouse down." Still the keepers went about their duties as best they were able in the true tradition of the service.

They also had acquired neighbors on their little land mass. The U.S. Lifesaving Service had established a surfboat station in the lee of the island near the footbridge and the old boat house. A boat keeper was in charge and whenever a vessel was in distress, a volunteer crew was summoned to put out to sea. It was a dangerous place to launch a surfboat when the seas were boiling. But the code demanded: "They had to go out, but they didn't have to return." A similar motto was maintained when the Coast Guard took over the Lifesaving Service in 1915.

At long last, it was decided to abandon the aging lighthouse. Funds were allotted for a totally new structure at the opposite end of the islet well away from the crumbling finger of land that had housed the original station. There was a sigh of relief by the keepers when the decision was made by the Lighthouse Establishment. The constant worry of the eroding narrow strip of land collapsing would at last be over. Designed by Carl Leick, the new, frame lighthouse would dwarf the tower at the west end of the islet. It would be a sister lighthouse to the new one built at Ediz Hook (Port Angeles) on the Strait of Juan de Fuca.

Commissioned in 1908-09, the gleaming white structure was fitted with a new lens of the fourth order with three bullseyes, five panels, three with bullseyes and two drum panels set in a bath of mercury. It was manufactured by Barbier, Benard and Turenne, of Paris, France. In addition, the attached fog signal house was fitted with a first class compressed air siren, replacing the old Daboll. These improvements gained favor with the maritime fraternity and it appeared the jinxed islet had entered a trouble-free era. In order to prevent any chance of forest fires, the few trees still left standing on the isle were cut into firewood.

For the next quarter century, the new lighthouse, dwelling, oil houses and other outbuildings, performed well with considerably less repair than was demanded at the first lighthouse. The old lighthouse remained at the opposite end of the isle, forlorn and abandoned but still shouldering the worst the Pacific could throw it's way.

Ironically, the saga of lighthouses bearing the name Arago was not yet ended. Further erosion on the main part of the island demanded a third lighthouse. This time it would not be an iron, skeleton tower or a frame sentinel, but a modern building of reinforced concrete which would be one of the last such structures built on the Pacific Coast under the U.S. Lighthouse Service. Built in 1933-34 by local contractor Jake Hillstrom, the tower and connecting fog signal building would be staunch in every respect. The octagonal-shaped tower was 44 feet above the ground and well over 100 feet above the water. The lens was transferred from the former lighthouse. At the same time, the lighting apparatus was electrified and the old oil lamps retired.

The 1908 lighthouse was moved a short distance from its previous position, and as it was still well preserved, the tower section was removed and the remainder of the structure used as the keepers office. For a short while there were three lighthouses on the tiny islet. The original still stood much to the surprise of everyone who thought it would fall into the ocean decades earlier. In 1937, dynamite was purposely placed in its confines and it was blown to pieces leaving only a pile of bricks and some rusted metal. Some of the rubble remains at this writing.

The concrete lighthouse is still active today. The station was automated in the spring of 1966. Its light source is a 1,000 watt quartz iodine electric globe shining 24 hours a day through the fourth order classic lens. All of the generators and compressors that formerly operated the fog horns, have been removed from the foghorn house in favor of an automated electric impulse fog signal outside the building. The former keepers residence has been razed as have all other outside installations. The lighthouse and attached fog house is the only unit left standing on the islet. Despite its solidarity, it makes an impressive subject for camera or artist when viewed from the mainland.

The beacon is visible for more than 20 miles at sea, rated at 270,000 candlepower. Radio innovations elsewhere have reduced the hours of activity for the foghorn from April through October. There is a radio beacon connected within the lighthouse which is in constant operation. No one lives on the island anymore but a gate blocks trespass across the footbridge. The bridge, to this day, is a chore to maintain.

Coast Guard units at Charleston, home of the ANT (Aids to Navigation Team) monitor the station and its environs by remote electronic surveillance 24 hours a day. When on-site, human intervention is required, computer analysis can not only identify the problems, but estimate the manpower required to affect the solution, advise of any special tools likely to be needed, and recommend what spare parts to bring along. Its almost like the lighthouse is operated by the hands of ghosts. What a change from the yesteryears!

Part of the old lighthouse reservation on the mainland opposite the isle, off limits to the public, is connected with an ancient Indian burial ground. It was sacred to the local tribes before the white invasion. It is still occasionally used to this day. Instead of the old practices of canoe burials, old human remains have been interred in traditional graves but this practice, in turn, has given way to casting the ashes of the dead into the sea from the graveyard cliff.

For many years, the cemetery was desecrated by thoughtless pioneers much to the chagrin of the Native Americans. The descendants of the early Indians have been very protective of the site.

"Arago #3—built in 1934. Utility building, on the brink, was dismantled by the Coast Guard in mid-1980's before it fell into the sea.

With Lighthouse Island, and the land directly opposite the isle, the gravesite has been kept free of public trespass except by special permission of the Coast Guard.

Another much debated matter faced the Coast Guard. Mrs. Margaret F. Brainard, in 1950, requested that her late husband Henry Millon Brainard, a former surfman with the Coast Guard, be eulogized with a monument on what is called Lighthouse Point. This is on the mainland side opposite the isle, near the footbridge. Brainard, though not on duty at the time of his drowning off Arago Point in 1947, served the Coast Guard in the late 1920's. His part Indian father was drowned in almost the same place years earlier and his son had requested that at his death, his ashes be spread at sea in the same area off Arago Point. After his body was recovered that request was carried out.

Enter Mrs. Brainard. She was determined that a marker be placed on mainland Coast Guard property. Stacks of correspondence followed even reaching Washington D.C. and Congress for granting of the unprecedented request. Despite numerous rejections that such practices were not acceptable, the woman persisted. She eventually gained the permission she wanted to place the plaque on government property.

Looking down on Lighthouse Island from a Coast Guard helicopter is a fascinating sight. It is a battleground of nature, beautiful to look at but presenting a pin-cushion of obstacles all about the tiny bit of land. Perhaps the most feared by mariners is Baltimore Rock, a half mile northwest of the isle. This is an inundated razor-sharp barrier that bears the name of an ill-fated sailing schooner that was snatched by the reef's fangs and destroyed in 1860. During the U.S. Coast Survey of 1861, the forepart of the ill-fated vessel broke the surface in grim warning to other ships. Her stern half was swept up on the beach westward of Tunnel Point. In 1873, a steamer struck the barrier and narrowly escaped sinking after backing off and making for port with deep water in her bilges.

Shipwrecks have been frequent in and around the entrance to Coos Bay through the years. Without doubt, the most disastrous was that of the iron-hulled 1045 ton, 220 foot steamship *Czarina*. She had been built in England in 1883. Not only was it tragic, but the drama involved numerous personalities and a large share of frustration over the inability of the surfmen to save the victims. Time and again the life-saving crew were repelled by the raging surf.

Crowds gathered on the storm-swept beach watching the wretched men on the *Czarina* clinging desperately to the shrouds of the sinking vessel awaiting rescue that never came.

Cape Arago lighthouse was not involved in the *Czarina* tragedy, though the ship was familiar to the keepers, having often passed by the sentinel. The ill-fated freighter was outbound from Marshfield for San Francisco on January 12, 1910. She was carrying a cargo of coal and lumber valued at $100,000. Owned by the Southern Pacific Company of San Francisco, the ship was in command of Captain Charles Duggan with a 23 man crew. Nobody realized that on that gloomy winter day the steamer would be making her final voyage, nor that of all those on board only the first engineer, Harry Kintzel, would survive the harrowing hours that were to follow.

Departing port at 11:15 in the morning, the *Czarina* approached the bar which was white with froth from the snarling swells. From the watch tower of the surfboat station on the inner bay shore of the north spit, the lookout had his eyes riveted on the vessel wondering why she would risk the bar crossing under such adverse conditions.

Voluminous seas soon placed the ship in jeopardy. Course was altered a few points northward and then again changed, resulting in a vice-like position. With a sickening thud her keel hit the reef near the south spit. Green, hissing seas swept her entire length. Sensing his desperate position, the captain blasted the ship's whistle repeatedly, the shrill sound carried on the wings of the strong winds to the ears of those at the Lifesaving station. Action was immediate. Captain W. A. Magee rounded up his crew to launch the surfboat. Contact was established with the bar tug *Astoria* to assist. By the time the rescue squad reached the scene, the *Czarina* had broken her grip on the rocks and drifted across the bar and into the outer breakers northward of the bar entrance.

By this time, the entrance was so rough that the skipper of the *Astoria* deemed it inadvisable to attempt crossing the bar because of the danger to his own vessel and to the fact that a steam schooner, bar-bound on the outside, was standing by the stricken vessel, but well offshore. The situation remained tenuous all through the night. By the pale light of dawn, the ship had foundered with only her masts and funnel protruding above the irascible surf. The entire crew of *Czarina,* and one passenger, were desperately clinging to the rigging. They were blue with cold and praying for help to come. From the rigging they looked down on the inundated deck of the wreck where the cascading breakers had ripped out the davits, destroyed the lifeboats and turned everything into a battering ram of wreckage.

The lumber cargo had parted the gripes and was tossed about like a mass of ten-pins. It was a scene of devastation. The seas gradually tore the ship to pieces. Pinned to the bottom by the sheer weight of her flooded engine and cargo holds, the main engine and boilers were like handcuffs. Hung up on a perch several hundred yards off the beach, the *Czarina's* anchor had gripped the bottom and held fast as the awful seas continued to cream the decks with venomous fury.

While the surfmen waited on the beach with their equipment at the ready-the surfboat, line throwing gun and breeches buoy-they were helpless to act despite agitation and actual threats by onlookers. Several attempts were made to launch the boat but each time the breakers repelled the effort and Captain Clarence W. Boice refused to further risk the lives of his crew.

The steam schooner, *Nan Smith,* standing by, made a brave attempt to enter the dangerous waters but was repelled before getting anywhere near the wreck without herself becoming a casualty.

One by one the exhausted victims dropped from the rigging and were swallowed by the churning seas. Among them was First Engineer Kintzel who was bashed around among the wreckage until his strength gave out. For two hours he endured in his soggy lifejacket when suddenly a huge swell swept him back onto the wreck.

With feeble strength, he managed to lash himself to a plank that was eventually swept toward the beach. Surfmen risked their lives by venturing into the wild surf and pulling the survivor to safety. That he recovered from the experience was indeed a miracle, being the lone survivor of *Czarina*.

Boice, who had proven himself a brave rescuer, was now being labeled a coward by some of the onlookers on the beach. But he stuck to his decision not to launch out again until the surf moderated. The surf didn't moderate. Every minute was precious. In a vane attempt, the Lyle gun was fired toward the wreck with a six ounce charge of powder, and though it was fitted with 700 yards of line, it fell 200 yards short of its target. A second try also fell way short after emptying the faking box. By now, the beach was littered with lumber.

As another night came on, fires were built on the beach in case any survivors remained on the wreck. But the seas had already snapped the masts, toppled the stack and leveled virtually everything remaining above the surf. Though there were some reports of seeing possible survivors among the wreckage, by 10 A.M. all hope had been abandoned for saving any others. The seas remained treacherous and high.

A lengthy hearing followed the tragedy. Boice was blamed for ineffective rescue efforts, the charges coming from several sources. He was labeled a coward. His resignation as keeper of the Coos Bay Lifesaving Station was accepted. Later, he was restored to a lesser role back at the Coquille River Station from which he had first come.

Many coasting vessels came to grief in the Coos Bay area including the steam schooner *Julia H. Ray* on January 26, 1889; the whaleback steamer *Charles W. Wetmore*, September 8, 1892; steamer *Arago*, October 20, 1896 with a loss of 13 lives; ocean barge *Chinook* loaded with 4,000 pounds of dynamite in April 1907; four-masted schooner *Marconi*, March 23, 1909; gas schooner *Osprey*, November 1912; passenger steamer *Santa Clara* under Captain August Lofstedt with a loss of 16 lives, November 2, 1915. But there were more.

There was the fire that swept the sleek passenger liner *Congress* offshore in 1916; the wreck of the steamer *Columbia* in 1924; sinking of the U.S. Corps of Engineers hopper dredge *Wm. T. Rossell* in 1957, the loss of the *MS Alaska Cedar* in 1962. And there were many more.

All the while, Cape Arago Light beamed its warning and sounded its foghorn in an effort to hold down the number of wrecks at the marine crossroads of the south central Oregon coast.

South jetty, Coquille River and homeward-bound fishing boat in from the Pacific Ocean, viewed from Coquille River Lighthouse. Rick Webber, a visitor from New Jersey said, "Here I get to look at a 'real' ocean."

Among the best known and most popular keepers of the Cape Arago Light Station were Captain Frederick Amundsen and Captain William Denning. Captain Denning was in the Lighthouse Service from 1903-1936 serving both at Arago and Heceta lighthouses.

It was a sad day for fanciers of lighthouses when the Cape Arago station succumbed to automation on April 15, 1966.

Chapter 5
Umpqua River Lighthouse

There were high hopes, in the early years, that the Umpqua River would be the major port of entry in the Pacific Northwest. The town of Scottsburg, about 30 miles up the river was developing rapidly and already served as a port of call. With all this going, it was no mistake that the mouth of the Umpqua River was chosen as the site for one of the first lighthouses built in Oregon and this, two years before Oregon became a state.

UMPQUA RIVER LIGHTHOUSE
Location:
43°40'N 124°12'W
Nearest town: Winchester Bay
Built: 1894
Type: White conical tower
Height above water: 165ft
Height above ground: 65ft
Light source: Incandescent
    oil vapor
Beam: White and red
Optics: 1st Order
Power: 29,000cp
Seen: 19 miles

NOTE: Classic data is from *Light List* 1934.
U.S. Dept. of Commerce, Lighthouse Service
and reflects details then in effect.

Settlements had sprung up along the river banks where giant stands of timber waited to be cut for the booming San Francisco market. Pristine and beautiful, that picturesque country had long been a favorite fishing and hunting ground for the coastal Indians who had remained undisturbed in their surroundings for centuries.

Following the California goldrush, ambitious pioneers came northward to search out lumber resources. The Umpqua proved a treasure trove of green gold. The mouth of the river was relatively wide and deep, but the river bar was rather narrow and always a concern for the coastal sailing schooner skippers in transit.

The first appropriation for the Umpqua River Light Station was made on March 3, 1851 when a sum of $15,000 was set aside by Congress for a lighthouse and fog signal. On April 23, 1852, J.

Umpqua River Lighthouse is one of the few lights along the Pacific Coast that emits both white and red flashes.

Butterfield, Commissioner of the General Land Office in Washington D.C., wrote a letter to Jno. B. Preston, Surveyor General, in Oregon City. He was transmitting a copy of a communication from the Secretary of the Treasury to the Secretary of the Interior dated October 1, 1851. This had to do with sites designated for lighthouses on the Pacific Northwest coast at Cape Flattery, New Dungeness, Cape Disappointment and Umpqua River.

Title paper for the Umpqua Lighthouse Reservation at the mouth of the river contained 33 acres and was issued October 1, 1851. On August 3, 1854, an additional $10,000 was appropriated for the proposed station. Another sum of $19,942 was allotted in 1856, then $5,055 more in 1857, and a balance of $2.93 carried to the lighthouse surplus fund of the Treasury.

The District Inspector for lighthouses was instructed by the Lighthouse Board to lose no time in commencing the erection of the Umpqua River lighthouse. The instructions read in part:

> ...and it is expected, from the urgent instructions from this office, and the zeal and energy of the officer-in-charge, that it will be built as soon as the necessary materials can be collected at the site. The illuminating apparatus and lantern for Umpqua was shipped to the Pacific Coast in July last [1855].

The 1857 report of the Light-House Board stated, "the lighthouse at the mouth of the Umpqua has been built, and the light will be exhibited early in the present fall." On December 27, 1859, the year Oregon became a state, President Buchanan signed the order withdrawing the lighthouse site and surrounding property from sale.

Construction was difficult in that sparsely populated corner of the world. Bricks and lime came by sea but timber was from the immediate area. Regrettably, the site chosen for the lighthouse at the river's south entrance, was on sand near the river bank. Sand is no material upon which a lighthouse should be erected. That engineering error spelled the doom of the lighthouse after only four years of service.

During a severe gale on February 8, 1861, the foundation was undermined and partially washed away to such an extent as to cause grave concern. There was so much worry that the keepers feared the entire structure would collapse, possibly with them in it. Inspection of the quarters supported their fears and abandonment of the facility was promptly ordered.

The lighting apparatus was successfully removed and while laborers were at work dismantling the iron lantern house, the tower began swaying violently and the men scrambled for their lives. Minutes later the tower came crashing down. The entrance to the Umpqua River was left without a lighthouse. Despite pleas for the rebuilding of the beacon, three decades would pass with no lighthouse and nothing more than a few spar buoys marking the channel into the river. Shipwreck was frequent and maritime commerce kept away from the river when an alternate port was available.

Early Oregon preachers often used a passage from the Bible as an illustration for the fall of a lighthouse compared with a human life.

> And the rains descended and the floods came, and
> the winds blew and beat upon the house; and it fell: and
> great was the fall of it.
>
> —Matthew 7:27

The Light-House Board, with its questioned vision, announced in its 1864 Report that the best interests of commerce would be served by establishing a new light at Cape Arago, instead of re-erecting the one at Umpqua River. That did not set well with the settlers along the river. Funds were not easy to come by in those years for government projects on the Pacific Coast. As mentioned in the previous chapter, Cape Arago lighthouse was not considered a first-class station.

As business increased on the Umpqua River, the community of Gardiner became a beehive of activity. Appeals from Gardiner, and elsewhere, for a new lighthouse, echoed louder but continued to fall on deaf ears. Finally, by an act of Congress on October 2, 1888, a $50,000 appropriation was made for the purchase of a new site and the construction of a light station on the headlands above the mouth of the Umpqua. This was sufficiently inland to prevent a repetition of the grievous fate of the pioneer beacon.

Evidently the lesson was well learned as the station tower was placed farther back from the river and ocean than any other lighthouse built on Oregon's seacoast.

A thorough survey of the land was made in 1890, at which time the drawings and specifications for the buildings were in an advanced state of preparation. At this time it was announced that a sister lighthouse would be built at Heceta Head during the same period.

Bids were received April 21, 1891, for construction of the keepers dwellings, barn, oil houses, cistern, tower and metal work. A contract for $5,020, lowest bid for the metal work was accepted,

In the early days, one could call the Umpqua Lighthouse
Reservation a community of its own. Although the original
keepers' dwellings are gone in this view, the coziness is apparent with placement of dependent's duplexes and utility
buildings close to the lighthouse.

but the aggregate of the lowest bids for the remaining structures
exceeded the available monies. New bids had to be called. The metal
work was completed March 21, 1892, and was transported to the
mouth of the Umpqua River by the Lighthouse Tender *Manzanita*.
The glass for the lantern house was also delivered by sea.

In the interim, with slight modifications, bids for the remaining
projects were received. Lowest for the tower at $12,000 was accepted
in October 1891. By the end of fiscal year ending June 30, 1892, the
work was progressing, the contractor having had all his material on
hand. The stone was cut and concrete and rubble foundation was laid.

About that same time, a bid of $17,879 was accepted for the
dwellings and other outbuildings. Unfortunately, that contractor later
notified the government he would be unable to go on with the work.
The bondsmen were apprised of the situation but they declined to have
anything to do with the matter on the grounds that shortly after the
contract was made, they (the bondsmen) had served notice of their
wish to withdraw from the bond.

Uncle Sam, in turn, notified them that they would be responsible
for all damages and loss resulting from the failure of the contractor to
finish the contract. As a result, bids were solicited once again and the

Umpqua River Lighthouse during construction in early 1890's. This tower is made of brick then finished with a cement-plaster overlay. It replaced an earlier lighthouse that collapsed due to coastal erosion three decades earlier.

lowest came in at $20,250. It was accepted.

The contractor for the erection of the tower completed his work on August 30, 1892. The builder of the dwellings and other outbuildings finished his work on January 14, 1893. When installation of the lighting apparatus was underway a disappointing discovery was made. The pedestal which was to support the lens was not the proper height by more than 15 inches. This presented a delay until the wrong could be rectified.

Overcost for the construction of the station ran $2,400. Also, a temporary watchman at the facility had not been paid. Meanwhile, the Attorney General was still trying to collect $2,371 from the delinquent bondsmen to make these final payments. The Light-House

Board was finally forced to request Congress to cough up an additional sum to remedy this nagging embarrassment.

The special appropriation for $2,371 was received on August 18, 1894 and shortly, the keepers arrived to man the station. The delayed "light up" heralded in the new year as the fixture was placed in operation December 31, 1894. The special oil lamps sent out brilliant shafts of light through the huge two-ton prismatic First-Order Fresnel lens.

Some final details at the station involved the finishing touches on the galvanized oil houses and installation of furnaces for heating the dwellings, as well as erecting station fences.

In the interim, the court case of the *United States vs. Contractors Smith & Burton,* and their bondsmen, continued. The judgment for the sum of $4,000 the full amount of the bond remained unsatisfied. On January 3, 1898, an offer of Smith & Burton, prompted the Treasury Department, to accept $628, and costs, in all $690 in settlement of the judgment of $4000.

In 1906, a new 1,600 foot road was built from the station to the main boat landing on the beach, making access to the lighthouse (located three-quarters of a mile south of the mouth of the river) much easier. The construction had been done under the eagle eye of Major James C. Post of the U.S. Army Corps of Engineers, 13th District, Portland. The reservation encompassed some 558 acres. The main supply line was by small steamer from Gardiner or by wagon along the beach from Coos Bay or by one of the visiting lighthouse tenders.

The tower was of brick with a work room attached. The focal plane of the light was 165 feet above sea level and 59 feet above the ground—65 feet to the top of the dome. The tower wall, at its base, was five feet thick, including the air space between the double walls, and 21 inches thick at the parapet.

Scintillating in its brilliance, the Parisian manufactured lens was more than 72-inches in diameter inside the glass, with 16 sides, prisms, hand ground and polished. Glass panes in the lantern house were 5/16th of an inch thick. The lantern house and dome were of iron construction. A lightning rod was a brass spindle with a platinum point. The watch room was occupied by the pedestal of the lens and revolving apparatus. The characteristic of the light was white and red alternating flashes. Lens parts consisted of eight lower panels, 24 middle panels and eight upper panels. The revolving machinery was actuated by clockwork and weights which dropped through the trunk of the tower for 34 feet before rewinding was required. The light was produced by a Funck mineral oil float lamp and oil storage houses were located 28 feet in the rear of the workroom.

The original keepers dwellings were of frame construction each with six rooms. The cistern had a 10,000 gallon capacity. It was built of brick, then cemented inside and out.

Duty at the new Umpqua Light Station was considered "desired duty" by those Civil Service employees who were assigned there. It was nestled among beautiful surroundings and best of all, had no fog signal to tend or to disturb sleep. Many happy keepers and their families found contentment on that reservation.

On August 20, 1935, four years before the U.S. Coast Guard took over the Lighthouse Service, 110 acres of the lighthouse reservation were turned over to the State of Oregon under revocable license to be used for a public park. There was also a proposal to sell 110 acres to private parties, but that proposal met with firm objections of the Assistant Secretary of Commerce, on September 4, 1936, on the grounds that adequate protection of the station's water supply and protection from fire was dependent on existing supervision by the Oregon State Park authorities. On May 21, 1938, the Director of Procurement reserved part of that 110 acres for the Treasury Department for use by the U.S. Coast Guard.

The State of Oregon purchased the land for park purposes for a mere $1,000. Through the years Umpqua Lighthouse State Park has been one of the most attractive tourist meccas on the coast. It is one of the most visited coastal parks and is maintained in conjunction with the neighboring Coast Guard property.

Douglas County has taken over one of the former Coast Guard buildings for a museum. The greatest attraction however, continues to be the original first order lens in the lantern of the lighthouse, which still reflects and refracts its beauty, with some 1,000 prisms. It was manufactured by Barbier & Cie of Paris in 1890 and revolves on Adiprene coated brass chariot wheels powered, at this writing, by a 120 volt AC electric motor and gear assembly.

The lens has seen a century of service but of course it is no longer lit with oil lamps. And the clockwork and weights were long ago removed. The lighthouse was automated in the 1960's but is watched over by service personnel connected with the Coast Guard Station at nearby Winchester Bay and the Aids to Navigation team headquartered at Charleston on Coos Bay. Rotating four times each minute, the lens is illuminated by a 1,000 watt quartz iodine globe and, every 15 seconds, produces a characteristic of two white flashes at 400,000 candlepower and one red flash at 200,000 candlepower

The once dangerous Umpqua River bar has been tamed by
the construction of three jetties at the river's mouth. Both
lighthouse (arrow) and jetties are significant aids to navigation at this harbor entrance.

which are visible about 20 miles seaward.

In recent years, the Coast Guard considered removing the huge
classic lens and replacing it with a more economical aero marine
(DCB) type optic, similar to those placed in many lighthouses across
the country. When word leaked out of the plan, the citizens of near
by Reedsport, Winchester Bay and Gardiner rose up en masse and
demanded that the classic fixture remain.

Leaders of the group enlisted the assistance of congressmen and
senators. The Coast Guard finally relented and agreed to retain the
lens despite the fact that the 24 hour-a-day usage had caused frequent
breakdowns by the worn down brass chariot wheels. Under the old
Lighthouse Service, the light only operated from an hour before
sunset till an hour after sunrise. When not operating, a curtain was
wrapped around the optic to protect it from sun rays. When
automation came, with no attendants on duty, the Coast Guard elected
to operate its lights 24 hours a day with a standby light, usually on
the gallery of the lighthouse, in case of failure by the main beacon.

The local communities were justly proud of their victorious
campaign to retain the classic fixture and celebrated the occasion with
a special ceremony. Observing the situation at this writing, it appears
the historic optic will remain a permanent fixture.

Though many of the old station outbuildings, including the
original keepers dwellings were long ago razed (1950's), the tower
and work room remain the same as when originally built. The
lighthouse was placed on the *National Register of Historic Places* in

1978, but at this writing the tower is only open to the public on special occasions, though that is subject to change.

On visiting Umpqua Lighthouse State Park today, it is hard to imagine that Indians once roamed that acreage for hundreds of years. In fact, when the original ill-starred Umpqua lighthouse was under construction on the sand, curious Indians came around to "check it out," some showing mild hostility over the intrusion into "their" domain. A few of their number agitated the white construction workers by stealing tools and supplies. Skirmishes occasionally broke out during the construction period. Had it not been for nearby Fort Umpqua, and the superior weaponry of the new settlers, the Indians might have tried to reclaim their lands despite the earlier treaties which most of the Indians didn't really understand.

It was the numerous wrecks and strandings on the Umpqua bar that spawned demands for a lighthouse. It was no secret that the losses were far greater during the periods when no beacon was in operation. During 1850-55 there were frequent losses. The sailing vessels *Bostonian,* on October 1, 1850; *Caleb Curtis,* 1850; *Almira,* January 9, 1852; *Nassau,* July 22, 1852; *Achilles,* 1852, *Roanoke,* February 2, 1853; *Oregon,* 1854; *Loo Choo,* July 15, 1856 were all casualties in the years just before the lighthouse was built. The steamer *Bully Washington* was brought to the Umpqua River by Captain Sylvester Hinsdale to serve between Winchester Bay and Scottsburg in 1853. Her boilers blew up just off Scottsburg on December 18, 1857, the same year the pioneer lighthouse went into service. Though that wreck had nothing to do with the lighthouse, it did slow river traffic. Her remains were visible in the river just below the Scottsburg Bridge right up until recent times.

One of the first known shipwrecks in Oregon involved the British sailing schooner *Sea Otter* of 170 tons. She is alleged to have wrecked just south of the mouth of the Umpqua, August 22, 1808, all but three of her crew perishing. What next happened seems more as folklore. The story goes that the survivors hiked over half the continent to reach the Red River in Louisiana Territory. If true, this was an incredible journey just three years after the Lewis & Clark expedition returned from the mouth of the Columbia River.

After the lighthouse was undermined and collapsed in 1861, shipwrecks increased. The sailing vessel *Ork* was lost November 4, 1864; steamer *Enterprise,* February 20, 1873; sailing vessels, *Meldon,* March 16, 1873; *Bobolink,* October 1873; *Florence,* October 9, 1875; *Sparrow,* December 4, 1875. The SS *Tacoma* hit a reef four miles north of the bar, January 29, 1883 and ten men were swept to their deaths. As the ship broke up and the survivors struggled ashore, they were assisted by settlers from Gardiner.

Before the new lighthouse was completed, the steam tug *Fearless* crossed out over the bar and suddenly disappeared after being last sighted just north of the entrance. Three whistle blasts were the only indication of trouble until her pilot house drifted up river with the tide. Seven crewmen drowned in that tragedy.

The lighthouse keepers and their families were eye witnesses to the first major shipwreck to occur after the new lighthouse went into operation in 1894. The victim was the steam schooner *Bandorille* that had been serving dogholes along the Pacific Coast for six years. It was on November 21, 1895, that Captain J. J. Winant attempted to take her outbound across a churning Umpqua bar with a partial cargo of freight for Florence, on the Siuslaw River. The vessel safely passed the first line of breakers but was then hit by two "widow makers." These crashing waves disabled her steering abilities by dislodging her rudder. While trying to make emergency repairs, Captain Winant was swept overboard. The *Bandorille* healed into the surf just south of the entrance and stranded on the shoals 800 feet offshore. The lifesaving crew responded and was successful in rescuing the remaining ten crewmen by breeches buoy. The captain's body was also recovered but artificial respiration failed to revive him. The vessel broke up within days under the constant battering of King Neptune.

The *SS Truckee*, stranded on the north spit of the Umpqua November 18, 1897. Following that wreck, the schooner *Alpha* was lost on February 3, 1907, but after that, there was a long period when no major tragedies occurred. The coastal lumber barge *Washtucna* met her demise August 17, 1922 and two years later a most unusual twin-shipwreck occurred on the same day. The lumber steam schooners *G.C. Lindauer* and the *Admiral Nicholson* were both outbound when they were swept ashore on May 16, 1924. Though the crews of both ships were rescued, the beaches were littered with lumber washed from their holds as the two ships broke up. Locals had a bonanza and much of the salvaged timber was used to build trestles for the north jetty which was under construction at the time. The *Lindauer*, a 23 year old coaster, was bound for San Francisco from Reedsport when she got into trouble. The steel-hulled *Admiral Nicholson* attempted to tow her free but succeeded in grounding herself at almost the same spot. The *Lindauer* was soon broken up but the stouter *Nicholson* was eventually salvaged by the C. K. West Company. Because the shipping market was too low to warrant

Umpqua River Lighthouse

reconstruction, she was sold for scrap.

These were among the last of the coastwise lumber fleet to meet disaster in the Umpqua region. A general decline of coastwise shipping started in the late 1920's and continued down to a mere trickle after World War II. Oregon's coastal lumber ports, once busy at all hours of the day loading the fleet of steam schooners, underwent a painful and slow death as truck transport took over the shipping business.

Deep-sea shipping also slowed, thus traditional lighthouses once so important, played a lesser role because there were fewer ships and those stood further out to sea with the advent of RADAR and LORAN. For the most part, assistance cases for the Coast Guard stations now involve mostly fishing vessels. There has never been a lack of wrecks in that category despite the many navigational innovations. It is also the fishing fleets that insist in the continuing operation of the lighthouses. Never a year passes without the Umpqua River Coast Guard Station (based at Winchester Bay) receiving numerous calls for help from the fishermen home ported there.

Scottsburg, the earliest settlement on the Umpqua River, once showed promise of becoming a really big town but the years have reduced it to only a small whistle stop. Gardiner, the major seaport in the early days, still has an historic flavor but its docks have not catered to deep-sea ships for many decades. The huge pulp mill there, the principal industry with its accompanying aroma has changed owners several times in recent years, and its continued operation is an open question. Reedsport is now the thriving metropolis and the population hub of the lower Umpqua.

Jetties were absolutely necessary to control the shifting shoals at the narrow Umpqua entrance. Many a navigator has given thanks for the lighthouse, the jetties, and to the Coast Guard Search and Rescue unit at Winchester Bay.

The only black mark standing against the rescue units goes back to 1883 after the wreck of the steam collier *Tacoma*. The vessel was bound for San Francisco from Puget Sound with 3,500 tons of coal in her holds. A faulty compass and a thick fog were responsible for an erroneous course when the ship crunched onto a reef four miles north of the Umpqua River. Captain George D. Koatz, and a few seamen, managed to launch a lifeboat and row to shore for help. As a result, three tugboats were summoned to the scene but by the time they got there, the seas had risen to great heights and the tugs were unable to approach the vessel.

The lifesaving crew was on the beach opposite the *Tacoma* but the keeper of the surfboat (the man in charge), refused to risk the lives of his men. Perhaps more so, he feared for his own life. In the mounting surf he seemed frozen in his tracks. In spite of facing charges of cowardice right on the beach, he refused to reconsider. In desperation, a volunteer group was organized and heroically braved the angry surf and succeeded in rescuing 18 men on the collier.

Those waiting on the battered steamer were in such a state of panic by the time the surfboat arrived, Chief Engineer Grant was forced to threaten them with a pistol to maintain order. After the rescue boat cleared the hulk with as many survivors as it could handle without swamping, the situation on the *Tacoma* worsened. The seas swept the ship with vengeance. One battered lifeboat remained. With herculean strength, fearing the surfboat would never be able to return for them, the remaining men managed to lower the boat into the raging water. It promptly capsized and all ten souls, including Chief Engineer Grant were drowned.

As a result of the failure of the keeper of the surfboat to respond, he was reprimanded and dismissed from the United States Lifesaving Service for cowardice and dereliction of duty.

Undoubtedly many similar tragedies like that of the *Tacoma* were averted by the presence of the lighthouse. But circumstances have occurred through human or mechanical error beyond the help of any aid to navigation.

Not many times has the Umpqua light gone out except for the period between the first and second lighthouses. However, on February 24, 1958, the Fresnel was darkened when an overheated stove in the workroom caused a fire inside the tower.

Again in November 1983, due to trouble in the rotating mechanism, a $7,000 repair job was undertaken, but it failed to fix the difficulty. An auxiliary light, mounted on the gallery (catwalk) was hooked up as an emergency measure. The Coast Guard wanted to replace the classic lens and its troublesome mechanism as earlier mentioned, but when forced to reconsider, a local contract was let and The Brass Connection, a firm in Reedsport won the $7,000 contract to install stainless steel bands for the guide rings, and to fit wheels for the load-bearing track of the carriage.

Additionally, a $1,797 contract was awarded to Molded Chemical Products of Kirkland, Washington. That firm was to manufacture the wheels for the load-bearing tracks and guide wheels. Adiprene, a clear, hard rubber-like substance, was applied to extend the life of the old wheels while the new ones were made. On January 14, 1985, after being dark for over a year, the eight foot high lens was once more in operation.

Located a short distance from Highway 101, south of Winchester Bay, the lighthouse overlooks the mouth of the Umpqua River and the Oregon Dunes National Recreation Area. It has become both a landmark and seamark to all those who pass by. And for those camping in the state park and seeing the track of red and white swaths of light blazing the night sky, it's a great time to spin yarns of the sea.

*　　　*　　　*

In the late summer of 1994, lighthouse lovers from far and wide gathered to mark the 100th Anniversary of Umpqua Lighthouse.

Though the official lighting was in December of 1894, summer weather made for a better celebration. The folks of Reedsport, Gardiner, Winchester Bay and environs have always held their lighthouse" in high esteem.

Chapter 6
Heceta Head Lighthouse

Since it was first discovered, navigators have always given Heceta Head a wide berth for there are treacherous fangs of basalt ready to pierce the hull of any ship unfortunate enough to get caught. Perhaps that is why the classic lens in the lantern house atop the tower produces the most powerful marine light on the Oregon Coast. This is a light that has become famous for its scintillating beauty.

HECETA HEAD LIGHTHOUSE
Location:
44°8'N 124°8'W
Nearest town: Florence
Built: 1894
Type: White conical tower
Height above water: 205ft
Height above ground: 56ft
Light source: Incandescent oil lamp
Beam: White
Optics: 1st Order
Power: 170,000cp
Seen: 21 miles

NOTE: Classic data is from *Light List 1934*.
U.S. Dept. of Commerce, Lighthouse Service
and reflects details then in effect.

Without doubt, the natural setting where stands this lighthouse is one of the most awe-inspiring to be found anywhere in the world. There are probably multi-millions of snapshots in the books of tourists and locals that have captured the fantastic setting. Many of these pictures have been snapped from Sea Lion Caves, a mile southward, or from Devils Elbow State Park. Artists also find this light the ultimate subject for the brush.

Much attention is also focused on what is today called "Heceta House," the former vintage keepers dwelling now utilized by Lane Community College but under ownership of the U.S. Forest Service.

The Coast Guard is only concerned with the lighthouse as an active aid to navigation. The surrounding area to the south is part of a popular state park. In 1978, the lighthouse, dwelling, garages and

oil houses were all placed on the *National Register of Historic Places*. History abounds at Heceta Head. The promontory carries the name of Don Bruno de Heceta, Portuguese explorer and navigator in the service of Spain. (A Spanish pronunciation would be *Hay-Cee-tuh* but this seems to have been corrupted to *Heck-kah-tuh*.) He set forth from San Blas, in Mexico, to explore the Northwest Coast in 1775, and carried a 45 man crew and provisions for a year. It was intended as a secret voyage with calls at San Diego and Monterey missions and then northward to the 65th parallel. He had orders to land often, take possession, erect a cross and plant a bottle containing a record of the act of possession.

Rough seas, contrary weather and a crew suffering from scurvy, prompted Heceta's vessel, the *Santiago,* to fall short of her mark. His counterpart Quadra, in the small consort *Sonora,* got separated from the flagship. The *Sonora* proceeded as far as Sitka, but Heceta's compassion for his miserable crew made him come about, but not until after he found the location of the Columbia River. Unfortunately, he did not enter the river. He also allegedly sighted the headland that bears his name, remarking as he sailed by, "the water was shallow some distance offshore."

When the U.S. Coast Survey sounded the area in 1862, it sustained Heceta's findings. George Davidson, author of the *Pacific Coast Pilot,* officially placed the name Heceta on the promontory and also on the bank offshore.

In the discovery years, Spain, England, Russia and United States vied for control of the Pacific Northwest, but upstart Uncle Sam won everything below the 49th parallel. The coastline of Oregon was haunting and pristine in those early years but totally void of navigation aids.

One of the most instrumental vessels in helping to locate the vitally needed sites, the U.S. Coast Survey ship *Fauntleroy,* was put to work in the wake of a Congressional bill creating Oregon Territory that was signed August 13, 1848. Unfortunately, Heceta Head was overlooked. It was not tagged for one of the 16 lighthouse sites suggested along the Pacific Coast. In fact, it was not considered even though it was just 13 miles northward from the Siuslaw River, which showed promise as a portal of commerce. Further, the Coast Survey annual report of 1851 failed to show any river between the Alsea and the Umpqua on its accompanying map.

Not until 1877, when the ship *Alexander Duncan* crossed the Siuslaw bar and anchored off the little settlement of Florence, four miles upriver, did the word spread about the commercial potential of the immediate area. Still, another decade was to pass before serious talk of a lighthouse was more than a whisper in government circles. Finally, in 1888, a bill was introduced to provide $80,000 for construction of a first-class light station at Heceta Head. It would serve as both a coastal and landfall beacon. The bill was approved by the Light-House Board and passed the Senate February 25, 1889. Obviously, board member Vice Admiral S. C. Rowan was somewhat divided in his opinion concerning the proposed station. He wrote:

> It does not appear that a harbor light is needed by the sparse commerce of this river. But it is quite evident that a coast light is required to divide the dark space between Cape Arago and Cape Foulweather.

Final surveys were made in 1890. A wagon road was hacked out of the wilderness and payments were made on a parcel of land needed for the reservation that was not already government-owned.

A portion of the headland was included in a homestead claim filed by Welcome E. Warren and his wife Dolly. They had filed a claim for 164 acres in 1888 that included Cape Creek which flowed through their acreage. The government reserved 19 acres of Warren's claim in an order signed by President Benjamin Harrison, July 18, 1891. The couple received in payment $825 for the land and water rights to a spring above the station. At the same time, the Department of the Interior set aside a tract of 239 acres for a lighthouse reservation. Much of the acreage was not essential but was set aside to prevent encroachment.

William Cox, owner of a nearby ranch, signed an indenture permitting government right-of-way through his property. By April 12, 1892, a seven mile wagon road was completed.

As late as 1941, the Siuslaw National Forest requested transfer of unused lighthouse property to the Forest Service and the Coast Guard agreed to the transfer as did the Department of Interior. Therefore, in 1943, the Executive Order of 1891 was revoked and the new order adopted.

Building both Umpqua and Heceta lighthouses with similar architectural plans aided the project. These plans included the tower, oil houses, barn, head keepers dwelling and the assistant keepers duplex. Initial work was begun in 1892 with low bid for metal work being $5,000. The tower and oil houses were $13,700 and the keepers dwellings and barn $26,470. The principal contractor was H. M. Montgomery & Company of Portland. The firm put 56 men to work on the project. Laborers earned $2 a day and worked a ten-hour shift.

When winter rains came, the wagon road was soon a quagmire. Moving and hauling tools and materials from Cape Cove up to the building site was often difficult. The cut lumber came from mills in Florence and Mapleton and was moved to the mouth of the Siuslaw where a tug towed it to the waters off Cape Cove where it was offloaded in bundles onto the beach.

Some of the building material was lost in the rough surf. The tug *Lillian,* owned by Meyer & Kyle was the privately-owned vessel most involved with delivery of materials. Bricks, lime and cement came by ship from San Francisco to Florence. The *Lillian* then towed it to the mouth of the Siuslaw, where teamsters loaded it onto horse-drawn wagons for the trip down the beach to the Cox ranch. This was an arduous undertaking at best and the road often impassable. George Prescott, who owned the team, was also enlisted to haul such items as dynamite and blasting materials.

As the work progressed, the lighthouse tender *Columbine* brought finishing materials from the Tongue Point base near Astoria. These included windows, finished lumber and general supplies, plus the rock for the base of the tower from the Clackamas River quarry. That cargo was unloaded on the Siuslaw and hauled from there by wagon.

Given the assignment of bringing the crates with the lighting apparatus was the lighthouse tender *Manzanita.* She dropped her anchor off Cape Cove as her crew lightered the boxes through the surf to the beach. It was a delicate and somewhat dangerous undertaking. The great lens and clockwork components were valued at more than $12,000—about the same as the cost of the tower. Much of it was susceptible to breakage. If the pulling boat should broach, it could spill the freight and the boat's occupants into the surf. But the landing was carried out with a minimum of trouble due to superb seamanship and special attention to the work by all hands.

Unlike most of the lighting equipment ordered for American lighthouses during that era, the apparatus for Heceta Head was of British manufacture. It was supplied by the firm of Chance Brothers. Previously the contracts had gone to French makers in Paris. The sparkling creation of glass and brass had to be assembled piece by piece and was composed of eight panels, each prism two inches thick, for a total of 640 prisms. The lens rode on brass chariot wheels. The carriage turned by clockwork as weights descended down through the trunk of the tower about 35 feet. Keepers had to rewind the weights with a crank handle at intervals to keep the two-ton apparatus

Keeper's dwelling at Heceta Head Lighthouse seen though the "Needles Eye." In later years the top of the formation eroded leaving only a pinnacle. Picture made about 1925.

revolving. This operating system was similar to the French method. The light source was a five wick lamp and was visible 20 miles at sea. The first fuel was coal oil (kerosene).

After passing all tests, the light was officially turned on March 30, 1894. This was several months ahead of the sister light at Umpqua River. The result was dazzling. The nearby communities gathered to cheer the event, many of the locals having had a hand in the project.

Principal keeper and "potentate" of the lighthouse was Andrew P. C. Hald who was transferred from his role as keeper of the Cape Meares lighthouse near Tillamook. Assisted by Eugene M. Walters and John M. Cowan, the latter who would later put in several years at Cape Flattery Light on Tatoosh Island off the Northwest Washington coast.

For some unexplained reason, the tenure of duty of the early keepers was rather short. Salaries for the head keeper was $800 annually and for assistants $600 and $550, not a wage that would tend to make one wealthy.

Because of the settlers and building crew people in the area, a post office, "Heceta, Oregon," had been established in 1891. With the completion of the lighthouse, a school was established in a one-room frame structure.

Olaf L. Hansen, who became first assistant keeper in the fall of 1896, additionally established himself as a prime member of the community. Though later transferred to another station, he came back in 1904 and became principal keeper remaining in that role until 1920. He, in addition to operating the lighthouse became postmaster and a member of the local school board. (It has not been determined that the post office was actually located at the lighthouse). A native Norwegian, he got his start with the Lighthouse Service on the tender *Manzanita* after a seagoing career that began at age 14. At Heceta, he brought a new bride, where they reared one boy and five girls. He also established a homestead on Mercer Lake near Florence. Olaf Hansen was also to see duty at both Tillamook Rock and Cape Disappointment Light Stations before he retired from the service.

Other personnel who spent several years of duty at Heceta were Frank DeRoy appointed as an assistant in 1913. He became Head Keeper on Hansen's departure in 1920. Robert Bay was an assistant from 1918-1930. Charles Walters was an assistant from 1919 until 1930.

Bob DeRoy, Frank's son, who spent his boyhood years at Heceta and at Warrior Rock, (Columbia River side of Sauvie Island) Light Stations, has many fond memories of his adventures on those reservations. On recent visits to Heceta, he claimed to have seen many changes in the contour of the beach due to erosion from winter storms. For instance, the Needle's Eye, a strange bit of strata on the beach that had a hole in the middle is no longer there. It was a favorite spot from which to frame a photo of the lighthouse. Also he noted several more trees presently growing on the headland.

It is claimed that in 1910, the five-wick burner in the light was replaced by a gas-powered Bunsen Burner but Bob DeRoy refuted that claim. Whether true or false, there was no argument over the innovation of indoor plumbing in 1916 thus ending the often cold and rainy night trips to the proverbial "Chic Sales" in the backyard.

Charles Stonefield, pioneer homesteader and farmer near Heceta Head, was a close friend of the keepers and often hauled supplies for them from Florence with his team and wagon. This was a 13 mile, all-day journey. He also held a contract for supplying fire wood for the station.

Those who lived at and around the lighthouse reservation were a

99

Heceta Head Lighthouse with its 1st Order optic has always been a proud sentinel on the Oregon Coast.

happy, industrious society. It was not uncommon to socialize at picnics, barn dances, card games or on fishing and hunting junkets. There were even two marriages at the lighthouse dwelling. Ben Bunch, a young farmer, married 16 year old Thelma Hansen, one of the keeper's daughters. Thelma Bay, an assistant keeper's daughter, found for herself a local man as well. Both weddings were attended by just about everyone for miles around.

Another big event at Heceta involved "boat day" with the arrival of the little Lighthouse Tender *Rose.* The ship brought supplies and sometimes mail from the station in Astoria. Goods had to be landed by boat through the surf and lighthouse personnel always prayed for good weather and flat seas.

The Hansen clan, so long associated with the Heceta lighthouse, were later transferred to Willapa Bay lighthouse. There was no small amount of sadness at their departure. After a decade at Willapa Bay, Olaf Hansen terminated his 36 year lighthouse career.

During Frank DeRoy's stint as head keeper, he wielded the whip in getting the station spruced up to the highest degree which won him the coveted gold star award for the best in the district. This merit placed him in a desired status among Civil Service employees. When DeRoy and his family transferred to Warrior Rock lighthouse in 1925, Clifford B. "Cap" Hermann, took over the light. A veteran of the service, "Cap" began his long career in 1905. He did duty at Cape Flattery, Lime Kiln, Cape Arago and Destruction Island as well as Heceta.

During his years at the lighthouse, the nation was undergoing many changes, some of which rubbed off at the reservation. The invention of the automobile touched the local area, and road building along the coast was progressing. The old wagon road was being replaced by a highway. New faces were common in that scenic country as many laborers were on hand to build the Cape Creek Bridge, tunnel and road connections. A new, larger schoolhouse had to be erected to educate the children of the workers.

The big boom ended when the construction projects were finished in 1932 in the throes of the nationwide depression. But at least another vital portion of the Oregon Coast Highway had been completed and the trip to Florence was no longer a difficult journey for lighthouse personnel.

Florence, which has always had a close association with Heceta Head lighthouse, may have been born of the sea. Was the community named for an Oregon statesman of the 1850's, or was it named for a wrecked ship? The literature is not clear. Folklore has it that a

101

The walk up the driveway from the keeper's dwelling to the
lighthouse is steep, as researcher Bert Webber discovers.
On an unknown date the hand-rail was added and eventually
the driveway was graveled. The power line came about
when the lighthouse was electrified.

Heceta Head Lighthouse on its shelf neatly carved from the
wilderness, and the keepers dwelling. The scene is at low
tide.

Two old-timer light keepers, Harry Waters and Frank DeRoy while they were assigned to Heceta Head.

Frank DeRoy, a Keeper at Heceta Head Lighthouse, and his wife Jenny.

member of the Duncan family, while foraging for firewood on the beach, discovered a ship's name board imprinted FLORENCE. Was this from the 430-ton bark *Florence* that had been abandoned on November 18, 1875 by Captain S. A. Dayton, of San Francisco, and his crew of eight? The ship was out of Port Discovery on the Strait of Juan de Fuca bound for San Francisco with a huge load of dimension lumber when she was taken by a severe storm, became waterlogged, and went down. This was about 20 miles south of the Umpqua River.* The ship was never found, but from the yarn, we learn that a nameboard washed ashore to be beachcombed. A few bodies of the missing crew washed up near Cape Perpetua about 50 miles north of

*According to Lewis & Dryden, the *Florence* sank 40 miles off the Umpqua River on November 17, 1875 and there was one survivor—Daniel Deary.

the abandonment. The ship was valued at $5,000 and the cargo at $3,000 according to Isadore Burns, the owner, who sadly reported to the U. S. Customs Service that he had no insurance.

The story goes that the ship's nameboard was nailed to a post of the nearby settlement and for want of a better name, the townsfolk picked up on "Florence." A post office with that name opened there on December 15, 1879.

In 1934, a major innovation took place at the station with electrification. The former oil lamps were retired after more than four decades and the chores of the keepers were minimized. The lens was then lighted by a 500 watt electric globe which increased the intensity to more than one million candlepower—many times greater than afforded by the oil flame. The new power plant was cause for a minor celebration for best of all, the keepers would no longer have to wind the clockwork weights or clean the smut from the lamps. The comfort of the station dwellings was also greatly enhanced by some modernization.

Cap Hermann was still master of the lighthouse when it was electrified. With the improvement and the decreased workload, one of the keepers was eliminated. Five years later, in 1939, when the Coast Guard took over the Lighthouse Service, the Civil Service keepers were offered an option. They could retire or join the Coast Guard under the Treasury Department. The majority being up in years, terminated their services but some of the younger men elected to join and receive Coast Guard status and benefits.

In 1940, contractor Rufus Johnson of Mapleton was awarded a contract to raze the head keepers dwelling, at which time the attendants moved into the duplex assistant keepers place. In later years the residence would become known as "Heceta House." That action occurred a few months before Pearl Harbor and declaration of war by the United States. This event—war—had a profound effect on the Oregon Coast. Fears of a Japanese invasion ran rampant. Heceta Head became a beehive of activity with as many as 75 Coast Guardsmen assigned there at its peak. The Hermanns remained in charge of the light under Coast Guard status. A Beach Patrol Detachment maintained walking tours (guard reconnaissance) on all beaches 24 hours a day and several patrol dogs were sent to accompany the "sand pounders."

On January 30, 1950, the beloved Cap Hermann and his wife reached retirement age. Fittingly, his last assignment had been Heceta Head, and at age 70, he rounded out an amazing 49 years of lighthouse service. His was the longest, continuous duty of any

The keepers quarters in the 1920's. The concrete block in yard in foreground was used for mounting horses as well as unloading supplies from farm wagons which backed up to it.

lighthouse personnel in the Pacific Northwest and perhaps among the longest in the nation. He was a recipient of the coveted Gallatin Medal for his outstanding achievement. The couple moved to Tillamook to round out their years. Though the duty was over, many enjoyable memories accompanied them both through retirement.

After Hermann's departure, Coast Guard personnel came and went in continual turnover—the day of the traditional lighthouse keeper was beginning to fade. Only a handful of the old keepers had remained after the Coast Guard assumed the responsibility for maintaining aids to navigation.

Still there was one of the old crowd that had stayed on. He was Oswald "Ossie" Allik, a quiet, pleasant Estonian native who came to this country as a young man and joined the Lighthouse Service. His first assignment was to the Columbia River Lightship. Later, he was transferred to Tillamook Rock lighthouse as an assistant keeper. He put in 20 years on that lonely bastion of rock, his final years as head keeper. When that sentinel was abandoned by the Coast Guard in 1957, Allik doused the light for the final time and moved to Heceta Head lighthouse where he was given the role as the last keeper to remain until that light succumbed to automation. He and his wife, Alice, moved into the old keepers duplex dwelling and remained there until 1963 when, along with the automation of the light, he retired. Thus he had the distinction of being the final keeper of both

Tillamook Rock and Heceta Head lighthouses. He turned off the switch for the final time at Heceta on July 20, 1963.

One by one the lighthouses on the Pacific Coast dismissed their attendants with the new era of automation. It was a distressing period for the historic old buildings. Though fences were placed about the towers, hippies moved on to the grounds and did dastardly deeds in the 1960's. The Coast Guard did not maintain the sentinels in the apple-pie order as when attendants were present.

With no need to keep Heceta lighthouse reservation intact, the Coast Guard elected to keep only 2.2 acres, including the lighthouse and the old oil houses. The remainder of the land was declared surplus including the former classic dwelling.

The state of Oregon eventually took over the reservation adjoining Devils Elbow State Park property. Several other nearby tracts were either donated or turned over to the state to expand the park. In (spring) 1966, the U. S. Forest Service was given jurisdiction over the park properties as part of the huge Siuslaw National Forest. That government agency in turn leased the old keepers dwelling to Lane Community College after other plans, such as turning it into a maritime museum, failed.

Various caretakers moved into the residence and eventually its deteriorating condition demanded a major restoration, qualifying as it did for the *National Register of Historic Places*. The Waldport Ranger District of the Siuslaw National Forest was the overseer for the project and careful research was undertaken to see that the building was restored to its original appearance. It was a costly undertaking, but the end result was gratifying. "Heceta House" began to assume its role in history.

For some reason, down through the years, the rumor got started that the residence was haunted. Its wraith was allegedly a ghostly 1890's woman, reputed to be the wife of an assistant keeper whose child died at a young age. The tale was built up in recent years when caretakers claimed that weird, unexplained things were happening inside the house.

A *Ouija* board reputedly revealed the name of the ghost as "Rue;" that she returned at intervals searching for her child. It is said there was once a headstone on the premises, which long ago vanished under the heavy underbrush, and that it was there that the child had been interred. Others claimed that Rue was the child come back.

Whatever the superstition, the Alliks were constantly bombarded with questions about the ghost in their final years of tenancy. Of the

106

Fishboat **WN4291L** went ashore between Seaside and Tillamook Head in the fog and was unable to send a distress signal. Despite efforts of the owners, boat was lost.

thousands of visitors that toured the lighthouse property many of them
asked about the ghost. Alice Allik was infuriated by the persistent
ghost seekers and denied vehemently that there was any substance to
it. She often declared:

> I've lived here for more than five years and I've never
> once seen a ghost or anything that looked like a ghost.

When Ossie was asked the same question, he would just smirk.
He wouldn't say yes and he wouldn't say no. But in his friendly
fashion, with tongue-in-cheek, he only shrugged his shoulders and
said, "Who knows?"

A few years after his retirement, Oswald Allik died of a heart
attack north of Lincoln City after stopping to help a victim of an
automobile accident whose car had gone over an embankment. He, at
the time, was a resident of Portland but retained a summer home on
the coast close to the ocean as his anchor to the past.

As for the rumor of the ghost, it refused to die. Unlike most
lighthouses with their traditional ghosts, the Heceta phantom has
always been associated with the residence, not the light tower. A
national television commentator in recent years listed Heceta House as
one of the ten most haunted houses in the United States. Of course,
that shot-in-the-arm skyrocketed the story to new heights. People are
fascinated with ghosts, and writers capitalize on that fact. The

107

television industry used the house and facets of its ghostly reputation for a nationally televised movie, and local film makers have made several shorts about Heceta House and its ghostly past.

During the time that Harry Tammen and his wife were caretakers of Heceta House, the story gained further impetus, especially during the reconstruction of the edifice. They insisted that the strange noises, screams, doors and windows ajar and such things as a silk stocking left in the attic where rat poison had previously been, were indications that the ghost was certainly present.

Lane Community College students and construction workers also reported unexplained occurrences. One worker declared that unseen hands misplaced his tools and that he actually witnessed the reflection of an old lady in the window glass of the attic. This frightened him so much that he quit work for a few days.*

The Tammens also reported a sound, like a broom sweeping, while sleeping one night only to discover the next day, broken glass swept up in a neat pile in the attic when nobody had been there for a long period of time. When they left their caretaking chores at Heceta House, Harry Tammen had become rather indifferent concerning the ghost and didn't want to discuss it further. His replacement, at this writing, Dick and Pat Kruse, have not been bothered by the wraith.

When the Heceta Lighthouse Station was built, there was little heavy vegetation on the acreage, a forest fire in earlier years having swept the area. The old station barn is long gone but it once provided plenty of room for the needs of the animals kept by the keepers. The original cisterns remain on the land and during World War II, when the large number of service men were present, two temporary barracks were built on the site of the razed keepers dwelling. The barracks were later torn down. One can easily see that many changes took place over the years.

Several of the heralded lighthouse keepers in the 13th District saw duty at Heceta Light at one time or another. Head keepers included Andrew Hald, Edward Durgan, Joseph Dunsen, Olaf Hansen, Frank DeRoy, Clifford Hermann, S. H. Elder, John A. Boyer and Oswald Allik.

Today, Heceta Head lighthouse maintains its original first order lens flashing every ten seconds, developing about 2.5 million candlepower by utilizing a 1,000 watt quartz-iodine electric globe. Some claim it develops up to 4.5 million candlepower but that rating seems questionable. Whatever the true reading, it is still the most

*When the author visited the ediface recently, he noted in the attic, that someone had assembled a replica of an old woman resembling the reputed ghost.

powerful of its kind (classic type) on the Oregon coast. The tower is 56 feet tall at the focal plane and 205 feet above sea level. The lens cage rides on adiprene lined brass chariot wheels and is powered by a 120 volt AC motor and gear assembly.

As earlier mentioned, deep sea ships and fishing vessels have traditionally given Heceta Head a wide clearance. Most of the shipwrecks in the area have occurred near and around the entrance to the Siuslaw River, 13 miles to the south. Credit Heceta light that fewer serious wrecks have occurred near its perimeter than at other lighthouses along the Oregon coast.

Long before the lighthouse was given a thought, the brig *Fawn* crashed ashore near Heceta Head in the winter of 1856. Four died, but Captain Bunker and three passengers were rescued by Indians. The sailing vessel was en route from San Francisco for Coos Bay but was carried far to the north by contrary winds.

And speaking of Indians, they roamed the lands on and around Heceta Head and on down to the Siuslaw River centuries before the arrival of the white man. Many shell mounds have been uncovered and the remains of an Indian pit house have been found around Cape Creek, just south of the lighthouse.

The schooner *Oliva Schultz* was wrecked off the Siuslaw River April 28, 1880, 14 years before the erection of the lighthouse. There were no survivors.

Near China Creek, just north of Heceta Head, heavy surf and minus tides in the summer of 1987 uncovered ballast rocks, burned timbers, twisted iron and brass spikes from a portion of the large coal carrying ship *Ocean King* which, in the spring of 1887, (just a century earlier) was sailing to San Pedro from Nanaimo, B. C. A strong southerly gale struck the vessel accompanied by raging seas 40 miles off Cape Blanco. She began to take on water rapidly when suddenly her pumps broke down. Drifting northward, Captain C. H. Sawyer and his crew held out for three more days before the desperate situation necessitated abandonment in the ship's boats.

For Captain Sawyer, it was a tearful decision. His command was a four-masted full-rigged ship of 2,434 tons, probably the largest square-rigger in the coasting trades at that date. She carried 3,850 tons of coal which would never reach its California destination. It was reported that the big ship had foundered with the loss of her entire crew. But evidently she broke up and a section came ashore near Heceta Head, where it was reported by George Davidson in his 1889 coast survey. Shifting sands must have shortly afterwards covered the evidence until the scouring of the beach in recent times. At the time of her loss, *Ocean King* was valued at $50,000 and her cargo at $15,000. Following many hours in the open boats, the captain and his crew were rescued at sea by the schooner *Angel Dolly.*

Then there was the stranding of the gas schooner *Anvil* at the north entrance to the Siuslaw, April 11, 1913. Time and again, as a regular passenger and cargo carrier in the coasting trades, she had passed close to Heceta Head lighthouse, and was well known to the keepers and to the populace of Florence. As a result of her stranding, it appeared that she would be a total wreck, but after her cargo was unloaded on the beach and while hundreds of spectators gathered to ponder the ship's fate, salvagers decided that it would be possible to get the wooden-hulled vessel afloat again. With a full tide and the assistance of a tug, the flat sands on which she rested reluctantly gave up its prey and the *Anvil* became one of the fortunate survivors. She was slowly pulled back to sea through the surf to the cheers of the onlookers. After repairs, the vessel was soon back operating on the coastal run much to the joy of the small bar ports that depended on her scheduled arrivals.

Certain kudos were forthcoming to some of the keepers who faithfully tended the light at Heceta Head. For instance, while serving as principal keeper, Clifford B. Hermann and his second assistant, Charles Waters, were commended for rescuing a boy who fell off the precipitous cliff above Sea Lion Caves. This incident occurred on March 27, 1927. The gallant rescue on the 500 foot cliff afforded working room on a narrow ledge only eight to 12 inches wide. The lad survived the ordeal.

On March 30, 1994, with minor fanfare, Heceta head Lighthouse marked its centennial – 100 years of continuous service. It is still the center of one of the world's most scenic seascape settings.

And finally, new light has been discovered regarding Heceta's ghost. It is alleged that a child of one of the keepers at the turn of the Century, died at a very young age and was buried somewhere behind the keeper's dwelling. Over the years, vegetation covered the grave which has never been found. The child was believed to have been of the Hald family. Thus, the tale of the child and its mother coming back in wraith form.*

---

* The death of the child was confirmed by a letter from Norman Jorgensen, El Cerrito, California. His mother's uncle was Andrew P. C. Hald, known as "APC," who had a wife names Sena. The tragic death of the child was due to drowning either in the station cistern or in the ocean according to Jorgensen's cousin Raymond Koontz, in his 90"s at this writing. "APC" Hald put in nearly four decades of lighthouse service. Earlier –1873 - 1879 – he made 14 voyages to the South Pacific in the brig *Nautilus.*

Chapter 7
Cleft of the Rock Lighthouse

On the picturesque north spur of prominent Cape Perpetua, sits a small privately-owned functioning lighthouse—the new kid on the block. As the only one of its kind on the Oregon coast, it has shown a medium range light since 1976 and was made official in 1979. That was just after the 200th anniversary of the indomitable Captain James Cook's discovery of Cape Perpetua on March 7, 1778, as he viewed it aboard his ship *HMS Resolution*.

CLEFT OF THE ROCK LIGHTHOUSE

(Private Aid)

Location:
44°17'5"N 124°6'5"W
Nearest town: Yachats
Built: 1976
Type: Square pyramidal gray
    tower
Height above water: 110ft
Height above ground: 34ft
Light Source: 1 electric bulb
    Quartz halogen
Beam: White and red
Optics: Acrylic bulls eye
Power: 80,000cp
Seen: 16 miles

NOTE: Base data from *Light List* 1983.
U.S. Dept. Transportation, Coast Guard.

With the reputation gained by Cook as the most celebrated navigator of his time, it is rather ironic that the only capes he placed on his charts on the northern Oregon coast were Cape Perpetua and Cape Foulweather. He completely overlooked the Columbia River. Though all the early charts, after Cook, carried Cape Perpetua, it was never considered a site for an aid to navigation until the present facility was erected. This was many years after the apex of coastwise shipping.

Cape Perpetua has the steepest rise directly above the shore of any headland along the Oregon coast—800 feet—a short distance from the beach and 1,000 feet at a distance of 0.8 mile.

Cleft of the Rock lighthouse, built on top of an ancient Indian shell mound on a tapering plateau, is 110 feet above sea level. The

CLEFT OF THE ROCK LIGHTHOUSE

lighthouse is dwarfed by the towering cape. The tower is a replica of the former Fiddle Reef lighthouse (*circa.* 1898). That lighthouse was located in Oak Bay near Victoria, B. C. (It has since been replaced by a minor navigation aid.) Cleft of the Rock's tower of redwood siding is pyramidal in configuration and is painted driftwood gray. The economical design was developed by Canadian lighthouse authorities around the turn of the century for being inexpensive and requiring minimum maintenance. That was in the wake of the Alaska gold rush when maritime commerce had increased enormously in the Pacific Northwest.

The unusual name for Cape Perpetua's beacon was taken from the hymn, "He Hideth My Soul In The Cleft of the Rock" (Fanny J. Crosby) which in turn was taken from Exodus 33:22. The piece of acreage on which the lighthouse and residence stand was, for countless years, a feasting, fishing and hunting area for coastal Indians. All over the grounds one can dig up ancient shell mounds where for centuries Indians feasted on muscles and clams brought up from the beaches. At one time, hundreds of red men inhabited a settlement at the mouth of the Yachats (Yah-Hots) River where the town of Yachats stands today. The Indians, mostly Siuslaw, Alsea and Yaquina, lived in a veritable paradise, separated from the world at large. With an abundance of fish, wild animals, fowl, berries and roots they had all they needed for survival and were among the world's best conservationists. They never took more than was needed and never wasted anything they acquired. The state's largest shell mound, 40 feet high, once stood at the present location of the Adobe Motel in Yachats. Many years ago the mounds were used to create roadbeds.

Cape Perpetua is basically an upheaval of basalt and is very old in content. It has a furrowed brow facing the sea, almost like a frowning giant. Much difficulty was experienced in the 1930's when a million dollar mile was blasted out of sheer, precipitous walls of rock as a portion of Coast Highway 101 rising to more than 300 feet above the sea. Even today, on the beach, one can find tools that were accidentally dropped, or pieces of metal utilized in the construction.

Cleft of the Rock lighthouse is located on acreage homesteaded by the late Art Carpenter in 1899. For a time the slopes were used for grazing livestock. Most of the cape is under jurisdiction of the Siuslaw National Forest, and a Visitors Center is located below the cape to the south, which features the theme "Forces of Nature." The interpretive structure affords a history of the area. During the First World War, huge stands of first growth spruce were cut to fashion

113

Cleft of the Rock Lighthouse (private) on Cape Perpetua was built atop an Indian shell mound (midden) where Indians feasted on mussels and clams for centuries.

If one looks southwest from Cleft of the Rocks Lighthouse, one sees only horizon for there is no land until one gets to Hawaii.

The square, redwood-sided pyramidal tower of Cleft of the Rock Lighthouse is 34 feet tall (110 feet above sea level). The tower is a replica of former Fiddle Reef Lighthouse, Oak Bay, near Victoria, B.C. In the lantern room is the beacon formerly used at Solander Island Lighthouse, an isolated post off the west coast of Vancouver Island, B.C. This is a power beam beacon producing 80,000 candlepower on white flashes and 12,000 cp on red. Below the lantern room, second deck, is the watch room and office. An experimental lens made by Paul Shirk of Waldport, Oregon, is in use at this writing affording excellent results at minimum cost.

The tower, topped
by the lantern
room, rises from
the rotunda in
Cleft of the Rock
Lighthouse

fighter planes. During the great depression, a Civilian Conservation Corps (CCC) camp was erected near where the visitors center is located today. The workers built many trails and constructed a lookout of stone on the high western slopes of the cape. In World War II, a lookout was maintained from the cape. A RADAR facility was installed there.

Today, the Cape Perpetua National Scenic Area is extremely popular with tourists. It offers camping, hiking trails, picnic grounds, sea coves and caves and blowholes. Devil's Churn is a big drawing card with the tourists.

The forces of nature have cut a deep fissure into the basaltic outcropping and the sea rushes into the narrow opening cascading all the way to the land end which culminates in a cave where sometimes breakers explode in picturesque geysers of spray.

116

Ocean breakers and tidal action ranging from ten feet plus, to three feet minus, scour the beaches and leave numerous tidal pools where many varieties of sea life eke out an existence.

Siuslaw Indian legend traced the origin of the tides to the summer of long draught and big fire:

> As the Shaman prayed to the Great Spirit for relief and food, Raven appeared with a solution. He would lead a small group of blindfolded men down the river to food by making the waters recede. His only instructions were to leave the blindfolds in place. If they looked, the water would immediately start to rise. As Raven led this group down the river, the smells of mussles, clams and small fish trapped in tidal pools came to them. One of the hungriest Indians could not resist and peeked. Raven saw this. He told the rest of the party that the water was starting to rise and that they could all look and gather food.

The movement of the tides has provided food ever since, according to the legend.

Seas charge into the Cape Perpetua seashore during the winter storms meeting the land mass in constant combat. The November hurricane of 1981 developed wind gusts in excess of 120 miles-an-hour inflicting considerable damage, especially to the surrounding forests.

Rains vary between the north and south slopes of the cape, anywhere from 60 to 100 inches a year. Slides sometimes occur and beach erosion is common. When the blasting was underway on Highway 101 across the face of Perpetua, a rock slide killed two construction workers, one of whom was buried under seven feet of rock. Until the highway was constructed, only a very narrow wagon road, built in 1914, afforded a perilous passage around the massive headland. That road followed the age-old Indian trail over the cape. The postman in the days of the wagon road had great difficulty in high winds. He was frequently forced to dismount from his horse and hang on to the animal's tail to keep from being blown hundreds of feet down the perpendicular cliff and into the boiling surf.

Cleft of the Rock lighthouse is 34 feet high. Its optic, a power beam medium range beacon, was formerly used by the Canadian Coast Guard at sea-girt Solander Island off the west coast of Vancouver Island. Of British manufacture, it was a product of Stone-Chance Ltd., Crawley, England. This firm was successor to the

Chance Brothers which many years earlier produced the lighting system for Heceta Head lighthouse. With a range of about 16 miles, the light source is a small halogen globe that through the acrylic bullseye produces about 80,000 candlepower. The standby light is a 375 millimeter glass drum lens previously used by the U. S. Coast Guard on Monterey Bay, California. Electronics expert Paul Shirk of Waldport, Oregon was instrumental in automating the Cleft of the Rock lighting apparatus.

Characteristic of the beacon is presently white and red alternating flashes every ten seconds. Parts and pieces of several old lighthouses are encompassed within the tower—sort of a pick-me-up latter-day sentinel—one of the last of its breed. Stair railings are from the original keepers dwelling at Yaquina Head lighthouse.

The stop watch for timing the revolving mechanism of the main light was used at Desdemona Sands lighthouse on the Columbia River. Brass oil cans from Tillamook Rock and Heceta Head recall former days.

French manufactured classic lenses are displayed in the "wreck room" one of which was salvaged from a junk yard several years ago. Post lamps that once lighted the waterways of Puget Sound and the Columbia River are to be seen. The original crank handle that was used to wind the weights that operated the beacon at Point Sur lighthouse (California) is also displayed.

A mini-bay extending westward from the lighthouse captures considerable flotsam and jetsam in its current system. Several dead animals and sea birds have been swept into what is known as Deadman Cove. The body of an unidentified sailor, possibly Russian, was discovered there from the catwalk of the lighthouse in 1980. Three weeks later, the jawbone of a woman was discovered in the same place. When contractors Hoen & Hamilton were building the lighthouse in 1976, they were constantly digging into remnants of Indian shell mounds. Occasional arrowheads would appear.

The crabbing fleet of Newport (Yaquina Bay) 25 miles northward, does a large share of its business in the waters around Cape Perpetua but deep-sea shipping remains well offshore with the exception of cargo vessels traveling to and from Coos Bay and Yaquina Bay. The ill-fated Japanese cargo ship *Blue Magpie* attempted to hug the shore the fateful night of November 19, 1983. Sighted traveling northward in the murk, the vessel's navigation lights were seen from Cleft of the Rock lighthouse. A few hours later, the ship was in dire trouble off the entrance to Yaquina Bay. Captain Kim Gab Bong, and his Korean crew, could not understand Coast

This bunk, in the "wreck room" of Cleft of the Rock Lighthouse, is from battleship USS *Oregon* that served with distinction in the Spanish-American War. This was a superior officer's bunk in a compartment near the wheel house. The American flag flew over the Yachats, Oregon post office. About the two ships in pictures: *left:* The S.S. *Umatilla* hit the reef, that was later named for the ship, on February 9, 1884. The ship was towed to port and rebuilt. *right:* The S.S. *Governor* sank in a collision off Point Wilson, Washington in 1921 —8 lives lost.

The lens from Solander Island Lighthouse, B. C. has been installed at Cleft of the Rock Lighthouse.

Guard warnings that the ship should not try to cross the bar. Instead, in a mad rush of water, the ship crashed into the outer side of the north jetty. That was the end of the *Blue Magpie* which immediately began to break up. In a remarkable nighttime rescue operation under the most adverse conditions, a Coast Guard rescue helicopter plucked all 19 survivors from the mangled vessel.

Two miles south of Cape Perpetua, the trim wooden-hulled fishing vessel *Debonair* crashed into the unrelenting rocks on October 31, 1981. An observer sighted the vessel heading directly toward her destruction when suddenly a figure of a man jumped overboard while the craft was still a few hundred yards from shore. Continuing her course, it was a resounding head-on impact for the *Debonair*—totally destroyed in the shadow of Gwyn Point. The mysterious man who leaped overboard was believed to have been the vessel's skipper, Gary Stevens, of Shelton, Washington. His body was not recovered and no explanation for the mystery has been found.

In the summer of 1982, six miles south of Cape Perpetua, the steel-hulled fishboat *Kim B.*, a 70 footer out of Eureka, ran aground near Ten Mile Creek. In that incident, the helmsman allegedly fell asleep at the wheel while the skipper was asleep in his bunk below. Despite salvage efforts, the rock obstructions on which the wreck lay soon bit into her hull and she shortly succumbed to the elements.

Seven miles due west of Cleft of the Rock lies the tugboat *L. H. Coolidge,* a 126 foot, 282-ton Upper Columbia River Navigation Company vessel. She got in trouble on the Coquille River bar in 1951, and was bashed against the jetty rocks. The famous salvage ship, *Salvage Chief,* which was able to free her, was towing the vessel to the Columbia River for repairs when the *Coolidge,* valued at $300,000, took the plunge in deep water off Cape Perpetua. This was on August 20, 1951. The towline had to be cut to save the *Salvage Chief.*

Anchor, a chocolate Labrador mix, was mascot of Cleft of the Rock lighthouse for ten years. A splendid water dog, she was on the beach under the perpendicular rock face of the cape, a quarter mile from the lighthouse, on January 2, 1987. The surf was seething, backed by one of the highest tides of the decade. Suddenly, a mammoth 25 foot sneaker wave erupted, slamming the dog against the cliff. The backwash carried her out to sea. Despite a long search the results were negative. Five days later she came home as she had done from the beginning but this time it was as a lifeless, watersoaked carcass carried into the rocks of Deadman Cove right below the lighthouse. Her grave faces the sea.

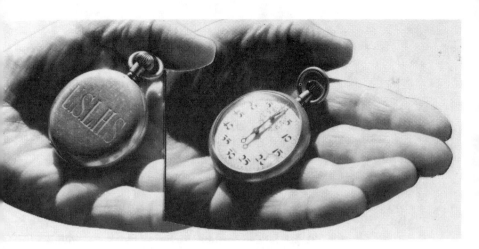

Stop watch used to check proper revolving sequence of lens at Cleft of the Rock Lighthouse. This watch is original equipment of former Desdemona Sands Lighthouse, long ago discontinued. The lighthouse was at the mouth of the Columbia River. Inscription on case is U.S.L.H.S. (United States Light House Service).

This crank, from Point Sur Lighthouse in California, is typical of the cranks supplied to all the lighthouses with systems that operated by weights. The clock-like motion of the mechanism kept the light revolving, thus the duty to "go wind up the weights" was of prime importance before the conversion to electricity.

On another occasion in recent years, a man intent on committing suicide drove his vehicle through the guard rail at full throttle and went plunging down 300 feet from the highest elevation of Highway 101 where it crosses the western face of the cape. As the car was smashed to pieces, the engine was thrown 25 yards in one direction and the man's body the same distance in the opposite direction. The following morning, a Coast Guard helicopter was summoned from the North Bend base to airlift the body out from an almost inaccessible spot. Due to the steep rock wall, the chopper could not get close enough to lower the stretcher. Neither could they put down on the sharp bolders at the surfline for lack of clearance for the main rotor blades. By moving the dead man out to the edge of the surf, the pilot was finally able to get into a position to lower the cable with a stretcher attached. In the haste to get there, a body bag had not been brought to the scene so the lifeless corpse, with its crushed skull, was airlifted in plain sight as scores of spectators gathered on the side of the highway, high on the cape to watch the traumatic procedure. The helicopter lowered the body to a parcel of land near the lighthouse where the coroner took over. Then the helicopter landed in the front yard of the lighthouse to drop off the victim's personal belongings which had been gathered up by the sheriff at the scene of the wrecked car.

A strange thing happened at the lighthouse in the fall of 1989. A woman visitor from Oklahoma was hypnotized by staring at the revolving beacon. She remained transfixed for nearly ten minutes completely oblivious of anything going on around her. At first it was thought she was having a stroke, but after her husband was summoned she came out of the trance and resumed her normal behavior.

*　　　　　*　　　　　*

Do lighthouses have ghosts? *You bet they do!* Whether one believes in such unnatural things or not, every lighthouse traditionally has some sort of a ghost, often in the category of poltergeists. Perhaps the stange occurrences can be attributed to the unusual configurations of lighthouse towers. Winds howl around the tall cylindrical towers often causing strange noises, and erratic shadows thrown by the revolving beams of light can create apparitions that appear amazingly ghostly. Never did this writer know a lighthouse keeper of the old school who flatly ruled out the presence of a lighthouse ghost, whether with tongue-in-cheek or by reality of mind. Most of the mysterious specters seemed to frequent the spiral iron staircases, usually on stormy nights, when the winds were howling outside. There are also many stories involving keepers in lonely outposts that have become mentally unbalanced and have done abnormal things with ghostly overtones. Privation and loneliness have frequently brought about unusual behavior in isolated places.

Yes, even Cleft of the Rock has a ghost, perhaps more in the order of a pranksome poltergeist. A vintage steering wheel on display in the rotunda of the light tower has sometimes turned on its own with no human hands nearby. Then again one can hear the voice of another family member when that member is not at home. At certain times, there are many unexplained noises heard, similar to those in other lighthouses. But, perhaps it's all in one's imagination.

*   *   *

Deep fissures cut in the basaltic rock below the lighthouse are often invaded by mighty breakers when the ocean is riled. When they thunder in like a herd of elephants and strike the bitter end, the shock can rattle the lighthouse like a minor earthquake.

Ocean waves are sometimes misunderstood. Temperature changes in the earth's atmosphere and the rotation of our planet cause the winds that blow across the ocean and on the vast Pacific where they have plenty of room to blow. As the wind travels across the surface of the ocean, some of its energy is transferred to the water. This causes waves and surface currents. Waves reflect the wind's transferred energy by passing through the water in a vertical, circular motion. Water particles within the wave do not move forward with the wave. It is the shape of the wave that moves as the energy is passed from one partical to the next. As the wind increases, so does the height of the wave. In deep, intercontinental ocean water, waves that would otherwise be twenty to thirty yards appart stretch into great undulating swells that can be a hundred or more yards between crests. Pushed by gale-force winds across thousands of miles, with the sea floor far enough below the surface to not interfere with the building process, giant combers in excess of a hundred feet from crest to trough are propelled mercilessly into anything in their path. However, as the sea bed rises toward the surface near land, the lower portion of the circular motion begins to drag on the bottom, slowing the base of the wave. With the crest still moving unchecked, it tumbles forward into the now slower moving trough, creating a surfer's paradise in certain areas.

Cape Perpetua is an excellent place to study the movement of waves, especially when the surf is high. Because of its geographical location on the earth's surface, the cape receives the maximum effect of the moon's gravitational pull on the ocean, which comes 50 minutes later each day. This has a profound effect on the tides which range normally from a ten foot high to a minus three foot low depending on the location of the moon. Wind direction and storms also effect the highs and lows.

Between the Pacific Northwest Coast and Hawaii is one of the world's longest stretches of open ocean not broken by a single island or parcel of land—about 2,400 miles.

Cape Perpetua is also passed closely by the migrant Gray whales on their annual trek between the Bering Sea and the west coast of Mexico, perhaps the longest such migration of any mammal, anywhere from 7,000 to 11,000 miles. A handful of the barnacled leviathans have a love affair with the Oregon coast, however, and reject the long migration, preferring instead to hang around the local waters.

Though Cleft of the Rock lighthouse may be a little out of step with some of the tall towers along the coast, the mariner, as earlier mentioned, is little concerned with architecture of the support structure or the keepers preference in landscaping. By night, he is only concerned with the light and its characteristic.

During the winter of 1987 there was a flood alert for Cape Perpetua. A mudslide had occurred inland and a quick check of the topography indicated that possible disaster was on the way. So a warning was issued to Cleft of the Rock lighthouse that it might be in the flood path. A flood of water and debris did go across Highway 101, but the contour of the cape allowed the torrent to pass through a gully and cascade harmlessly down to the rocks below. Slides often occur on the higher slopes of the cape and trees are frequently uprooted by the forces of nature. But after a few years, lush growth covers the abrasions.

In 1989, the Bandon Stamp Club of Bandon, Oregon, honored Cleft of the Rock lighthouse by placing a drawing of the sentinel on a cachet (envelope). Such souvenir covers excite collectors worldwide. Over a period of time, other Oregon lighthouses have been similarly portrayed.

Located near milepost 166 just off Highway 101, the lighthouse is 1.8 miles south of Yachats on the fringe of the Pacific. Though the lighthouse is not open to the general public, there is a good vista from where it can be viewed from a pullout on the coast highway.

Chapter 8
Yaquina Bay Lighthouse

No other lighthouse on the Oregon coast had such a short period of active service as did Yaquina Bay lighthouse. Miraculous is the fact that the frame structure has remained all these years as a monument to the past despite years of abuse and long periods of abandonment. Now, fully restored, it has become one of the leading tourist attractions for the city of Newport. It is probably the oldest standing building in the city. Like the king of all it surveys, it rests in the center of a state park overlooking the entrance to Yaquina River bar.

YAQUINA BAY LIGHTHOUSE
Location:
44°00'N 124°W
Nearest Town: Newport
Built: 1871 Discontinued 1874
Type: Frame dwelling with
tower
Height above water: *
Height above ground: *
Light source: Whale oil lamp
Beam: White
Optics: 5th Order
Power: *
Seen: 11 miles

*Data not listed in government documents

Thanks to the friends of Yaquina Bay Lighthouse Association, a non-profit organization of volunteers who act as hosts to visitors, the restored lighthouse is kept in excellent condition. These folks work in conjunction with the Oregon State Parks to maintain the building. It has been furnished with period furniture and historical portrayals of the role of the lighthouse both as an aid to navigation and as a lifesaving station.

To better understand the unusual history of Yaquina Bay lighthouse, let us go back to the beginning. The location was originally part of the homestead of Lester and Sophronia Baldwin who were among the earliest white settlers in the area. The United States

125

Utility side of Old Yaquina Bay Lighthouse. *Top:* Picture made while occupied by U.S. Lifesaving Service. *Lower:* View in 1971. Both photographs made on foggy days.

government petitioned the Baldwins to sell 36 acres of prime headland property atop the north summit for the site of the lighthouse. It was ideally situated to act as both a harbor and seacoast light. The real estate transaction was completed in April 1871 for a sum of $500. Initial construction began a month later.

Little did those connected with the project realize that the active life of the finished product would be so short. As it turned out, it became a rather embarrassing situation for Uncle Sam, and moreso for the Light-House Board. Call it confusion, red tape, wasted money or just plain stupidity, it ended up a bit of a fiasco. With the completion of the lighthouse, its whale oil lamp was lit inside a Fifth Order lens on November 3, 1871. It was officially and forever extinguished on October 1, 1874. Why? Just four miles northward, shortly after establishment of Yaquina Bay lighthouse, a first-class lighthouse was erected on what today is known as Yaquina Head but at the time was listed on charts as "Cape Foulweather." (Of course the true Cape Foulweather is six miles north of Yaquina Head.) When the new lighthouse was completed in 1873, this light erased the need for a beacon at Yaquina Bay. Accordingly, its lighting apparatus was removed and the three year old lighthouse sat in relative abandonment.

Now let us look at the details of the construction of the neglected sentinel. A San Francisco metal expert, Joseph Bien, assembled the lantern house and the other metal work in the structure. Ben Simpson of Newport, won the contract to build the tower and connected dwelling. Obviously, he did a splendid job when one considers that the classic frame structure has stood over 120 years.

A capable lighthouse employee with a big family was assigned as the first keeper. In fact, he was the only keeper to hold the head keepers post at this station. He was Charles H. Peirce who formerly had been in charge of Cape Blanco lighthouse. The transfer was made as his wife Sarah figured the new location would be a better place to raise their children—all nine of them. A tenth was born while at Yaquina Bay lighthouse, thus there was never a lack of free labor, the offspring ranging in age from one to 21. Most became highly familiar with the chores of operating a lighthouse. Peirce received a salary of $1,000 annually, and the family was content with their new surroundings. It was not a happy day on October 1, 1874, when orders were received to terminate the lighthouse. Back went the Peirce clan to Cape Blanco.

With the commissioning of the Yaquina Head (Foulweather) Lighthouse the orphaned sentinel was to remain empty for 14 years. There was no maintenance, thus without tender, loving care, it fell into a state of disrepair. Oddly, there were no takers when Uncle

127

Charles H. Peirce
First and Only Keeper
Yaquina Bay Lighthouse

Charles Peirce, light keeper, with his wife, Sarah, brought their large family to the lighthouse and made it their home. He was originally from Boston and she from New York City. Peirce joined the U. S. Army in Boston in 1846. He and Mrs. Peirce would eventually have a large family and all would accompany him to his various duty stations. They moved to San Francisco in the early 1860's where he was appointed Captain in 1865. Later he, with his family, served at Fort Steilacoom in Washington Territory then transferred to Alaska's Fort Tongass shortly after Alaska was purchased from Russia. Captain Peirce was honorably discharged from the Army in 1870. He served in the U. S. Lighthouse Establishment at Cape Blanco then was appointed to the new Yaquina Bay Lighthouse when it opened. He brought his wife and family of nine children with him. (A tenth child was born in the new lighthouse in 1872.) When this lighthouse was closed on October I, 1874, he, with his clan, went back to duty at Cape Blanco.

Sam offered the edifice for sale in 1877. It is hard to imagine today that there would not have been a ready buyer to purchase the finely crafted structure. A few pioneers made token offers but they were so ridiculous that the government elected to hang on to the building. Because money to fix an abandoned building in faraway Oregon was short, only minor efforts were made to keep the roof from leaking and to do other necessary repair work.

With the completion of the Oregon Pacific Railway between Corvallis and Yaquina City in 1885, there was talk of relighting Yaquina Bay Light, but the plan never came to fruition. The repairs made at the time were with the thought in mind that the beacon would shine again but this did not happen. Finally in 1888, the U. S. Army Corps of Engineers was granted permission to utilize the facility for living quarters for the crew that would construct the north jetty at the Yaquina Bay bar entrance. The initial work and additional contracts, which lasted until 1896, kept the edifice in use. The jetty work was in charge of James S. Polhemus, assistant U. S. Engineer, but when the crew moved out, the lighthouse was again abandoned for several more years.

In 1906, the U. S. Lifesaving Station, established at South Beach in 1896, petitioned the government for permission to occupy the dwelling and tower for crew quarters and a lookout station. The location was ideal for keeping constant vigilance over the vessels coming and going across the bar. When the Coast Guard took over that branch of the service in 1915, the facility was still in use, in fact, they continued to utilize the structure until 1933, when new quarters were constructed inside the bay.

In 1911, the Yaquina Bay Mutual Telephone Company was granted permission for an easement through the property. That same year, R. A. Bensell, president of the Newport Bathing House Company, was granted permission to construct and operate bath houses for public use some 500 feet southwest of the lighthouse. Newport by that year had become a popular destination for summer tourists. All the while the lighthouse remained a topic of conversation and as usual, many stories revolved about its future. During the periods of abandonment, many ghost stories were spread, but a fictitious story written by Lischen Miller, in an 1899 issue of *Pacific Monthly*, entitled "The Haunted Lighthouse," labeled the place forever as a mysterious topic for conversation. The writer was the sister of poet laureate Joaquin Miller. The majority of readers, who enjoyed the tale, believed that the old lighthouse was really haunted, and the reputation attached to the edifice has not faded to this day.

Picture from old post card view—U.S.L.S surfboat crossing a breaker near Yaquina bar entrance.

U.S. Lifesaving craft and crew attached to the Yaquina Bay Station undergoes drill in preparation for the real thing in the early part of the century.

The Haunted Lighthouse
Lischen Miller (1858-1915)

Situated at Yaquina, is an old deserted lighthouse. Its weather-beaten walls are wrapped in mystery. Of an afternoon when the fog comes drifting in, it is the loneliest place in the world. At times those who chance to be in the vicinity hear a moaning sound like the cry of one in pain, and sometimes a frenzied call for help pierces the deathlike stillness of the waning day. A light gleams from the lantern tower where no lamps were ever trimmed.

In the days when Newport was but a handful of cabins, across the bar there was a sloop, grotesquely rigged and without a name. Her skipper was a beetle-browed ruffian with a scar across his cheek from mouth to ear. A boat was lowered, and in it a man about forty years of age, accompanied by a young girl, were rowed ashore. He explained that he had encountered rough weather, and to his daughter the voyage proved most trying. If, therefore, accommodations could be secured, he wished to leave her until he returned in a fortnight.

Muriel was a delicate-looking, fair-haired girl still in her teens. She spent many hours each day idling with a sketch book and pencil in that grassy hollow in the hill. The fortnight lengthened to a month yet no sign of a sail rose above the horizon. It was in August that a party of pleasure seekers came over the Coast Range and they were not long in discovering Muriel. She joined them in their ceaseless excursions and was made one of the group that gathered nightly around the campfire.

The Cape Foulweather light had just been completed, and the lighthouse upon the bluff above Newport was deserted. Some member of the camping party proposed that they pay it a visit. With much merry talk and laughter, they climbed the hill. Harold Welch unlocked the door and they went into the empty hall that echoed dismally to the sound of human voices. Stairs led up to a small landing from which a little room, evidently a linen closet, opened. It was well furnished and its only unoccupied wall was finished with a simple wainscoting. "Why," cried one, "this house seems to be falling to pieces."

He pulled at a section and it came away and behind was a heavy piece of sheet iron. He moved it to one side and peered into the aperture. It went straight back then dropped abruptly into a soundless well. "Who knows what it is"?

"Smugglers," suggested somebody, and they all laughed. But they were strangely nervous and excited. There was something uncanny in the atmosphere that oppressed them with an unaccountable sense of dread. So they hurried out leaving the dark closet open and they passed out through the lower hall into the gray fog.

Harold Welch stopped to lock the door, but Muriel laid her hand on his arm. "I must go back," she said. "I–I dropped my handkerchief in the hall upstairs. I am going alone," she said.

Perhaps because her slightest wish was beginning to be his law of life, he reluctantly obeyed her. He had just caught up with the stragglers of the party when the somber stillness of the darkening day was rent by a shriek so wild and weird that they who heard it felt the blood freeze in their veins.

"Muriel, we are coming! Don't be afraid." But they got no reply. In a few minutes they were pouring into the house, then up the stairs and there, on the floor, they found a pool of warm, red blood. There were blood drips in the hall and on the landing and in the linen closet they picked up a blood-stained handkerchief. But there was nothing else. The iron door had been replaced and the panel in the wainscot closed, and try as they might, they could not open it.

"It will be a dreadful blow to her father," remarked the landlady where Muriel stayed. "I don't want to be the one to break it to him."

And she had her wish for neither the sloop nor any of its crew ever again sailed into Yaquina Bay.

131

The tale of the haunted lighthouse and of Muriel has stood the test of time. To this day, Coast Guardsmen who man the lookout tower just to the south of the lighthouse, occasionally tell of strange happenings about the premises by nightfall. Claims of apparitions, strange noises and a light inside the aging edifice, when nobody was inside, have all run their course.

In 1934, after the Coast Guard moved out of the old building, it maintained only a skeleton lookout tower next to the lighthouse. The Oregon State Highway Commission became the proprietor of the empty building and the reservation property. Little interest was shown in the lighthouse over the next few years and once it again it reverted to a neglected status, the ghost stories gained new impetus. Twelve years after receiving custodianship, the Commission scheduled it for demolition. The state considered it nothing more than a dire hazard and unsafe for further habitation.

Civic pride came to the fore. The people were determined that *no way* would they allow the state to demolish the oldest standing frame lighthouse on the Oregon Coast. In many citizen's eyes it was the landmark of their community. A caretaker, who had been living in the edifice, constantly complained of his uncomfortable quarters insisting that it was not weatherproof and sadly in need of repairs. His remarks added incentive to raze the structure. Local opposition won out. In 1948, the Lincoln County Historical Society was formed. Its basic purpose was to save the lighthouse.

But the state had a mind-set to tear it down. Its state highway engineers declared it unsafe for public use and insisted that a minimum of $15,000 was necessary just to meet the lowest standards. As no money was available and the building was considered, by the state, to be a hazard—*tear it down*. In desperation, the historical society tried to raise money for the repairs. Tax money was also sought but rejected in ballot measures five successive times. The case appeared hopeless going into December 1951, and it was reported that a wrecking crew had been dispatched. Preparations were made for the finale. As luck would have it, one last extension was granted. Credit must go to L. E. Warford, an Ohio industrialist who had grown up in Albany, Oregon, and spent many happy vacation days on Yaquina Bay. Well acquainted with the old lighthouse, he spearheaded a campaign to get national recognition for the structure by tying it into early Oregon history. He rallied support from ex-Oregon Governor Douglas McKay, then Secretary of the Interior, and to a degree from ex-President Herbert Hoover.

At last, in 1955, the Highway Commission was compelled to

reverse its demolition plans and to recognize the lighthouse as historical enough to preserve. Engineers gave it another inspection and could probably "see the light" shining once again in the tower if a few thousand dollars were approved for immediate repairs. The historical society kept pushing for additional funds and erected an historical sign on the premises. in 1956, the site was dedicated at a public ceremony with Senator Richard L. Newberger giving the principal address. The lighthouse was finally saved thanks to the "push" from L. E. Warford and the persistent efforts of the Lincoln County Historical Society.

For 18 years the structure was under lease to the society for use as a county museum. In the early 1970's, a study by the Oregon State Parks Department determined that the lighthouse could probably be restored under the Historical Preservation Program. Closure followed and restoration began in 1974. Complete refurbishing followed and here it is today being thoroughly enjoyed by about one million people a year.

As the years rolled on, the lighthouse was constantly improved as was the park surrounding it. With government backing, the edifice was accepted on the *National Register of Historic Places*. The Friends of Yaquina Bay Lighthouse Association was organized to assist the Oregon State Parks Department in the enhancement and improvement of educational and interpretation functions. The Lincoln County Historical Society was satisfied that all details were worked out properly before relinquishing operation of the lighthouse to Oregon State Parks.

The Bandon Stamp Club in its Coos Stamporama, featured Yaquina Bay Lighthouse on a special stamped envelope issued May 19, 1985.

As an active lighthouse, its history was neither brilliant nor of long duration. The sentinel had a sister at Ediz Hook (Port Angeles) on the Strait of Juan de Fuca (circa 1866). Though its years of activity lasted until 1908, when it was torn down, the Yaquina Bay Lighthouse continues to live on. Its one and only keeper, Charles H. Pierce, was a Civil War Captain on the Union Side. He served with honor, as he did during his tenure as a lighthouse keeper at the Oregon stations. he adhered to the instructions and rules of the Lighthouse Service with the same precision as when he was a military man.

Instructions and Directions to Lighthouse and Light Vessel Keepers for 1871

The light-house shall be lighted an hour before sunset, the keepers provided with a lighting lamp, will ascend to the lantern in the tower and commence lighting the lamp—so that the light may have its full effect by the time twilight ends. Lighthouse lights are to be kept burning brightly, free from smoke during each entire night from sunset to sunrise. Lightkeepers are required to keep a careful watch and see that the lights under their care are properly trimmed throughout each night; and during thick and stormy weather those keepers who have no assistants must watch the light during the entire night.

The Lincoln County Historical Society, and its Friends group, has refurbished the lighthouse as it appears today. Sarah Peirce had running water in her 1871 kitchen but the water "ran" only from the nozzle of the pitcher-pump into her dishpan.

On the sign:

OREGON HISTORY

OLD YAQUINA BAY LIGHTHOUSE
Retained for Scenic & Historic Int-
erest & Marker Referring to
Capt. Cook's Voyage 1778 Placed
Opposite, by State Parks Admini-
stration in 1955. During Yaquina Bay
Centennial Observance Sept. 1956 State
Marker was Dedicated at Public Meet-
ing Auspices Lincoln County Historical
Society, Hon. Richard L. Neuberger
Speaker.

Placed by Centennial Comm. & Lincoln County
1959

Once nearly hidden in unruly undergrowth, the old lighthouse was supposed to be torn down but with a major effort by the Lincoln County Historical Society, which was formed for the purpose of saving the old building, it was "retained for scenic & historic interest."

Yaquina Bay
Lighthouse
during its
abandonment in
the late 1890's.

The Lincoln County Historical Society launched drives for
funds for restoration of the lighthouse and pressured the
state for assistance. The beautifully restored and refurbished
lighthouse seen today is a result of that community effort.

Shipping is heavy on Yaquina Bay and at the bar, thus shipwreck is no stranger.

Ships, like some people have jinxed careers. One such vessel was the gas-powered, sloop-rigged cargo carrier *Condor*. From her construction in an Astoria shipyard in 1906, she had flitted in and out of Oregon river bar ports carrying varied cargoes. Her original schooner rig had been reduced to that of a clumsy sloop for easier handling, but her sometimes cranky gas engine had remained in place. As a coastal trader she was somewhat of an ugly duckling having earned a rather unsavory reputation for breaking down and running aground. Always the *Condor* came back for more, that is until November 17, 1912 when her short six year life abruptly ended.

Attempting to enter Yaquina Bay in command of veteran skipper W. H. Dority, the vessel suddenly lost her propeller and was rudely driven against the rocks near the end of Yaquina Bay's north jetty. Dority, his chief engineer George Waddell and mate George Mustoe faced possible drowning as the vessel's deck began to break up under their feet.

Spotted by the lookout at the Life Saving Station, the alarm bell was sounded and in quick dispatch the surf boat was on the way to the scene of the wreck. In the interim, the *Condor* was being unmercifully pounded by the seas combing the jetty rocks.

Joining in the rescue effort with the U. S. Lifesaving craft was the motor schooner *Mirene* which managed to toss a towline to the crew of the battered vessel. Despite herculean efforts, the line parted three times and in order to keep from going on the rocks, the surfboat went into action. Defying fate, the craft was jockyed into a highly dangerous position to perfect the rescue of three survivors. It was an heroic effort and it paid off as all were saved.

In a matter of hours the wooden-hulled *Condor* was splintered in pieces. Only a day before her demise, she and the *Mirene* had departerd Newport with cargo for Waldport on Alsea Bay, but the irascible bar at Waldport negated crossing so both vessels headed back to Newport. On returning over Yaquina bar, the *Condor* lost her screw. The rest is history. During the six years of operation, the U. S. Lifesaving Service had responded to no less than half-a-dozen calls for assistance by the *Condor's* crew—not an enviable epitah for a vessel of yesteryear.

*   *   *

One of the more tragic maritime disasters among the many recorded in and around Yaquina Bay ocurred February 24, 1935, well within view of the venerable Yaquina Head Lighthouse.

A series of bizarre incidents happened after the dredge *Melba*, out of Astoria, passed Yaquina head enroute to the Siuslaw River in tow of the tug *Melville,* skippered by Mike Lawless. Heavy seas were rising, the barometer dropping and gail winds were approaching by early morning. Breasting the headwinds and southerly swells, the tug and dredge plunmged into one sea after another leaving yeasty froth in their wakes. At 7 A.M., when opposite Alsea Bay, Lawless made a grave decision to come about in the teeth of the gale and head back to Yaquina Bay. When he got there, the seas were seething at the bar entrance.

The Coast guard was alerted to the situation and the motor lifeboat with her five man crew was standing by.

An alarming amount of water began to flood the hull of the dredge and the lives of the two men aboard her were in jeopardy. The tug was unable to handle the unwieldy dredge as her bow began rising and the stern settling until the aft section was inundated.

In a daring maneuver, the motor lifeboat *Yaquina* moved in among the wreckage, that had broken loose, to rescue the men, but in turn struck a large chunk of driftwood that knocked a large hole in her hull causing the engine to conk out. Dead in the water, the lifeboat got broadside of the swells and over she went throwing her crew into the brine. Crew members John Hart and Les Halsey were sighted struggling in the water as spectators from the shoreline gathered in their rain gear to watch the drama. Hart managed to swim to the jetty where he was rescued by onlookers who were by now risking their own lives.

Meantime, a prevailing ebb tide was carrying the battered partially sunken dredge and the lifeless *Yaquina* back across the bar where the latter craft slammed against the rocks on the north side of the jetty.

FIVE LOSE LIVES IN YAQUINA BAY

Coast Guardsmen Die in Rescue Attempt

Two In Dredge Crew Swept Into Boiling Sea

NEWPORT, Feb 26 (Special)—Five men are dead, a $20,000 coast-guard boat is battered and on the beach, and a $5000 dredge smashed to pieces as the result of the costliest and most tragic marine disaster ever to occur on Yaquina Bay.

By now, a second Coast Guard motor lifeboat, this one from the Depoe Bay Station, was speeding toward the disaster area. She was skippered by George Kistmaker. Among the churning waters she managed to get in close to the *Yaquina* endeavoring to pluck off Halsey who was still clinging to the wreck. A line was tossed to him and made fast to the impaled vessel. As the tow began, another voluminous swell swept both vessels toward the menacing rocks. Halsey let go his hold and scrambled up on the jetty, leaving the Depoe Bay craft no choice but to return to her station.

It was indeed a black day at Yaquina Bay. The dredge *Melba* went to Davy Jone's Locker; the *Yaquina* was seriously damaged; three Coast Guardsmen lost their lives and two civilians went down with the dredge.

Some observers estimated the seas on the bar were more than 40 feet high at times. Wreckage was everywhere washing up on the nearby beaches for weeks afterward. The heroic efforts of valiant men had failed. Still the lifesaving unit had lived up to the tradition of their service which insists, "You have to go out, but you don't have to come back."

Where an occasional Coast Guard rescue effort fails, the majority succeed. A typical example would be in the plight of the 104-foot oil exploration vessel *Morning Star*.

The Portland-based motor ship operating out of Newport, enveloped in a pea-soup fog, was thrust against the outer end of the north jetty of the Yaquina Bay bar at precisely 11:12 P.M. It was black as the ace of spades. Nerve-wretching was the scraping of the hull against the rock barrier, sending chills up the spines of the crew.

Captain W. M. Sanderhook quickly put the engine in full reverse and in the seven-hour ordeal that followed, one occupant of the *Morning Star* was to receive a broken arm and another a severe back injury. Seas were moderate but the fog persistent. The impact with the jetty rocks had seriously damaged the vessel on that frightful night of October 17, 1961. Seven men were aboard as the ship was returning to Newport after taking seismographic readings for Standard Oil Company, tantamount to possible oil drilling off the Oregon coast. Running at moderate speed, the vessel proved no opponent for the unrelenting stationary objects that formed the end of the jetty, her hull having suffered two sizable holes.

A distress call dispatched three Coast Guard rescue vessels which after probing through the fog amid radio exchanges and whistle signals, finally met the *Morning Star* floundering off Bell Buoy No. 1. There, six crewmen were evacuated shortly after midnight. The drama

TUESDAY, OCTOBER 17, 1961

VOL. CI — 57,590   OREGONIAN   Second Class Postage
Paid at Portland, Oregon

Vessel Hits Sea Jetty; 11 Rescued

Oil Exploration Ship Crashes Yaquina Rocks During Dense Fog

Picture on Page 7

NEWPORT (Special)—Coast Guardsmen early Monday rescued 11 crewmen off the floundering oil exploration vessel Morning Star after the 104-foot Portland - based - ship rammed the tip of the Yaquina Bay North Jetty in a dense fog.

Two crewmen were injured, but neither was hurt seriously. Coast Guardsmen saved the ship after a seven-hour struggle in moderately heavy seas. The ship was returning to harbor at Newport after taking seismographic readings for Standard Oil of California, one of five firms which has a permit to explore for oil off the Oregon Coast.

The ship was running at moderate speed, using its radar to navigate [...]

taken to the Pacific Community Hospital. John Russo, Bridal Veil, suffered a broken left arm. It was put in a cast and he was released early Monday. Charles Curtis, who suffered a back injury, was being held for observation. He lives at 2116 SE Yamhill St., Portland.

The Coast Guard said it appeared the damaged ship might be repaired at the Georgia-Pacific drydock at Toledo or beached at Newport for repairs.

---

continued. Portable pumps were placed aboard the stricken vessel that had already swallowed tons of water.

Suddenly a sneaker swell rolled the *Morning Star* on her beam ends and it appeared she might sink with the remainder of her crew still aboard. Chief bos'n Giles Vanderhoof, in charge of the rescue effort, appeared pessimistic about ultimate success. Fearing the worst, Sandercock asked the 52-foot motor lifeboat men to remove the remaining crewmen and in quick response, the rescue craft performed an admirable bit of seamanship and managed to pluck the survivors from their various perches.

In turn, three Coast Guardsmen were placed aboard the listing wreck and they managed to make a line fast between both vessels. Despite the waterlogged condition of the *Morning Star*, a tenuous battle raged in an epic battle of men against the sea.

The beacon at Yaquina Head Lighthouse was stabbing the fog but the beam was unable to penetrate therefore was of no assistance to the troubled vessels.

It was a risky business at best, but the 52-footer managed to tow the oil exploration vessel into calm waters within the bay. Remarkably, the *Morning Star* and all her crew, as well as 22 service men of the Coast Guard, survived the ordeal. The badly damaged ship was later repaired and returned to service.

On that occasion they had to go out but they all came back.

The wreck of the Japanese cargo carrier, *Blue Magpie* might not have happened if the ship's skipper, a Korean, had better understood English thus being better able to heed Coast Guard warnings. The wreck was in 1983 at the north jetty of Yaquina bar. Coast Guard search and rescue helicopter crews saved all 39 crewmen during a dangerous wind storm.

When the *Blue Magpie* of 3,801 tons, passed Cleft of the Rock Lighthouse, (see page 118), those at the light knew the ship was riding high and was unusually close to the shore. They had no way of knowing what would happen next, but a short time later, the 350-foot freighter crashed into the north jetty at the entrance of Yaquina Bay. The sea was heavy, the night black, and on striking the jetty rocks the ship broke into three sections. Out poured 3,000 gallons of the estimated 75,000 gallons of Bunker C crude oil as well as diesel fuel.

There was a crew of 19 Koreans on board. They were all taken off with difficulty by Coast Guard helicopters that fought 40-to-50-mile winds with a sea running 15 to 25 feet. The Coast Guard had advised the ship's captain, Kim Gab Bong, not to enter the harbor until there was improvement in the conditions. But he attempted an entry anyway. It was later learned that the ship's captain spoke almost no English. The accident occurred about 1 mile off shore. The ship was Japanese owned but registered in Panama. Official reports said that the bow was on the jetty, the midsection had sunk and the stern was mostly inundated.

Of course when anything as exciting as a shipwreck occurs within sight of land, people by the thousands show up almost out of nowhere to gawk at the unusual scene. The wreck of *Blue Magpie* was no different.

Wanting to minimize risk to other vessels, the Coast Guard closed the entrance to the harbor.

The freighter was out of Long Beach enroute to Vancouver, B.C. when she sought refuge in Yaquina Bay all to no avail.

Classic 4th order fixed Fresnel lens utilized for four decades at Semiamhoo Lighthouse near Blaine, Washington. This lens was rescued from a Seattle junk yard. It is similar to the one originally used at Desdemona Sands Lighthouse. The lens was made by the French firm Barbier, Bernard and Turenne.

Top: Yaquina Head Coast Guard Lighthouse reservation as it appeared in 1970. Camera faces southeast. *Lower:* Camera faces northwest in this 1956 view. Presently, all buildings other than the tower and work room are gone. The road is paved with a large public parking lot near the tower.

Chapter 9
Yaquina Head Lighthouse

Considerable confusion centers around the Yaquina Head Lighthouse. Was it constructed in the wrong place or not? A number of writers have labeled it the misplaced lighthouse.

The confusion involves geography and the misplacing of names on the early maps. Yaquina Head was actually labled Cape Foulweather by most citizens in the early years, although the *List of Lights and Fog Signals, Pacific Coast of the United States,* a government document, lists it as Yaquina Head Lighthouse in its 1896 edition.

```
YAQUINA HEAD LIGHTHOUSE
Location:
44°41'N  124°5'W
Nearest town: Newport
Built: 1873
Type: White conical tower
Height above water: 162ft
Height above ground: 93ft
Light source: 1 electric
       incandescent bulb
Beam: White
Optics: 1st Order
Power: 23,000cp
Seen: 19 miles

NOTE: Classic data is from Light List 1934.
U.S. Dept. of Commerce, Lighthouse Service
and reflects details then in effect.
```

A rumor has long persisted that the son of the contractor that built the station stated in confidence, that his father had told him that due to the extreme difficulty of getting building materials up the steep bluffs of what we know today as Cape Foulweather, the materials were off-loaded at more readily accessible Yaquina Head, seven miles south of Cape Foulweather. This excellent folklore is extinguished by the most reliable source of all, George Davidson's 1889 *Pacific Coast Pilot.* He wrote:

> In the published list of the Light-House Board this light
> [Yaquina] is designated Cape Foulweather [Yaquina Head].

Thus it was carried in the early lists as Cape Foulweather but in the 1896 *Light List* dropped the Cape Foulweather and henceforth utilized only Yaquina Head as the designation.*

With all these factors now firmly established, Yaquina Head, a first-class light station was constructed, and constructed well with skilled workers. The tower stands today in all its splendor, one of the Pacific Coast's finest towering lights. This lighthouse is a daily destination for scores of visitors who also take in the surrounding grounds and beaches. The lighthouse reservation, managed by the Bureau of Land Management, Department of the Interior, is a mecca for viewing the sea bird refuge and the variety of sea life along the shore and at sea.

The sentinel stands proudly 162 feet above the ocean beach. This white, conical tower is on a flat piece of acreage projecting at the west extremity of the head four miles north of the entrance to Yaquina Bay. On May 1, 1966, the lighthouse was automated thus ending a long period of station attendants dating from 1873, when the classic First Order lens was lighted with oil lamps.

The original lens is still in place but like all the other coastal lighthouses, it is now illuminated by a 1,000 watt quartz iodine electric globe. This bulb flashes on then off every 20 seconds with two second flash, two second eclipse, two second flash, 14 second eclipse and is visible more than 19 nautical miles, in clear weather, from its lofty perch. The ornate tower is 93 feet tall—the tallest on the Oregon coast.

The lens does not rotate but is fixed with only the light bulb flashing. This modern globe produces approximately 131,000 candlepower, many times that of the oil lantern that was installed years ago.

The optic was manufactured by Barbier & Fenestre of Paris, France in 1868. When completed, its parts were shipped around the Horn. This lens has six prismatic panels with two and a half panels acting as reflectors. A radio beacon is also at this station.

The 19.35 acre reservation was surveyed by U. S. Engineer J. S. Polhemus. The site was reserved by a document signed by President Andrew Johnson on June 8, 1866, but the question comes to mind once again, was the site approved for Cape Foulweather, (near Otter

---

*Davidson, with the U.S. Coast & Geodetic Survey, was an expert in his field and gives a complete description of every detail of the Yaquina area as well as every other maritime geography and topography of the Pacific Coast. Davidson's work was the "Bible" of pre-20th century West Coast navigation. He further stated, "On 1st of October 1874, the Fifth Order light which had been chosen [for] the 'North Point' of the Yaquina [Bay] entrance, was discontinued.

Crest) or Yaquina Head?

In order to rectify the situation many who lived in the immediate area at the time of construction reputedly referred to Yaquina Head as Cape Foulweather, but nobody seems to have challenged the mistake. Complainers, as well as population was sparse on the Oregon coast in the 1870's.

Metal work for the tower was manufactured in Philadelphia and the bricks originated in San Francisco. Many of the supplies and materials had to be landed in a craggy cove below a steep cliff on the south side of the site. Tidal and wave conditions had to be right as the lightering process was a dangerous occupation. Once landed on the rocks, small derricks were employed to hoist the cargo up to the plateau. During the operation, one of the construction crew was blown off the cliff but his oil skins acted a little like a parachute in the strong wind somewhat cushioning his fall. He lit in a heap but suffered only minor injuries.

Another unfortunate accident occurred when two lighters capsized in the rough seas near the landing. All the cargo was lost. Later, a section of the lens was smashed while being unloaded at the landing and had to be replaced.

Considerable credit is due those early engineers and builders who did the construction between 1871 and 1873. That was a long time ago. The mode of transport and communications were primitive at best compared with what we take for granted today, and with all the troubles the workers faced and how they handled them is remarkable. There was no loss of life during the construction period. One rumor persisted for many years that a workman fell off a scaffolding into the hollow between the double masonry walls of the rising tower. The extreme difficulty of retrieving the body was such that he was left entombed and eventually sealed in a walled crypt. Such a story has never been substantiated, but it is still told today. Perhaps this yarn gives impetus to the persistent claim of a ghost heard traversing the 114 steps of the iron circular staircase late in the night.

As the tower and dwellings took shape, the place was a beehive of activity with carpenters, iron workers, masons and laborers working ten to twelve hours each day. The steps leading from the landing had to be hacked out of solid rock. It is said that mules were also employed to move some of the heavy materials, and that when the wind blew hard, which was often the case, the beasts of burden would balk. Still the work continued unabated, and the workers were presumably pleased that they were not on the more difficult steeps of the real Cape Foulweather.

There was considerable rejoicing when the station was completed and the light officially turned on, August 20, 1873. It was a masterpiece of construction, this 93 foot tower which at that date may have been the tallest structure in the state of Oregon.

The commodious two-story frame keepers dwelling, the oil houses, outbuildings and cistern were all solidly built. The station opened a new era for the Yaquina area which showed great potential for the maritime future. In fact, there were bright hopes, for a time, that Yaquina Bay would become one of the major seaports in the Pacific Northwest. Alas, some unfortunate incidents occurred.

When the Oregon Pacific Railroad terminated at Yaquina City in 1885, offering a direct link to the Willamette Valley, namely Corvallis, there was wild celebration when the final spike was driven and the steam train came rolling in. The company had acquired a passenger ship that would offer service from Yaquina City direct to San Francisco. It would make connections with the train. For the first time, Yaquina Bay was able to offer genuine competition with the Columbia River.

The refurbished liner was the SS *Yaquina City,* brought out to the Pacific Coast by the Oregon Development Company. This was a subsidiary of the Oregon Pacific Railroad Company. Under an earlier name, SS *Western Texas,* she had been employed several years in the Gulf trade. With new owners and a new lease on life, the vessel made her grand entry. After several successful voyages, suddenly by fate or sabotage, that sea-link suffered a major setback when on December 4, 1887, the *Yaquina City,* while crossing the Yaquina bar, mysteriously slipped her rudder cable and drove up hard on the sands at the river entrance.

Though all hands reached safety, the vessel was caught in the vice of pounding breakers and soon began to break up. Salvage efforts proved futile and the citizens of Yaquina City and Newport gathered on the beach to mourn the loss of "their" liner. She went to pieces in only eight days.

Undaunted by the tragedy, the company, with collected insurance on their lost vessel, decided to give it another go. This time they purchased an even larger, more luxurious liner. She was the SS *Caracas,* built in 1881 by the famous Cramp shipyard in Philadelphia for the New York-West Indies service. Registering 1,200 tons, the steamer was 257 feet long with a 34 foot beam and had excellent accommodations for a large number of passengers.

Under Captain Lord, the vessel sailed for the Pacific Coast, and like her predecessor, on arrival at San Francisco underwent refurbish-

> ### Report of the Light-House Board
> #### 1881
> *Cape Foulweather.– Yaquina head, on westerly end of Cape Foulweather, Oregon.* As this station was again damaged by winter storms, materials were purchased and sent forward in the spring and the damages were repaired. The buildings were also repainted.

ing. She also emerged with a new name, the SS *Yaquina Bay.*

On her inaugural voyage, she passed through the Golden Gate and made a good run up the coast. Gleaming under her new coat of paint, and with flags flying, she entered Yaquina Bay still under the command of Captain Lord. The date was December 9, 1888. It was just one year since the demise of her forerunner. Accepting a tow to insure a safe bar crossing, she trailed behind the tug while the passengers prepared for their debarkation at Yaquina City. A heavy bar swell caused considerable strain on the hawser and suddenly it snapped and the steamer found herself in watery shackles unable to get free. Before long she was hung up on the shoals not far from the grave of the *Yaquina City.*

Despite the full thrust of her engines and a wildly spinning propeller, the liner was hopelessly aground. Nor could the tug relieve the stranded victim. Prompt rescue operations were undertaken and the passengers and crew were removed without casualty. But the *Yaquina Bay* was irretrievably lost!

The financial strain and loss of business on behalf of the owners, plus the highly unusual circumstances surrounding the loss of the two liners a year apart and in nearly the same place, forced the company out of the passenger ship business.

Cries of foul play followed declaring that the ships had been purposely wrecked by payoffs from Columbia River shipping interests. Charges of negligence surfaced, but no proof could be established.

All through the tragic drama involving the two liners, the light in the tower at the discontinued Yaquina Bay lighthouse remained in darkness, the structure acting only as a daymark. The light at Yaquina Head was in service but useless to prevent shipwrecks such as these.

Perhaps no keeper of Yaquina Head lighthouse had a longer tenure than John Zenor. He was stocky, curly-headed individual who spent 22 years at the post after transferring from Ediz Hook Light Station at Port Angeles, Washington. His career with lighthouses began at Umpqua River in 1928. After a short stint at Grays Harbor Light Station learning the rudiments of electricity in lighthouses as a replacement for oil lamps, he was assigned to Yaquina Head which in

Yaquina Head Outstanding Natural Area, administered by Bureau of Land Management of the U. S. Dept. of the Interior, provides safe refuge for varities of birds, seals, sea lions, even crabs and starfish. Descriptive data about all the inhabitants of these rocks and intertidal pools, as well as telescopes through which to view them, are in the present outdoor visitor's area. This picture was made many years before the B.L.M. received its mandate over the area.

his mind was a great relief after Ediz Hook. He hated the latter station with a passion due to the incessant fog. Nor was he reticent in claiming that once he retired from lighthouse duty, he never again wanted to step foot inside any lighthouse.

It is somewhat strange that one with that philosophy would put in so many years tending the light, and to leave the service with an unblemished record. His main complaint with Yaquina Head was the strong winds that often swept across the reservation.

When he began his career, oil lamps were in use and he, of course, was pleased when the traditional chores of maintaining oil lamps ended. Going through the evolution at Yaquina Head he saw his station reduced from a three-man to a two-man operation.

Zenor spent much of his time hosting visitors, some 14,196 in 1931 alone, and often saw them get blown around the premises in the strong winds. (At this writing in 1992, the wind is still blowing.) But he always maintained that he appreciated the fact that he didn't have to deal with excessive amounts of fog.

One claim made by the head keeper was that he firmly believed the huge lens at the lighthouse was cut five degrees off center, which in his eyes had a slightly negative effect on the beam of light. Undoubtedly, the French manufacturers would have rejected his reasoning. The same lens has been in use since the station was established in 1873. According to the late keeper, the beam was set for a distance of 19 miles and hit about ten feet above the water on the bridge of a passing ship.

Activity reached an apex at the lighthouse during World War II, when Zenor was suddenly surrounded by a host of Coast Guard personnel. He had elected to sign on with that service in 1939, but retained his status as a lighthouse keeper. Some 16 service men were attached to the station following the declaration of war. A 24-hour weather station was established and the Beach Patrol Detachment carried out constant lookouts for a possible enemy invasion of the beaches stretching to the north and south. The patrolmen and the lookouts in the lighthouse were required to be especially alert for submarines. Many rumors were heard but proved to be false for the sea often plays strange tricks on the imagination but every report had to be treated seriously.

As is the case with all visitors, Zenor was often bombarded with questions about the lighthouse ghost, a rumor that had persisted since the early years. He, with candor and in a low voice would tell of the apparition: "Someone unseen would come in and go up the spiral stairs on certain dark nights," he revealed, but then he went on the say, "that following World War II, the visits of the ghost seemed to subside." Be that as it may, the tales of the apparition have never completely faded and probably never will as long as the tower stands. Zenor did conclude that many of those who had been at the station had witnessed the presence of the wraith by nightfall. Sometimes he would hike the stairs to check the lantern room after hearing the ghost go up and down the staircase.

Despite Zenor's sometimes dissatisfaction with lighthouse life, he had a compassionate heart. During World War II he befriended many young Coast Guardsmen stationed at the facility and he is known to have arranged a Christmas dinner at the lighthouse for the men, their wives and girlfriends. During the war one had to know a secret password, that was changed every day, to enter the tower.

A veteran of the First World War, Zenor devoted 33 years to government service. When he retired from his duties at Yaquina Head in 1954, he rounded out his days at his home at Otter Crest, a few miles north of the aid to navigation he had tended for two decades. In his usual quiet-spoken manner, he accepted his retirement in stride spending much of his time caring for his rhododendron garden. Until the last, he insisted he "could never understand peoples' interest in lighthouses."

The original light keepers dwelling at Yaquina Head was torn down when the Coast Guard took over and was replaced by two new bungalow type dwellings for the service personnel. When the station was automated, the living quarters were vacated and fell into disrepair. The buildings were often occupied by hippies, some of whom were vandals.

After a plan for using one of the buildings as a visitor's center collapsed, the Field family, Larry, Alice and Helen were awarded a contract to dismantle them for the materials in 1984. The grounds were then left with no structures except the lighthouse and attached work room.

A quarry which for years operated at the eastern end of Yaquina Head, a half mile from the lighthouse, produced rock for county roads until 1983. After a number of years of negotiation, the federal government purchased those holdings to be converted into a park with tourist attractions. (There had always been concern, particularly by preservationists, about the cavernous hole the quarrymen had dug into the headland. Some expressed grave concern over the damage the diggings had inflicted on the headland and to the ecology.)

Out at the lighthouse, viewing platforms were built on the western side of the tower where visitors can better observe the seabirds

The Abandoned Quarry

For many years, Yaquina Head was the nearest place on the coast where hard rock, essential for building purposes, could be found thus for about 58 years (approx. 1925-1983), quarry operators blasted and dug rock on private property. Yaquina Head was declared an Outstanding Natural Area in 1980 by an Act of Congress and assigned to the Bureau of Land Management. One of the first duties of BLM was to require a stop to quarry operations. Major cleaning of the headland followed and has been finished. The BLM has plans for reclamation of the quarried land so eventually, in BLM words, "you'll hardly know that quarrying occurred."

and mammals that frequent the area. Murres are sometimes so thick on the seastacks just offshore that they form a virtual mattress of feathers.

There have been numerous shipwrecks on and around the entrance to Yaquina Bay, but none has attracted more attention of the public, the conservationists, and the press than that of the Korean-manned Panamanian registered Japanese cargo vessel *Blue Magpie.* The story of this shipwreck appears in Chapter 8.

The World War II built, concrete-hulled ship *John Aspin* is a sunken wreck on Yaquina Reef. That 5,000 ton ex-Army transport, built at Tampa Florida in 1944, parted her towing cable while being taken from Cathlamet to Newport for use as a revetment for a commercial dock. She went down a half mile from the outer end of the north jetty, beyond recovery, on April 22, 1948.

Other wrecks in the area that have been of concern in times past are the schooner *Caroline Medeau* on the bar, April 5, 1876, three years after Yaquina Head lighthouse was commissioned.

The oyster schooner *Cornelia Terry* ended her days on the bar, outbound with oysters for San Francisco October 13, 1864.

The steam schooner *J. Marhoffer* caught fire just north of Yaquina Head, the wreck drifting into a small bay in May 1910. By depositing her boiler on the rocks, the name for the bay became Boiler Bay. The boiler can be seen today at low tide.

Here is the true story of the wreck and that timeless boiler that marks the spot.

It was early afternoon May 19, 1910. The venerable steam schooner *J. Marhoffer,* Captain Gustave Peterson, was steaming northward off Yaquina head at a speed of nine knots. The first (chief) engineer was off watch and asleep in his cabin. His assistant was in the engine room fiddling with a new gasoline blow torch. After he pumped it to high pressure, it suddenly exploded and threw a curtain

153

Stately tower of Yaquina Head Lighthouse and workroom are all that remain
of cluster of buildings at this early lighthouse reserve. *Left inset:* Dedication on
concrete monument at left, rear of
tower.

of gas into parts of the oil-soaked engine room. Quickly, the entire compartment became a flaming inferno, the smoke well visible to the keepers at the lighthouse. But the vessel continued at top speed. Hastily the captain and chief engineer ordered the engine room flooded but the valves and pumps, already turned red hot by the conflagration, would not budge.

"Abandon ship!" was the next order that reverberated over the decks of the 600 ton vessel. Peterson, a veteran steam-schooner man, was reluctant to leave his three-year-old Grays Harbor-built lumber carrier but would later have no choice. The fire was out of control. He ordered the helm almost due east and headed for the rock-ribbed shore that was about three miles away.

Despite her protests, the skipper ordered his wife into the first lifeboat which was in charge of the mate. The furiouslly burning wooden-hulled vessel was now a flaming torch. Before the boat was lowered, the mate seized the shipmaster's mascot dog and tossed him into the sea. When the lifeboat was in the water, the mate retrieved the dog. On nearing shore, the boat was turned by the breakers and listed heavy to starboard but managed to gain the beach.

Striking foul ground in the breakers, the flaming *Marhoffer* was finally abandoned by Peterson and the remainder of the crew for fear of explosions.

Captain Otto Wellander, and his lifesaving crew from Yaquina Bay, was well underway to the scene after the first alert, but it was early settler Grandma Wisniewski who first sighted the survivors in the life boat and ran to the beach waving her red sweater. They mistook the signal as a warning against a dangerous landing spot and pulled away, finally landing at Whale Cove.

The second lifeboat, having considerable trouble in the surf, capsized near Fogerty Creek (now a state park). The already injured ship's cook was thrown overboard and drowned.

When the rescue party arrived several hours later, only the forecastle and a portion of the *J. Marhoffer's* stern remained intact. Heavy surf soon made scrap of the remaining parts. The boiler, warped by heat, came in among the rocks and cradled itself, remaining to this day as a gravemarker for one of the coast's stalwart steam schooners of a bygone era. A hawsepipe from the wreck, dragged up the cliff, remains adjacent to Highway 101, gradually rusting away.

One of the oldest wrecks in the vicinity was that of the Peruvian bark *Joseph Warren,* swept on her beam ends by a tremendous storm that caused the drowning of four crew members. The vessel drifted at the mercy of the seas for 13 days, her decks swept clean of deck houses and rigging. The derelict came ashore, just south of Yaquina Bay, in late November 1864. The gaunt survivors struggled ashore.

The oyster schooner, *Lizzie,* slipped her anchor near Yaquina bar and stranded near the river's south entrance February 16, 1876.

The steam schooner *Ona* met her demise on the bar, July 26, 1883 and earlier the same year, the schooner *Phoebe Fay* was abandoned in sinking condition off Cape Foulweather.

The handsome barkentine *Quickstep* foundered south of Yaquina Head, November 25, 1904. In more recent years, several commercial fishboats have been wrecked on and off the Yaquina shores some with loss of life.

Through it all, the Yaquina Head lighthouse has continued to shine its beacon to help prevent accidents, and certainly the toll in lives and property through the years would have been far greater without its presence. In the poetic words of Robert Louis Stevenson, one can almost picture the grace and symmetry of the tower:

> Eternal granite hewn from living isle
> And dowled with brute iron, rears a tower
> That from its wet foundation to its crown
> Of glittering glass, stands,
> In the sweep of winds,
> Immovable, immortal, eminent.

On many occasions in recent years, the lighthouse has served as a backdrop for television programs, advertising campaigns and movies. Perhaps one such production that left its "mark" on the tower was a segment of the Nancy Drew mystery series. The lighthouse was transformed into a ghostly, abandoned tower complete with artificial cobwebs and strange sound effects that probably made the traditional ghost green with envy.

A large cast of players and producers were present during the filming that included the stars Monte Markham and Jean Rasey.

The Coast Guard granted permission for the use of the facility with the provisal that the show not conflict with the operation of the beacon and that the tower be returned to applepie order after the filming was completed. The first order was obeyed, but the latter was sadly neglected. This forced the Coast Guard to threaten a law suit to get the tower restored both on the interior and exterior, a requirement the delinquent producers were finally forced to fulfill.

On the lighthouse grounds in recent years, archeological teams from graduate-level institutions have been given permission to explore

Office of the U. S. Light–House Inspector
THIRTEENTH DISTRICT
Portland Oregon

I September 1893

Subject:

CIRCULAR ORDER TO THE LIGHT-HOUSE KEEPERS OF THE 13TH DISTRICT

The regulations governing the uniform of Officers and men, of the U.S.Light-House Service, as set forth in a pamphlet sent to you will be strictly adhered to.

Every appointed keeper or assistant keeper must be in the prescribed uniform on or before January 1894. Failure to comply with this order will be reported to the Light-House Board with the recommendation for the dismissal of the delinquent.

This order does not apply to the laborers, temporary employed at the lighthouses. When a laborer is appointed acting assistant keeper he will at once comply with the regulations.

Every keeper at the light-stations will sign this order and the chief keeper will inform this office that the order is thoroughly understood.

O. W. FARENHOLT
Commander, U. S. N.
Inspector 13th L. H. District

Signed:

R.Petersen   Keeper

H. P. Score   1st Ass't

Alex K. Pesonen   2nd Ass't

Axel Rustad

Joseph Burchall

This order was received at Tillamook Rock Lighthouse and was signed by all the personnel stationed there at that time.

for Indian Artifacts in shell mounds and middens deep in the earth.

The native Americans roamed the head hundreds of years before white men ever set eyes on the Oregon coast.

On January 15, 1980, lightning struck Yaquina Head lighthouse and knocked out the electrical system. Coast Guardsman Jerry Hebert from Aids to Navigation Team at Charleston, and some assistants, worked throughout the night to restore the service.

Apparently the only living thing that ever attacked the lighthouse was a wild duck that was evidently confused by the beacon in 1932. The enraged feathered-friend turned enemy, dived into the beam and shattered a lantern pane and chipped a lens prism. It was his final flight.

Cape Meares Lighthouse (left) in an early time photograph. Note the workroom faces opposite direction from new room recently constructured. Abandoned Lighthouse in 1971 with Dale Webber on platform (top), with new automatic DCB beacon in rear.

Chapter 10
Cape Meares Lighthouse

The original Cape Meares lighthouse, which celebrated its 100th anniversary on January 1, 1990, is now the main attraction of an Oregon State Park. It is ten miles west of the city of Tillamook on a county road off highway 101 and is at the north end of the Three Capes Scenic Loop Drive. Cape Meares, like its neighboring lighthouses, is no longer active with resident personnel. Its duties are performed by a utilitarian boxlike structure with an exposed DCB (aero marine type beacon). The old lighthouse, a good distance west of the DCB, has been retained as an historic attraction in a parklike setting that attracts scores of visitors the year round.

```
CAPE MEARES LIGHTHOUSE
Location:
45°29' N  123°59'W
Nearest town: Bayocean
Built: 1890
Type: White octagonal, pyramidal
     tower
Height above water: 217ft
Height above ground: 38ft
Light source: Oil vapor
     incandescent
Beam: White and red
Optics: 1st Order
Power: 13,000cp
Seen: 21 miles

NOTE: Classic data is from Light List 1934.
U.S. Dept. of Commerce, Lighthouse Service
and reflects details then in effect.
```

The pioneer sentinel and station outbuildings required a year to complete. When built, it was equipped with a First Order Fresnel optic. Funded by the government on a recommendation by the U.S. Light-House Board as early as 1886, the light was not officially illuminated until January 1, 1890.

Authorization for the project was signed by President Grover Cleveland but with all the intervening circumstances and long delays, President Benjamin Harrison was in office when the lighthouse became operative.

The Notice to Mariners No. 71 in the year 1889 read:

> Notice is hereby given that, on or about January 1, 1890, a fixed white light of the first order, varied by a red flash every minute, will be shown from the structure recently erected on the extreme westerly end of Cape Meares, Oregon. The light will illuminate the entire horizon. The focal plane is 223 feet above mean sealevel, and the light may be seen in clear weather, from the deck of a vessel 15 feet above the sea, 21½ nautical miles. The light is shown from a black lantern surmounting a low white tower in form of a frustum of an octagonal pyramid. Two brown oil houses (distant 65 feet) and a keeper's dwelling painted white with lead colored trimmings and brown roofs (distant 1,000 feet) stand to the eastward of the tower. The approximate geographical position of the lighthouse, as taken from the charts of the U.S. Coast and Geodetic Survey is as follows:
>
> Latitude 48° 28' (52") North
>
> Longitude 123° 58' (30") West
>
> Magnetic bearings and distances of prominent objects are approximately as follows:
>
> Tillamook Rock Light-House N.N.W. ¼ W., 27½ nautical miles
>
> Cape Lookout, S. by E. 9 nautical miles
>
> Cape Foulweather (Yaquina Head) Light is the next light to the southward, distant 49 miles
>
> By order of the Light-House Board
David B. Harmony
RearAdmiral
Chairman
Office of the Light-House Board
Washington, D.C. December 2, 1889

Built under the direction of the U.S. Army Corps of Engineers, the Willamette Iron Works of Portland, Oregon won the contract for the sheet iron which was to be the basic material for this lighthouse. Coastal vessels hauled the supplies and materials to Tillamook Bay from where they were transported overland by wagons with a great amount of hard labor. Delivery was made March 1, 1889 at a cost of $7,800.

General contractor Charles B. Duhrkoop was the foreman supervisor. He was present when the bricks for the lighthouse were kilned on the site, and timber was cut from the surrounding forests. His stipend was $2,900 when the station was completed. This included

Cape Meares Lighthouse before workroom was added in 1895.

encasing the 40 foot tower in iron plates, a specification unlike any other lighthouse on the Oregon coast. It was never revealed whether or not the exposure to severe weather while on this job had an effect on the chief builder, but Duhrkoop, a native German, died of pneumonia at his Portland home on January 9, 1893 just three years after the Cape Meares station was established.

Lighthouse keeping at Cape Meares, though somewhat isolated in the early days, had its pleasant side. Twin sturdy dwellings, each 2½ stories, commodious and comfortable, housed the keepers and their families. Much of their food was grown on the reservation in fertile gardens well watered by the frequent rains. Cows and chickens were also in evidence.

Though Duhrkoop was responsible for the building of the light tower, Richard Seaman of Portland won the contract for the construction of the dwellings, the oil houses and barn. He also bid the grading for the property and the road. His work came to $26,000. He was paid in three installments. From all reports, the dwellers were well pleased with their premises.

About once a month, weather and tides permitting, personnel would make the long trip to Tillamook City. Horses and wagons were used to go from the lighthouse to the bay, and by high tide, a pulling

Charles B.
Duhrkoop.

boat was rowed and poled across the bay to town for staples and other supplies. High tides were necessary due to the fact that a large portion of Tillamook Bay virtually turned to mudflats when the tide was out. The return trip also had to await the proper tides, therefore the entire round trip would be a day's effort—eight hours or even longer —if the wagon road from the lighthouse to the bay was a quagmire.*

The gem of every lighthouse is its optic and Cape Meares had a beauty. It's lens was composed of hundreds of prisms, ground and polished. It was a fixture said to have been one of only two eight-sided lenses in the country when first installed. The lens, carriage and allied accessories weighed about two tons. Manufacturer was Henry LaPaute of Paris in 1887. It was shipped around the Horn in crates and then brought to the location by a lighthouse tender and landed below the precipitous headland on which the sentinel stood. It must have been a nail-biting effort just to hoist the crates up to the level, one at a time, with a hand-operated crane made from spruce trees cut on the cape.

After the lighting apparatus was installed, a five-wick kerosene lamp provided the light source. The focal plane was 223 feet above sea level and visible more than 21 miles. An advanced light source was installed at the lighthouse in 1910 when Cape Meares, along with other Oregon beacons, were fitted with the more efficient incan-

---

*After 1912, when the town of Bayocean came into being, general shopping was done there. A road from Tillamook City was not opened until 1928 after which Bayocean sported a Texaco gas station.

descent oil vapor lamps. These were commonly referred to as an IOV. The IOV offered a cleaner and more brilliant flame. The rotation of the lens was achieved by weights and rollers in a race. If and when the revolving mechanism failed, keepers were required to turn the huge lens by hand and at the specified speed, for as long as it took to get the clock-works reactivated.

In 1934, the station was blessed with the addition of electricity. Two Kohler generators were installed for power and the traditional oil lamps were eliminated, but a spare was kept "just in case."

Automation came to the lighthouse on April 1, 1963 at which time the historic structure was abandoned in favor of the present 17 foot tall concrete block house (that has all the romantic qualities of a privy).

A number of articles have appeared over the years suggesting that the lighthouse on Cape Meares was built there by mistake, that the tower was intended to have been installed on Cape Lookout nine miles south. Research, however, concludes that the lighthouse is exactly where the surveyor, George W. Freeman, U. S. Lighthouse Establishment, planned it to be. Perhaps the so-called error was initiated on July 6, 1788, when Captain John Meares, master of the *Felice Adventurer,* while sailing southward along the shores of present Tillamook County, sighted a feature that he named on his charts as "Cape Lookout" and accordingly gave a description and drew an illustration of that promontory.

Decades later, the U.S. Coast Survey chart makers somehow mistakenly placed the name Cape Lookout on its charts of 1850 and 1853 at another cape about ten miles south of Cape Meares' original location. The error was later realized, but George Davidson, the knowledgeable author of *Pacific Coast Pilot,* and an officer with the Coast Survey, decided in 1857 that the mistake could not be corrected. His reasoning was because the name "Cape Lookout" had already become widely associated with the position given on previous navigation charts. He, in turn, officially affixed the name Cape Meares to the original Cape Lookout.

Despite his well-meaning effort, the confusion about these capes among historians, has lasted to the present time.

The site of the present Cape Lookout, by far the more prominent location from a navigational standpoint, was surveyed and recorded then set aside for a lighthouse.

And the land at Cape Meares was also surveyed and recorded. In addition, a special study entitled *Report on a Location of Wagon Road from Tillamook Bay to Cape Meares Light House Reser.* in August

Tillamook Bay, Bayocean, Cape Meares area

1887, was also prepared by George Freeman. This "road report" when studied carefully, identifies elevations, a spring on Cape Meares, and the specific route of the wagon road. These can be seen easily by visiting the places Freeman mentioned, for his sites are still there. Consider the place where George Freeman would build a dock in Tillamook Bay for the lighthouse tender *Manzanita* to off-load supplies, then the distance from that location to Cape Meares lighthouse. These can be visited today and could not possibly be associated with any plan to put the lighthouse on Cape Lookout.

Another unique factor has to do with George Freeman's detailed description of the spring for supplying fresh water to the lighthouse. He wrote in his *Report on Survey of Cape Meares, Or* in August 1887, "The spring is 373 feet above mean sea level..." and the "proposed lighthouse site is as far west as is safe in my judgement to go, this point...is 216 feet above mean sea level." Piped water from the spring would gravity-flow for use at the lighthouse. (In the book *Bayocean*, we see that the engineer hired to build a water system for the community ascended Cape Meares where he tapped the spring, then sent the piped water using gravity pressure, all the way to the town.)

164

Postoffice operated in lighthouse

For awhile, the Barnegat post office, which was located in the vicinity of the present Cape Meares community, across from what later was the resort town of Bayocean on Tillamook Spit, was operated from the Cape Meares Lighthouse. Most postal historians seem to have missed the fact that a U. S. Post Office actually operated from within the U. S. Lighthouse Establishment's reservation at the Cape Meares Lighthouse.

Evidence that the post office was in the lighthouse appears in *The Tillamook Headlight,* September 13, 1900:

Our post office has been moved to the light house...Mr. Grosheim is acting postmaster.

In the *Headlight* May 2, 1901:

Our postmaster [Mr. Grossheim]...will leave the lighthouse for a few weeks vacation to see civilization once more.

— Data courtesy of Tillamook Pioneer Museum

In 1889, the Light-House Board ordered work for the aid to navigation to get underway.

For years, the Cape Lookout property remained a lighthouse preserve but never had an aid to navigation on it. On September 3, 1935, the U. S. Lighthouse Service gave the property to the State of Oregon, thus was the beginning of Cape Lookout State Park.

The citizens of Tillamook City were pleased that the lighthouse was erected at Cape Meares as it was to become an important guidepost on the sea road to their bay, as well as a powerful signal to ships in the coastwise trade.

Anthony W. Miller, was appointed the first head keeper of the Cape Meares facility. He was assisted by Andrew Hold and Henry York. Other principal keepers through the years included George Hunt, Harry D. Mahler, George H. Higgins and Thomas P. Ford. Miller only remained at his post for three years before transferring, but Hunt was at the helm of Cape Meares light for 11 years. There was an interlude when a woman was acting head keeper for a single month, July 11, 1903 until August 14, 1903, while awaiting the arrival of Harry Mahler. She was Mrs. August Hunt, the wife of George Hunt who had served as head keeper from January 30, 1892 until 1903.

Christmas Day wedding bells rang at the lighthouse in 1901.

Cape Meares Lighthouse with workroom.

Second assistant keeper George H. Higgins, a short, serious man, won the hand of Amelia M. Freeman, daughter of Tillamook pioneer L. G. Freeman. She wore a lovely lace gown and flowing veil while the spouse, with his handle-bar mustache and blue uniform with brass buttons, starched collar and white necktie, was in his lighthouse best. The marriage proved a good one and the bride, a few inches taller than her husband, settled down to "light housekeeping." They had four children, three born at the station. Finances were helped in May 1903 when George was elevated to first assistant keeper, and finally in 1907, to principal keeper. For reasons unknown, he retired from the Lighthouse Service two years later.

The station was a prime attraction in the "land of cheese, trees and ocean breeze," the logo phrase for Tillamook County. During the summer months there were frequent visitors to the lighthouse. Folks were always given a friendly reception and an inspection of the facilities. The reservation offered stately forests, fabulous seascapes, wildflowers and an ancient contorted spruce tree known as the "octopus tree."

166

Children reared at the station were resourceful. They were educated in a one-room schoolhouse built in the tall timber. A potbellied stove furnished the heat and the teacher, Mrs. Endicott, boarded with the Mahler family at the keepers quarters. Mode of travel between the dwelling and the school was frequently on horseback, three to a horse, along the north trail about a mile from the lighthouse.

In the early part of the century, the students were the two daughters of assistant keeper Sam Morris and two daughters and a son belonging to the Mahlers. The lighthouse kids not only learned to make their own fun but also became indoctrinated into the chores of keeping the light.

Considerable white and black paint was necessary in maintaining the light tower inasmuch as the exterior was iron-plated. The salt air was no deterrent to rust and the keepers, who were often scraping and applying red lead to troubled spots, were pleased that the tower was not one of the tall variety. The workroom abutting the tower was not erected until 1895. This 12 x 17 foot addition was of masonry construction and enhanced the appearance of the tower. When the workroom was added, an iron staircase led down to the structure from a high bank replacing the earlier wooden staircase.

Two oil houses were east of the tower, far enough away to prevent damage in case of fire. They held 3,240 gallons of kerosene, in five gallon cans, and were carefully placed behind 15 inch-thick walls, each house measuring 12 x 15 feet. It required considerable coal oil to fire the five-wick lamp every night.

Automation came to the lighthouse in 1963 with an impact similar to that when electricity was introduced in 1934. During the latter year, the oil houses were dismantled. With the advent of automation, the Coast Guard decided to replace the traditional lighthouse with an exposed aero marine type (DCB) beacon atop a utilitarian structure to minimize the responsibilities of maintaining a lighthouse without attendants.

There was talk of removing the entire tower, in fact, the old workroom was removed and the lighthouse stood in abandonment with its plates gathering rust.

Again it was the local citizenry that took up the cause to save the lighthouse. The Coast Guard finally relented and leased the property, and the aging tower to Tillamook County on November 6, 1964. A low key ceremony was conducted to mark the event.

On July 2, 1968, Tillamook County transferred the property to the Oregon State Parks Department of the Oregon State Highway

Mrs. August Hunt
Boyington who became
Acting Keeper at Cape
Meares on death of her
husband Mr. Hunt. She
married Mr. Boyington who
was also a Keeper.

Commission. During the vacancy, the keepers dwellings had been hippie-occupied from time to time, vandalized, and were seriously deteriorated. On one occasion, vandals broke into the tower and stole the precious bullseye prisms out of the classic optic. Because of general deterioration, the dwellings had to be torn down as they presented a safety hazard. With those buildings gone, all that remained on the reservation, outside of the new DCB replacement light, was a tower that had been sadly neglected, its iron plates now ruddy with rust.

Allotted state funds permitted a turnabout in an unfortunate situation. In 1978, a new workroom, a replica of the original, was erected to connect with the tower. But instead of placing it on the east side where the original room was located, it was built on the south side to permit easier access for visitors. The tower was scraped then repainted along with some repairs, and volunteers were organized to host the facility for scores of summer visitors.

The tower was officially opened to the public on Memorial Day 1980. Though an effort was made to recover the missing bullseye prisms from the big lens, only one was returned. Thus the lens, at this writing, still has holes at the focal plane.

The old lighthouse serves as an historical attraction within a state park and is no longer an aid to navigation. The state maintains the surrounding area to the ultimate, all of which focuses on the little lighthouse so long the pride of Tillamook County.

The functioning DCB unit had been scheduled to be discontinued by the Coast Guard in 1986. It would have been carried out had it not been for a flurry of protests from the commercial fishermen whose home port is Tillamook Bay. They depended on this light which is on 24 hours a day and puts out close to 2 million candlepower. (An old *Light List* noted that the Fresnel lens produced 13,000 candlepower at one time, then when upgraded, put out 160,000 candlepower on its red flash and 18,000 candlepower on the white sector of the lens without a bullseye.)

As of 1938, Cape Meares has been a wild life refuge especially for nesting seabirds. The surrounding vertical cliffs provide protected rookeries for numerous species. The forests above the cape also afford refuge for birds and animals amid the great Sitka spruce, Western hemlock and fir which covers 138 acres. Among the forest is the Octopus tree. It has a diameter of ten feet at its base but with no central trunk, tentacles three to five feet thick branch out just above the ground like a giant sea creature.

The "little iron giant of Cape Meares," as the lighthouse has been called, offered considerable assistance to maritime commerce in the days of coastwise shipping before the advent of navigational innovations. But no matter how effective a lighthouse, shipwreck still occurs wherever there is a heavy concentration of shipping.

The coastal schooner *Gracia,* 166 tons, flirted with the dangerous coastal outcrops at the base of Cape Meares December 12, 1893, just three years after the lighthouse was established. The crew was rescued but the vessel and her cargo were a total loss.

Most of the wrecks occurred around the treacherous Tillamook bar. This is a narrow entrance that can become easily riled under adverse conditions. Remains of the schooner *Lila & Mattie,* which was disabled on the bar in 1897, still lie in the shallows in the bay.

The three-masted schooner *Ida Schnauer* was wrecked on the bar, June 17, 1908 after slipping her anchor cable. That wreck occurred just three weeks after the installation of the U. S. Lifesaving Station at Barview on the bay.

The rescue crew was kept busy. On one occasion, the commercial yacht *Bayocean,* with about 100 passengers on board, became stranded in the bay on the mud flats, in the fog, at low tide, when her skipper couldn't see to turn in time for his run to his private dock at the budding resort community of Bayocean. The weekly trip from Portland saw the ship depending on the lights on Tillamook Rock and at Cape Meares for bearings in its dash for Tillamook Bay. With the ship aground and all those passengers on board, the Lifesaving Service feared it would have its hands full. But on investigation, it was determined the only danger was with disgruntled people who wanted off the ship, but who would just have to stay put until the tide came in when the pilot could take another shot at the dock. We will discuss Bayocean (town) shortly.

Four persons perished when the gas schooner *Phoenix* attempted to come about on the rough bar November 5, 1923. She became a total loss.

The big tug *Tyee* was snatched by a huge "widow maker" on the bar in December of 1940, the driving force ripping off her pilot house and taking the lives of two crewmen. The rest of the crew hung on when the hull flipped over and the diesel engine dropped out and sank in the depths. They were eventually rescued. The inverted hull lay on the beach for along time but was eventually righted in a novel salvage effort. It was refloated and rebuilt as the tug *Sandra Foss*.

The gas powered halibut schooner *Vida* lost her rudder while crossing the bar April 28, 1912 and was driven up on the north spit, a total loss. The lifesaving crew rescued the six man crew. The *Vida* was just one of many commercial fishing vessels wrecked in and around Tillamook Bay through the years. Even as this is being written, the 72 foot fishing vessel *Miss Anngel* is aground on the shoals, after her helmsman fell asleep at the wheel. A Coast Guard crew rescued the four aboard after which salvage efforts were begun on the crabber-dragger.

Cape Meares light is located five miles south of the Tillamook bar entrance and its powerful beam, even in this age, is very important to Tillamook based fishing boats.

From Cape Meares to the north is a low, gravel and sand spit. On the Kincheloe Point (north) end, there are tree-covered sand dunes 40 to 50 feet high. This spit forms the west shore of Tillamook Bay. (On the ocean side, the beach was once very wide and flat, but today high tide laps the dune. The once grand beach, over 100 yards wide and almost 5 miles long, eroded away.) On a number of occasions starting in the late 1930's, high, winter, storm-driven breakers crashed over and washed away the spit. The road was lost. The water line that fed fresh spring water from near the top of Cape Meares to the town of Bayocean was knocked out. The great storm of November 1952 completely demolished the spit leaving a gap one mile wide where the sea poured directly into Tillamook Bay. All the oyster beds there were covered with shifting sand and ruined—buried. Kincheloe Point and adjacent land now appeared as an island. Prior to the washout, many expensive homes slid off their foundations (built on sand!) and fell into the ocean.

170

Cape Meares
Lighthouse as it
appears today.

The town of Bayocean had been a planned real estate development. Due to man-caused erosion initiated by short-sightedness of politicians about jetty construction, the town fell into the sea over a thirty year period. The town, which had a three-story hotel, school, newspaper, post office, voting precinct, a Port District, and dozens of homes, had been collapsing a little at a time so when the big break happened there was not much left to damage. One of the west's grandest indoor swimming pools, The Natatorium, that had been built right on the beach, was one of the first buildings to go. Only the school house and four homes were moved off the spit in time. (The school is today's Community Hall in the village of Cape Meares.)

Because the people of Tillamook (city) feared the ocean would roar right up their city streets, now that the spit was gone, as well as the commercial wipe-out of the oyster farms in the bay, the Army Corps of Engineers was directed to "fix the spit." The present break-water from Pitcher Point became the new link between the so-called "main land" and Kincheloe Point. Oregon authors Bert and Margie

171

The Classic Cape
Meares Lighthouse.
See also the
photograph on
cover of book.

Webber have an award-winning book about this, *BAYOCEAN: The Oregon Town that Fell Into the Sea.*

Many historians believe that Tillamook Bay is what Captain Robert Gray referred to as "Murderer's Harbor" on his voyage along the northwest coast in 1788. In attempting to enter, the sloop *Lady Washington* stranded on the sands and for awhile was in danger but obviously was able to float free. The natives at first appeared friendly and brought fish, crab and berries to the seafarers which were gratefully received. As usual for the period, some of the crew were suffering from scurvy. A detail of the seamen were sent ashore to cut grass for the animals on board. A black lad named Marcus, who had joined the ship in the Falklands, thoughtlessly left his cutlass standing in the sand after cutting the grass with the weapon. An Indian attempted to steal it. Marcus tried to recover it but was met by the fury of a host of Indians, and killed. The rest of the white party narrowly escaped to their ship where only Gray and two others had remained. The Indians in their canoes pursued the party and a battle followed in which some of the Indians were shot. Marcus was the only victim among the ship's crew.

The *Lady Washington* immediately put to sea with bad recollections of the bay which for a brief period was thought by Gray to be the fabled "River of the West." A few years later he discovered the real "River of the West," the Columbia.

172

Chapter 11
Tillamook Rock Lighthouse

Tillamook Rock Lighthouse, one of the three most famous, or infamous, sentinels in the nation's arsenal of aids to navigation, is finishing out its days as the world's only lighthouse-gravesite. Now, after 77 good years as a sentinel whose beam was a lifesaver, it has been turned into a columbarium.

> **TILLAMOOK ROCK LIGHTHOUSE**
> **Location: 45°56'N 124°01'**
> **Nearest town: On rock off shore**
> (Can be seen from Seaside, Cannon Beach and Ecola State Park)
> **Built: 1881** Discontinued 1957
> **Type: White square tower**
> **Height above water: 133ft**
> **Height above ground: 62ft**
> **Light source: Oil vapor incandescent**
> **Beam: White**
> **Optics: 1st Order**
> **Power: 48,000cp**
> **Seen: 18 miles**
> **Horn: Diaphragm**
> NOTE: Classic data is from *Light List* 1934. U.S. Dept. of Commerce, Lighthouse Service and reflects details then in effect.

Completely stripped of its interior furnishings down to the stone walls, the empty cavern is filled with racks to hold urns of ashes of the dead. The windows and portholes are cemented over and the lantern panes removed in favor of solid metal plates. Basically speaking, it is one huge crypt. The only interior reminder of a dramatic past is the circular iron staircase which in ghostly fashion winds up into the dark, sealed off lantern house.

Eternity at Sea, a company that now owns the sea-girt structure, has placed the lighthouse on the *National Register of Historic Places*. But one cannot tell, by viewing it from shore, that the rock's once grand sentinel is no longer a lighthouse, except at night, for the once powerful beam is missing. Except for the thousands of sea birds and seals and sea lions that flop up on the lower ledges to rest, all traces

Tillamook Rock and its lighthouse as it appeared in 1957 from the west. The focal plane of the light was 133 feet above sea level and sometimes winter seas inundated the lantern house and knocked the light out of order. Background is where the ship *Lupata (Lupatia)* crashed in an 1881 storm.

of life are gone. The site is unattended other than for unscheduled visits by the owners and brief spot-check visits by Fish and Wildlife personnel.

Before winter rains descend—the rock's annual shower bath—the lighthouse is generally covered with white slime—bird droppings.

When the rebuilding to columbarium standards was completed, there was appropriate ceremony with guests being ferried back and forth by helicopter. Had not the local facility been purchased for the present purpose, the abandoned lighthouse would have been left to the elements.

While some adventurers have visited the rock, this is not advised. The rise and fall of the sea make landing from a boat nearly impossible and there are no hand-holds due to the slipperiness of the bird droppings. Further, Tillamook Rock is private, posted property.

For the dramatic history of the lighthouse let us go back to 1878. As Minots lighthouse was to Massachusetts and St. George Reef to California, so Tillamook Rock was to Oregon. Of the three, only Minots has been relighted. Perhaps no lighthouse in American history received more publicity through the years than did Tillamook Rock. Most of the publicity was due to the severe punishment and damage incurred by storms and raging seas bashing against the station. The first official act relating to the station was approved June 20, 1878:

> That the sum of $50,000 be and the same is hereby appropriated out of any monies in the Treasury not otherwise appropriated for the purpose of constructing a first-class lighthouse on Tillamook Head, Oregon.

The second act, approved June 16, 1880 read:

> For continuing the erection of a first-class lighthouse and steam fog signal on Tillamook Head, Oregon, $50,000.

The third act, approved March 3, 1881 read:

> For completing the erection of a first-class lighthouse and steam fog signal on the rock off Tillamook Head, Oregon, $25,000.

The original act of Congress placed the light on Tillamook Head, a precipitous 1,000 foot headland, 20 miles south of the Columbia River. The lofty elevation altered the thinking of the authorities when they found out that fog often obscured the summit, thus a lighthouse so elevated could not be seen by ships. But the fog, while blotting out the top of the head left the lower elevation clear. There was no other place on the headland to erect a lighthouse on its shear seaward face. Finally attention was turned toward isolated Tillamook Rock. This was a forlorn, barren, hunk of basaltic upheaval lying a mile and a quarter off the head. It was upon this menace to navigation that the Light-House Board decided that a lighthouse must be built regardless of the dangers involved. Had the engineers known in advance the difficulties they would encounter, they might have reconsidered.

Although the authorities wanted to get the work started in the winter of 1878-1879, there were two factors that delayed the project right from the start. First was the weather, very bad weather, weather so horrific that it created its own dangerously high tides. More than a few "old salts" have labeled Tillamook Rock as "...the place old Nor'easters go when they die." Second was the logistics of construction in a hazardous environment. Although the ports were searched, no vessel suitable for a trip to "the rock" for exploration could be located. Thus, the whole project went on "hold" until June of 1879 when a lighthouse engineer was finally transported to the site by a lighthouse tender. Perhaps as an omen of things to come, when

FIRST ORDER L.H. TILLAMOOK ROCK, OREGON

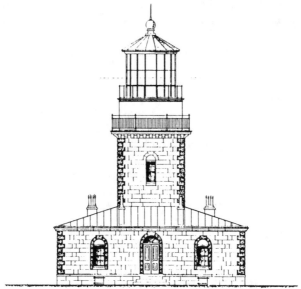

Elevation East Side

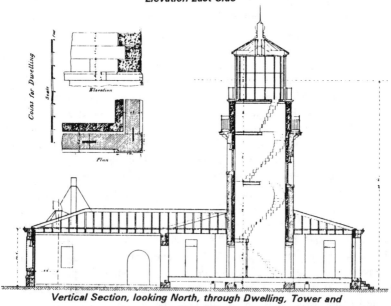

Coins for Dwelling

Elevation

Plan

Vertical Section, looking North, through Dwelling, Tower and Fog Signal Room

Office L. H. Engineer 13th Dist.
Portland, Oregon

L.H. Engineer

they arrived at the rock, monstrous seas made even considering a landing out of the question. The engineer did however, rule out the headland for a light and was of the opinion that despite the obvious obstacles, the rock could be conquered.

H. S. Wheeler, superintendent of construction, in a rather unusual command, was ordered on June 17, 1879 to proceed to Astoria and not return to the Lighthouse District Office in Portland until he had succeeded in landing and making a survey of the rock.

With no lighthouse tender available at the time, the services of the U. S. Revenue Cutter *Thomas Corwin* were secured. She crossed over the Columbia River bar June 22. When the ship arrived at the rock, the seas lapping at its base were pitching dangerously. Anchoring in the lee (such as it was) of the "island," a surfboat was launched and Wheeler began his survey. The craft approached the north side of the awesome, contorted crag. No landing site was discovered among the sheer cliffs jutting from beneath the sea. With great effort, they pulled around to the eastern shore which presented itself as the only possible landing point on the entire islet.

By getting in daringly close to the slimy outcrop and carefully timing the rise and fall of the swells, two men were able to jump from the boat to the rock. However, their efforts to conduct any kind of survey were thwarted by the steep, slippery slope. Almost as soon as they arrived it was time to go; an approaching squall threatened to strand or drown them both if they stayed. But, how to get back? The boat pulled in closer than good judgment allowed, but it was still too far for the frightened men to leap across the intervening space. The only way possible to get back off the rock was to jump into the frigid water then be pulled into the boat.

In spite of the heroics, Uncle Sam didn't get the message. Wheeler was instructed to repeat the effort. Again he was given transport to the rock via the *Corwin*. On that occasion he was able to

TILLAMOOK ROCK
Elevation (South Side) showing the Rock as it appeared originally

leap from the surfboat to the lower ledge of the cliffs, finally with great difficulty making a preliminary survey with a tape line. Here are his evaluations as they appeared in the Annual Report to the Light-House Board, as of June 30, 1879.

> An isolated basaltic rock, divided above low water level, into two very unequal parts by a wide fissure with vertical sides running east and west; stands 100 feet approximately above the sea and has a crest which is capable of being reduced so as to accommodate a structure not greater than 50 feet square... Apart from the rugged character of the headland, the tendency of the sea-face to land slides, and the great distance from the nearest supply point, the headland is too high for the site of a light-house in a locality visited by such dense fogs. The light should be placed as low as possible, and the rock is its proper site. Though the execution of the work will be a task of labor and difficulty, accompanied by great expense, yet the benefit which the commerce seeking the mouth of the Columbia River will derive from a light and fog-signal located there will warrant labor and expense involved.

The July 11, 1879 report to the Board gave plans and estimates for proposed buildings on the tiny islet. Though the early calculations were imperfect, partially because of the difficulties encountered on the rock, the necessity for getting the project underway appeared urgent.

The rock had a summit which leaned over like a melting chocolate drop. A huge blasting job would be required in order to provide a level building site. It was proposed that engines, derricks etc. be utilized in construction work and that it be arranged to send these to the rock with dispatch. Brick, cement, sand etc. would be gathered at a staging area in Astoria and readied for transport to the rock.

On August 31, the Oregon Secretary of State, under official seal, conveyed to the United States title and jurisdiction over Tillamook Rock. The edict was passed by the state legislature and signed by Oregon's governor W. W. Thayer on August 30, 1879.

Inasmuch as the early coastal Indians feared the rock and believed it home of a god, the men who made the initial landings for the lighthouse survey were probably the first humans to touch foot on the craggy upheaval.

All seemed in readiness. But it was deemed essential that a qualified surveyor and builder be sent to the rock to make a complete plan before construction began. That assignment was given to John R. Trewavas, a qualified master mason from Portland. He had played a major role in the construction of England's renowned Wolf Rock lighthouse off perilous Land's End.

He and an assistant named Cherry, attempted a landing from the *Corwin's* surfboat. Tragedy struck. Trewavas slipped and was swept into a churning mishmash of surf. Bravely, Cherry dived in after his companion but was unable to find him. Occupants in the boat were able to rescue Cherry, but Trewavas had disappeared and his body was never recovered. His drowning cast a pall of doom over the entire project.

When local newspapers received the tragic news, a public outcry reached all the way to Portland as well as the state capitol. A campaign was launched to abandon the project to avert further loss of life in what was labeled a foolhardy undertaking. But Uncle Sam would not be denied.

Charles A. Ballantyne who listed himself as "A. Ballantyne," had a reputation as a tenacious construction boss and was hired as Trewavas' replacement. The choice proved an excellent one. In addition to his building skills he was a born leader. His instructions were to organize a party of eight to ten skilled quarrymen, which was the most the budget could stand for the preliminary work.

Again, the *Corwin* was to be the transporter of personnel. In the interim, the adverse publicity made it virtually impossible to hire local laborers for an obviously dangerous undertaking. Ballantyne had to resort to secret recruitment of men unfamiliar with the rock. The service felt it necessary to keep the recruits away from Astoria so as not to be influenced by the prophets of doom. Accordingly, the laborers were housed aboard the cutter on September 24. However, southwesterly gales and an impassable bar delayed the passage indefinitely. The quarrymen were transferred from the ship to lighthouse keepers dwellings at Cape Disappointment.

Finally, on October 21, the *Corwin* was successful in putting four laborers on the rock along with hammers, drills, iron ring bolts, a small stove, provisions and a supply of canvas for temporary shelter. The landing was made with considerable trepidation, but the success of the effort provided the incentive for landing the rest of the quarrymen five days later when the seas subsided.

On that occasion a small derrick was landed, a piece at a time, so now work could get underway. The ocean remained moderate so the men lost no time in getting started. Back in town, the landings of men and supplies was of constant concern.

What did Ballantyne and his crew find in their surroundings?

On the bold, basaltic upheaval they found the water on the west, north and east sides to be from 25 to 40 fathoms deep, but shoaled from 16 to 18 fathoms on the south side over a limited area. Midway between the rock and the headland there was a small obstruction awash at high tide upon which the seas broke heavily. It was called Halfway Rock.

Tillamook Rock itself was void of all plant growth for there was no soil whatever. Springing from a basalt bench on the west side, the workers discovered a marked inclination seaward, rising to a height of 80 feet that terminated at its crest with a large rounded knob resembling the burl of a tree. The overhang was 25 feet long from west to east.

The north side was vertical above the bench near the water's edge. The east side was very steep and irregular. The south side was bounded by a deep fissure about 25 feet wide' that divided the rock in two. Waves broke violently in the fissure during storms throwing spray skyward like a geyser to the top of the rock. On occasion the green water reached the summit. The narrow spine of basalt on the south side of the fissure rose about 50 feet. All over the terrain were rocky needles and crevices, tantamount to the surface of the moon. For countless decades, sea lions, seals and sea birds were the lone inhabitants. When the first landings were made, the protective bulls were obviously agitated by the intruders. After awhile, however, the humans won this perch and the sea mammals departed in search of other rock haunts.

Landings by small boat at the base of the rock were considered so dangerous that even the idea had to be eliminated. A new form of getting personnel and supplies back and forth had to be developed. The method devised was unique. On arriving off the islet, the Revenue Cutter would moor to a spar buoy keeping the ship's head to the sea at a distance of some 300 feet from the rock. A surfboat was launched and after a crew of four strong seamen had taken their positions at the oars, two quarrymen jumped aboard and were rowed directly toward the rock on the north side of the eastern slope. Here the water was the closest to calm as it ever got. Cherry, one of the sailors who had earlier shown his bravery, watched for his opportunity and leaped ashore then scrambled up the slippery slope. He was immediately followed by quarryman Thomas Brown, thus accomplishing the first part of the plan.

180

After the men had reached a secure area safe from the pitching sea, the surfboat returned to the *Corwin*. Meanwhile on the ship, the end of a 4½ inch line had been secured to the mast. The other end was passed to the surfboat which delivered it to the men on the rock. Once ashore the line was run up the slope to an elevation of 85 feet and looped around a projecting ledge. The slack was then taken up on the ship.

The main line, known as the cable, was rigged with a large single block called a traveler, which moved fixed blocks, one at the ship and the other on the rock. The traveler was designed to be hauled back and forth along the cable from the deck of the ship by an endless line made fast to a hook on the traveler.

By that apparatus, men and materials could be transferred back and forth with a fair amount of security. The conveyance was a breeches buoy which was hooked to the line and used to transport the men. One vexing concern was apparent from the start—keeping the line taut. When the cutter rolled and pitched, the line would grow slack, often dragging the man in transit through the icy water, then snapping him airborne like a rubber band. Further, the *Corwin* had to frequently return to her base at Astoria. On her return, the cable and transfer apparatus would have to be re-assembled.

On December 18, 1879, Ballantyne, amid snow showers and squalls, was put aboard the steam tug *Mary Taylor,* in order to confer with Captain Denny, the vessel's master about instructions for off-loading a derrick. Another matter concerned how to physically transfer a substantially overweight quarryman from the ship to the rock. Unfortunately, when Ballantyne was to go back to the ship, all lines were slack and the construction foreman was dragged through the water. Wet and cold but undaunted, Ballantyne checked the details with the skipper unaware that the big quarryman was so frightened he had no intention of subjecting himself to a cold water bath. (We will reveal shortly how the quarryman was ultimately air-lifted to Tillamook Rock.) In the interim, a tackle gave way on the rock and two workers were slightly injured, narrowly averting a serious mishap.

The first two weeks of occupation demanded extremely hard labor. One of the first tasks was to erect shelters, then land tools and supplies. Next was the initial work to place iron bolts in the solid rock. All work was done in total exposure to the weather, for there were no caves, overhangs, or occupiable ledges anywhere on the rock which provided adequate shelter. Some of the crew wondered why they ever signed up for such a project.

The Story of the Corpulent Quarryman

There was no finer quarryman than Mr. Gruber. But getting him to agree to accept work on the lighthouse project had been a chore in itself.

Now on the ship facing the rock, Gruber observed the dunking the construction foreman, Ballentyne, had endured when Ballentyne was roped back to the ship from the rock. It turned out that Mr. Gruber was so frightened over the primitive method of personnel transfer between ship and rock, that he refused to leave the steamer. Mr. Gruber was afraid of the water. There was just no way he would agree to be dragged through the frigid Pacific Ocean regardless of how great the job might be. He would not budge.

It took considerable persuasion to change his mind. When it was discovered that Mr. Gruber's frame was too large to get into a breeches buoy, Ballentyne had suggested he be lashed to the top of it. Gruber panicked! None of that for him! Thus he sat out the day on the ship to be returned to Astoria. Back in port, a jumbo-sized cork life preserver was acquired.

Once again at the rock, with the life preserver lashed to a boatswain's chair, Mr. Gruber climbed in and was readied for his epic ride. Fortunately, despite his bulk, the man was landed on the rock without so much as getting even the soles of his shoes wet. Because he had been in the chair, instead of in a beeches buoy, he had freedom of movement during the transit. Even the sea cooperated as the swells of the ocean were such that the lines between the rock and the ship remained taut. Mr. Gruber was the first man to gain the rock in a completely dry condition. Everyone was relieved. Especially Mr. Gruber.

Their canvas A-tents were held down by ropes lashed through ringbolts imbedded in the rock. The shelters were drafty and leaky at best. A bench was cut in the basalt on the southwest side near the 90 foot level for a frame dwelling. It was only after many salt-water drenchings that this portion of the project was abandoned—the seas too frequently inundating that section of the rock after exploding skyward on impact with the butt end of the fissure. Only the north side afforded any protection from salt water geysers.

The frequent squalls, sharp, biting gales and rampaging seas made the very act of survival difficult. Under such conditions, forward progress on the project was almost a bonus. The rock was so hard and progress was so slow with traditional methods that giant, oversized cartridges of blasting powder were finally used. But then they discovered the charges had to be placed in deeper, hand-hewn crevices to be truly effective. A narrow ledge was finally hacked out to accommodate the main derrick. Then a crude pathway was chiseled out to reach an area 30 feet above the sea. Unshapely steps and footholds were made to go up the steep side to the 90 foot level. Day after day, the team worked on, carving and clawing, then blasting their way up that wretched upheaval. As bad as conditions were, they got worse. Much worse.

Came another January of storms when one of tremendous proportions swept the north Pacific. It raised voluminous seas that combed over the summit of Tillamook Rock. This seriously endangered the lives of the wretched little band of workers. Everyone and everything on the rock was in peril. Work was at a standstill. The storm reached its apex on January 7 while the crew was trying to get some much needed rest in their sodden, leaking tents. Bedding and clothing were soaked and there was near panic in the ranks. Except for the intrepidity of Ballantyne, the men would have left their shelter, which though exposed, was the safest place on the rock. Crashing seas had already swept away the supply shelter housing many of their tools.

Holes had been torn in their abode and the stove had sea water in the firebox. With forethought, the construction boss had stocked the quarters with hard bread, coffee and bacon, that being the total menu for several days. The crash of the seas was so great that it seemed at any time everyone would be carried to a watery grave. Rocks were flying about as the breakers tore off chunks and tossed them at will. From the second day of January until the 16th, the howling weather continued. During all that time, the wrathful Pacific seemingly beat the drums of doom as if trying to eradicate the crag that bore the name Tillamook and the parasites that clung to it. All that time there had been no contact with the mainland and grave concern was expressed as to whether the men had survived.

The seas were so rough that the storehouse, the provisions, the water tank, two spars, the roof of the blacksmith shop and the traveler line were all swept away.

Finally on January 18, the *Corwin* was able to approach the rock. Ballantyne signaled that he and his crew had survived the onslaught but they were in dire need of food and other provisions plus coal. The *Corwin* launched a surfboat and carried as much as possible to the rock. With great difficulty, by the use of ropes, the supplies were landed. But the spirits of the gaunt victims of the storm were raised the most when a big bag of mail was hoisted ashore. The *Mary Taylor* also approached later in the day and sent in all the provisions Captain Denny could spare.

By the following day, another southwest gale was blowing. Nevertheless, the workers managed slowly with their work. A slight moderation in the weather occurred on January 20. Then a week later the *Taylor* successfully landed an additional five workers. With the added man power, it didn't take much longer before a large sand blast was accomplished and a hole seven feet deep was drilled in a hard portion of the rock, then charged with 15 giant powder cartridges.

Undaunted by the worst King Neptune could dole out, Ballantyne had a remarkable ability for bolstering the spirits of his crew and vigorously pushed the work until May when he was ordered ashore. He was to superintend the construction of the appliances required for handling the stone and the heavier building materials. This included all the masonry.

By the time he returned to Tillamook Rock on May 31, his laborers had blasted away the entire hump of the summit. The top of the rock was now ready for construction of the lighthouse. By this time, work had been in progress for 224 days. What had been done was a monumental accomplishment under very adverse circumstances. This had been a battle of man against nature and man had won. During that period of time, the crest of the rock had been reduced by about 30 feet with the removal of 4,630 cubic yards of basalt. Had the site been larger, much of the stone needed for the tower could have been cut right there from the waste and stored on the site. This would have saved the cost of quarrying it elsewhere then hauling it from the mainland.

During the blasting operations, 12 to 15 pounds of giant No. 2

powder was used as a charge, the holes firmly tamped with sand, then the explosion made by the Bickford's triple tape fuse and cap fused with furminate of mercury.

By exploding charges of black powder of 100 pounds and more in the fissures, some 250 cubic yards of rock was blasted at a crack. The blasting utilized 1,231 pounds of black powder and 300 pounds of giant powder. Total equivalent of black powder was 4,231 pounds. The expenses as of June 1, 1880 including labor, powder, materials for quarters, temporary derricks and chartered tenders: $13,537. This was $2.86 for each cubic yard of rock removed.

The original derrick, that had been hoisted up on the rock, was a small frame, triangular, 20 foot high apparatus. It was fitted with a winch at the bottom and strengthened by cross-cleats at short intervals. When the construction boss returned to the rock on May 31, the ship he was on carried a second large boom derrick for raising stone and heavy equipment. Its mast was 45 feet high and the boom 75 feet long.

The timbers were towed out from Astoria and winched up on the rock. The needed iron fittings were landed via the traveler apparatus. Additional equipment, for the masons, included four ladder derricks, a donkey engine, boiler and winch for operating the derricks, and five water-tight casks for holding fresh water. There were three sling tubs for mortar transfer and a wooden cage for landing workers. Everything was put on the rock without damage, which in itself was an accomplishment of merit.

Sealed proposals for cut stone and building materials had been invited at Astoria on November 13, 1879. the requirements were:

> 1,000 cubic feet of first class Ashlar Stone (dressed)
> 1,000 cubic feet of Rubble Stone
> 100,000 well burnt brick
> 5,000 cubic feet of Pit Sand

After studying bids, the award went to Messers. Chalmers, Holmes & Jeffery of Portland, Oregon.

The sandstone came from the Bellingham area on Puget Sound and from a quarry near Astoria. Other stone was quarried at Mt. Tabor, then east of Portland, today a residential district in Portland. The bricks were carefully chosen to line the walls of the building and for the parapet walls as well.

A small wrecking vessel was chartered by the Light-House Board to transport the heavy building materials to Tillamook Rock. The stone, brick, cement, lime and allied materials were lifted from the vessel's deck by the large derrick on the rock, its boom easily bridging the watery abyss.

Calvin Nutting and Son, of San Francisco, won the bid for the iron lantern house on April 20, 1880. His price was $8,200. Nutting had to agree to deliver his product to the site.

A. & F. Brown of New York, was the successful bidder for the steam powered, first-class fog sirens. The cost was $5,100, boxed and delivered.

Smith Brothers & Watson, Portland, received the nod to manufacture locomotive type boilers. These would be 12½ feet long, at a cost of $3,550.

During construction, a variety of vessels were employed in the transport of personnel, supplies and equipment. First and foremost was the U. S. Revenue Cutter *Thomas Corwin,* Lt. (skipper) John Brann. The veteran U. S. Lighthouse Tender *Shubrick* (first lighthouse tender assigned to the Pacific Coast) was requested but could only provide occasional trips due to its responsibilities for keeping regular schedules for other lighthouses. Accordingly, the steam powered, schooner-rigged *Mary Taylor* Captain J. E. Denny, rendered yeoman service under charter by the Light-House Board. The 94 ton vessel was chartered for a sum of $1,650 per month and was engaged until May 20, 1880, the charter price having been reduced to $1,200 a month. Proving adequate for the difficult run to and from the rock, her services were invaluable. However, her later replacement was the steam schooner *George Harley,* Captain J. W. Dodge. Though slightly smaller, the *George Harley,* was better suited for carrying heavy materials, having been equipped as a wrecking vessel. She carried steam hoisting gear adequate for lifting heavy stone. In fact, Captain Dodge received special praise from the Light-House Board for his skillful handling of the heavy stone and heavy equipment—nothing having been damaged during the on-loading at mainland ports or off-loading at Tillamook Rock.

The masons on Tillamook Rock got ahead of delivery, so the sailing schooner *Emily Stevens* was chartered. Special hoisting gear was installed on her deck to enable the ship to do the work. She could carry 500 tons of cargo per trip. The agreed fee was $10 a ton.

Depending entirely on sail, the *Emily Stevens* had to time her departures from Astoria on favorable wind, tide and bar conditions. Square-sterned and well-founded, the vessel, in addition to her hoisting gear, used the now surplus donkey engine on the rock to assist in handling the cargo ashore.

Moorings were of the utmost importance in the cargo transfer operations. Difficult anchorage off the rock was a major concern. To hold the ships in position, spar buoys tethered to the sea floor, were fashioned of Oregon Spruce 45 feet long and 2.6 feet in diameter at the butt end. Mooring chains were 40 to 45 fathoms long with heavy sinkers attached. On arrival off the crag, a vessel would have her bow pointing seaward (west) and run out lines to three buoys. Additional bow and stern lines were sent to the rock where they were secured to ringbolts embedded deep in the basalt. The buoy sinkers weighed from 5,500 to 7,000 pounds.

After a vessel was properly moored, the derrick boom was swung out toward the craft, then the hoisting rope, after passing successfully through the blocks at the foot and top of the mast, and at the peak of the boom, was united with the fall of the ship. The fall was further led through a single block hung upon a bridle that connected the masts of the cargo carrier at their top, then were passed to the winch of the donkey engine on the deck. The hoisting rope carried a hook permanently lashed to it from which the articles to be transferred were suspended.

The lighthouse and connected fog signal building were erected 90 feet above the sea on a founding surface 80 x 45 feet. The original building was designed to accommodate four male keepers (no women or children were ever permitted) with ample space for a six month provision for coal and supplies.

The edifice of one story, 48 x 45 feet, had an extension 32 x 28 feet under the same roof for the fog siren equipment. The stone tower, 16 feet square, rising from the center of the building, supported an iron lantern and parapet which housed a First Order lens and lighting apparatus. The lighthouse beacon would display a white flash every five seconds. The walls, according to the official report, were the same thickness as those of the dwelling enclosing a wall 12 feet in diameter through which the circular staircase rose. The tower was 35½ feet high to the brick parapet extending upward another eight feet upon which rested the iron lantern house.

Duplicate boilers for the fog signals were arranged parallel to the north and south walls of the signal room with engines between them. All of this was interchangeable with appropriate valve fittings so either siren could be actuated by either boiler.

The sirens which were usually and knowingly called "blasters," sounded five seconds duration at intervals of 1½ minutes.

Rain water was collected from the roofs of the building and conducted to a brick-lined cistern, that had been excavated out of the solid rock on the north side. It had a capacity of 13,000 gallons. The siren, when operating with a pressure of 72 pounds of steam, consumed 130 gallons of water per hour.

Outstanding personalities instrumental in the construction of the lighthouse were:

H. S. Wheeler, Superintendent of Construction
Charles A. Ballantyne, Construction Foreman
Thomas Brown, Sub-Foreman
Con O'Brien, Machinist (engines for landing gear, etc.)
Major G. L. Gillespie, U.S.A., Lighthouse Engineer, 13th Distrist
Lt. E. M. Price, U.S.A., Army Corps of Engineers

Stone by stone and brick by brick the building rose affording a modicum of protection from the weather and seas for the laborers. The quarrymen, masons, engineers and iron workers all performed their jobs with dispatch even though the working conditions were far less than usually acceptable. After 525 days of labor, the celebrated day for the official opening approached. But something very bizarre occurred only a short time before the light was ready to shine. On several occasions, during the construction period, ships getting too near the rock were warned away in the fog by the men setting off blasting charges. However, one dark, stormy night during a southeast wind, the 1,300 ton British bark *Lupata**, Captain R. H. Raven, wandered off course and came dangerously near the rock. It was about 8 o'clock on January 2, 1881. The ship was so close that some of the workers claimed they could hear the commands of the captain and in the murk, see the dim glow of the running lights. Hastily, bonfires were kindled in addition to shouts and powder blasts in order to warn of impending danger. The warnings were heeded and the vessel veered away, but in the confusion, unknown to those on the rock, her course was changed eastward, causing a straight-on crash into the unrelenting outcrops off Tillamook Head.

Not until the following morning, when the murk cleared somewhat, did the men on the rock realize the disastrous results. Just above the surface, far in the distance, was a slanted topmast, rigging in disarray, and a few pieces of wreckage. That was all that remained of the ill-fated ship. Her entire crew (16) had perished. The only survivor was a young Australian shepherd dog found whimpering on the slippery rocks at the base of the headland. Most of the bodies were recovered. To add to the tragedy, it was learned that the ship's

---

*Some registers carry her name *Lupatia* as does Louis & Dryden. *Oregonian* disagrees.

master, Captain Irvine, had earlier perished at sea and the first mate, Haven, had assumed command. Bound for the Columbia River in ballast from Hiogo, the vessel's final resting place was less than two miles from Tillamook Rock.

The ironic conclusion to the *Lupata* tragedy was that the wreck occurred only 19 days before Tillamook Rock lighthouse became officially operative on January 21, 1881.

The United States government, labeled the establishment of Tillamook Rock lighthouse an outstanding "engineering triumph," accomplished under the most trying conditions. Despite the early public outcries to abandon the project, it was completed without the loss of a single life with the exception of surveyor John Trewavas.

As if a curse had been placed on the rock, its reputation was soon known from coast to coast. It has remained a mystery down to the present time how a lighthouse could absorb so much punishment from the forces of nature. The cost of repairs, alterations, maintenance and upgrading became a headache for both the U. S. Lighthouse Service and later the U. S. Coast Guard. Numerous keepers narrowly escaped death while maintaining the sentinel but the structure was built like a fortress and has stood the test of time.

It was a nostalgic event in 1957 when the Coast Guard closed the facility after 77 hectic years of active service. Tillamook Rock lighthouse had become too costly to operate. It had antiquated equipment and it was definitely difficult to get to. By 1957, it was no longer near the steamer lanes. The Coast Guard was relieved to be free of the responsibility. An innovative age of automation had arrived and old Tillamook light, which the press labeled as "Terrible Tilly," was put out to pasture.*

*NOTE: Readers are encouraged to obtain a copy of *Terrible Tilly, An Oregon Documentary; The Biography of a Lighthouse. See:* Bibliography.

Bob Gerloff,
fabled
assistant
keeper,
Tillamook Rock
Lighthouse

The first principal keeper assigned to Tillamook Rock was Albert Roeder who proudly took command of the $125,000 structure. He and his assistants were soon to learn that they were in a place of violence when gales struck the Oregon Coast sending monstrous waves against the rock and spraying the stone walls of the lighthouse. The iron roof was frequently holed by flying rock and debris. Windows were often broken and the lantern panes cracked or shattered 133 feet above normal water. Sometimes the fog signal trumpets were clogged with seaweed or pieces of basalt. Occasionally the entire structure was inundated by sea water. The derrick house

Report of the Light-House Board
1881

Tillamook Lighthouse on Tillamook Rck, 18 miles south of entrance to Columbia River, Oregon. - This station is practically finished. The small working party now there is building a brick engine and supply house on the northeast slope, a guard fence around the crest of the rock, a landing-wharf, an iron stairway connecting the wharf with the keepers' dwelling, and a tramway for raising supplies from the wharf to the supply house and to the fog-signal room. The corner-stone of the dwelling was laid on June 22, 1880 and on Jan. 8, following, the main building, tower and fog-signal annex were completed, the illuminating apparatus was adjusted and the working party withdrawn. On January 21 the light was exhibited for the first time and on February 11 the machinery of the fog-signals was in place, ready for service. The time actually consumed in construction, after the laying of the corner-stone was 201 days, and the time from the examination of the rock, June 26, 1879 to the first exhibition of the light, January 21, 1881, was 575 days. During this period but one life was lost, and no property was destroyed except by storms....

and long boom below the lighthouse on the eastern exposure were sometimes in the path of invading seas and the results were disastrous.

In 1886, a half ton mass of concrete filling was sheared off and thrown through the railing and into the ocean 90 feet below. In 1912, an overhanging chunk of rock weighing several tons was ripped from the western exposure causing such a grinding noise as to send the keepers into near panic for fear the lighthouse might be torn from its foundation.

The greatest concern of the keepers was when the lantern panes were smashed allowing sea water inside. On occasion the water ran down the staircase into the watch room, and then down the circular iron steps through the trunk of the tower to the rotunda. Nary a year passed without damage of some kind. Iron railings were often crushed by boulders. Outside tanks were knocked from their mounts. The roof often became like a sieve during heavy rains and repairs were constant.

At times there were long periods before a tender could bring supplies and mail to the weary keepers. Contact with the shore was out of the question until necessity demanded the laying of a cable from the mainland to the rock as a means of communication. The work was accomplished at a cost of $6,000, but a year later heavy sea parted it.

Old post card view of Tillamook Rock and Lighthouse, Oregon Coast.

Perhaps the most frightening experience for the keepers goes back to the storm of October 18, 1912. Head keeper William Dahlgren, one of the stalwart keepers of the light, was on duty during that storm. He had just finished checking the light and fog signal and came into the kitchen to warm himself against the stove and to smoke his pipe. Suddenly, just like an earthquake, his hair stood on end. The entire building shook. Plaster fell off the walls. The stove sent out billows of black smoke and soot. The other keepers, aroused from slumber came running into the kitchen in their underwear. None dared step outside into the howling storm. They had to wait it out until daybreak to find the cause. Just before midnight, as they stood around the stove, there was another terrible shocker and a grinding crash that sent all hands up the circular staircase of the tower to see if the beacon was still in operation. Several panes of glass had been knocked out and chunks of rock, seaweed and fish were inside the lantern room amid several inches of water. They worked for hours to clean up the mess and to get the lens back to proper rotation. There could be tempest-tossed mariners searching for the light. Not until daylight did the sleepless keepers find the cause of the first impact. A one hundred ton slab of basalt had been excavated from the west end of the rock and surging seas had altered the contorted face of the monolith.

Roy Dibb (left) and "Cap" Hermann, winners of the Gallitan Award for years of lighthouse service. Both served at Tillamook Rock.

Again in 1914, Dahlgren rallied his assistants when the station was immersed time and again for 15 hours. The fog signal house roof was badly holed. According to one account, to ease tensions, the head keeper removed his clothing and stood under the biggest leak. "Just the thing to pep up a man when he's feeling low," he is alleged to have told his amazed associates.

Continuing storms often took bites out of the lighthouse. Finally it was decided the constantly damaged iron roofs would have to be replaced. This was done with two-foot thick reinforced concrete. During that piece of reconstruction, a half-story was added to the dwelling section of the building. The "attic" addition, affording less than head room, provided storage and a place for a semblance of a library for the books that compassionate shore dwellers contributed to the isolated keepers. The rock in later years picked up an unfortunate name, Oregon's "Alcatraz" Prison. In 77 years of active duty only a handful of women were ever allowed to visit the rock and never overnight. The selected few were either wives of keepers or women on official business.

Undoubtedly, one of the most memorable storms to ever reap its vengeance on the rock occurred on October 21, 1934. Keepers William Hill, Henry Jenkins, Hugo Hansen and Werner Storm were present. It was as if the world was about to be flooded as in Noah's time. The entire Pacific Northwest was being battered but to the keepers it was as if the epicenter had zeroed in on Tillamook Rock. Winds well in excess of 100 miles per hour were blasting out of the southwest, whipping up portentous seas seemingly designed to destroy the lighthouse.

Hunks of basalt, 25 to 150 pounds each were stripped off the mass and thrown against the tower. Sixteen panels of glass were knocked out, the lantern house flooded with water and worst of all, the classic First Order Fresnel lens was smashed—glass from the splintered prisms covering the decking. Working at times in knee-deep water thrown up in geysers from below, the men worked feverishly to seal off the broken panes and set up an auxiliary light. Shards of glass cut Hansen's hand severely and despite a flood of blood, he labored with a tourniquet on his arm. Water flowed like a waterfall all the way down into the rotunda. Despite the best efforts of the men, no light was shown from the lantern house that night. Not until the following day were they able to install a fixed light inside an auxiliary 375 millimeter drum lens. The keepers were exhausted and the lighthouse was a shambles. Railings were flattened, sandstone blocks pitted, storage tanks torn lose, cowl resonators jammed, fog trumpets choked and rock fragments, dead seabirds, seaweed and kelp scattered about the outside cement walkways. All of the landing gear had been carried away. The derrick house was flooded and the boom literally sheared off. Iron bolts anchored three feet deep in the basalt core had been ripped out.

Though the seas moderated slightly, the storm continued for four more days and the frustrated keepers had no way to communicate with the mainland district office, as the cable had been severed. The situation was desperate. Ships were bar-bound inside the Columbia River.

It was the ingenuity of keeper Jenkins that bridged the gap. He contrived a makeshift short wave radio sending set out of spare parts, and after repeated unsuccessful efforts was finally picked up by a ham radio operator at Seaside, Henry Goetz, and he in turn alerted authorities.

The valiant effort of the keepers was soon front page news but it wasn't until October 27, that any vessel could approach the rock. Finally, the lighthouse tender *Manzanita* arrived and launched a surfboat carrying Lighthouse Superintendent E. C. Merrill and the tender's skipper Claude Asquith. These officers would survey the damage.

Without the traditional landing gear it was a touchy operation getting the men onto the rock, just like in the beginning. But with skillful maneuvering of the boat, the two men managed to leap onto the rock safely but not completely dry. The shaken visitors were appalled by the damage, carefully making a three hour inspection. Thousands of dollars would have to be expended to bring the station back to efficient operation. Merrill was quick to congratulate the keepers for their exceptional attention to their duties under the most trying conditions. In the interim, a line was made fast between the rock and the *Manzanita* and transport of personnel was resumed as in the construction years with a traveler catering to a breeches buoy. The inspectors were returned to the tender with greater confidence. Before leaving, the lacerated hand of Hansen was attended to

Communication was established with amateur radio station W7WR in Portland which coordinated operations between the lighthouse district headquarters, the Astoria supply base and the rock. Repair crews were sent to the site on the *Manzanita* and the extensive repair and alteration work began.

First consideration was replacement of the shattered optic. The entire lighting apparatus was replaced by a modern rotating beacon similar to those used at remote stations on the Great Lakes. The new unit was of American manufacture. The old incandescent oil vapor lamp was no more. Diesel engines were installed in the fog signal house for generating electricity for the light and for the station. A long row of batteries was set up as a backup.

To further protect the lantern from flying rocks and debris, a network of heavy cable was placed around the entire exterior iron housing to prevent breakage of lantern panes. Portholes set deep in the stone replaced all windows remaining on the west and southern exposures. New railings and tanks were installed. The derrick house was repaired and a new boom was installed plus numerous other repairs to get the station back to operating level

For several weeks the keepers had plenty of company. Transport of personnel and supplies was eased when the derrick, boom and hoisting machinery were restored.

The new light at Tillamook produced 75,000 candlepower visible in all directions. It was a double tier apparatus with eight separate lenses to afford the proper flashing characteristic.

Most of the early keepers at Tillamook had rather brief tenures of duty, one wondering if the nature of the place prompted requests for transfer. Albert Roeder, earlier mentioned as the first potentate of the rock, served in that capacity from only January 20, 1881 until May 5, 1881. He was replaced by George M. Rowe, who lasted slightly over

Tillamook Rock Lighthouse, its lower reaches awash.

Keepers on Tillamook Rock await arrival of the lighthouse tender.

a year from May 5, 1881 until August 14, 1882. Next came Fred B. Casper whose term as head keeper was from August 14, 1882 until December 5, 1882. C. D. Varnum took the reins from December 5, 1882 until May 29, 1884. After him came Joseph Horning, Charles H. Davis, George Hunt, Rasmus Peterson, Marinus A. Stream, Alexander K. Personen, Alex Rustad, George Stillwell, William T. Langlois and William Dahlgren. Except for Langlois and Dahlgren, none put in more than four years as keeper-in-charge. Dahlgren assumed control November 3, 1910 and evidently enjoyed his role for well over a decade.

In later years the best known keepers were George Wheeler and Oswald Allik. Allik, as mentioned earlier came to the rock as an assistant keeper. On Wheeler's retirement, he took over as head keeper, putting in a total of 20 years at the lonely station. When the Coast Guard abandoned the lighthouse in 1957, Allik turned off the light for the last time and was then transferred to Heceta Head lighthouse becoming its last keeper before the advent there of automation.

Isolation sometimes plays strange tricks on the human mind. On occasion, keepers became mentally unstable forcing immediate transfer or dismissal from the service. Four men living in close association day in and day out on a tiny mass of rock with restriction of movement during storm periods or long hours of fog, often caused misunderstandings, heated arguments and on occasion physical aggression. All such incidents had to be immediately reported to the district headquarters where the inspector would decide if requests for transfer were valid or if discipline was necessary. The head keeper was similar to the captain of a ship. All complaints went through him regardless of whether he was involved or not. In such isolated surroundings, many transfers were ordered due mainly to personality conflicts. When the head keeper was on leave, the first assistant keeper took the role of the principal keeper.

The majority of the arguments involved the operation and servicing of the fog signal apparatus. For instance, in 1929, first assistant Teofil Milkowski, in charge in the absence of the head keeper, got into a violent dispute with third assistant Ben. W. Franklin. Said Milkowski in his report to the district headquarters:

> I dean't want troble so I started out of the kitchen when Mr. Franklin struck me from the back on my ear and I turned arround and he grabbed me so we went at it and I gave him plenty.

Oswald Allik, career lighthouse keeper and all-around genial fellow, at his favorite station, Tillamook Rock.

Aladdin type standby lamp supplied to Tillamook Rock Lighthouse for emergency use following the devastating storm of November 1934 that threw the lighthouse into darkness.

After both sides were heard, the district inspector called for Franklin's immediate transfer just as soon as the next lighthouse tender arrived at the rock.

In later years, after the Coast Guard took over the Lighthouse Service, head keeper Allik gave some instructions to a young Coast Guard assistant who took offense to the order. He became so angry that he doubled up his fist as if to strike the older man. Allik in his usual gentle manner, turned his cheek toward the impetuous young man and declared:

> If it will make you feel better you have my permission to strike me.

Sheepishly, the irritated man backed off and after sulking for a

Early in its history, the only light at Tillamook Rock Lighthouse was from kerosene lanterns. These gave way to electric globes. Later, the electrical system was backed up with this room full of batteries. These were Exide wet cells and had to be attended weekly. Hanging at left (arrow), is rubber apron required to be worn by attendant who took hydrometer readings and added distilled water to the batteries when levels were low. A detailed record was kept on every battery.

brief period came back and apologized, eventually gaining a great respect for the keeper-in-charge.

During the earlier years at Tillamook Rock, long storm periods delayed vessel arrivals for lengthy periods and melancholy sometimes set in. For instance, on Thanksgiving 1913, the seas had been so rough for several days that the tender *Manzanita* was long overdue in bringing supplies and mail. On board was the traditional turkey that had been ordered weeks earlier.

It was obvious that the tender would not arrive for the holiday and with no turkey for Thanksgiving it appeared the menu of the day would be canned corned beef. As nightfall approached, the wicks were trimmed and the beacon set in motion. The wind was howling and the sea a mass of gray billows. During such conditions, as was often the case, birds in flight would become confused by the rotation of the light and the sharp beams sent out through the bullseyes of the lens. Some birds would dive directly toward the lantern house in true Kamikaze fashion.

On that occasion the victim was a duck that crashed into the lantern pane and fell dead on the platform below. The ever optimistic head keeper, Dahlgren, spotted the innate feathered friend and promptly rushed it to the kitchen where the keeper, who had the cooking duties, dressed the bird and shoved it into the oven. A few hours later the keepers dined on their Thanksgiving duck which they labeled a true gift from heaven.

After Pearl Harbor, some of the coastal lighthouses were either blacked out or dimmed out. Not so at Tillamook. Its light shined on. Ironically the Japanese submarine *I-25*, that shelled Fort Stevens on the night of June 21, 1942 knew its location by the light at Tillamook Rock.

It was the first time a military installation had been fired on in the continental United States since the War of 1812. Though the 17 shells fired at the fort did virtually no damage, it put the United States on red alert, once again fearing an invasion.* The guns at the fort did not return the submarine's barrage much to the anger of the soldiers assigned to all the three forts at the mouth of the Columbia River. For months afterward, the keepers at Tillamook Rock were ordered to keep a constant lookout for enemy submarines and to immediately report any sightings to the military authorities. (The Japanese Navy did not tell anyone they did not expect to be back.) It was fortunate that the enemy never shot at the lighthouse.

DRY RED LEAD was used for making paint. This storage box is an original from Tillamook Rock Lighthouse.

* *See: SILENT SIEGE-II: Japanese Attacks on North America in World War II. See* Bibliography.

201

Look up! ...up in the air! It's not a bird...not a plane! It's Jim Gibbs, author, riding the breeches buoy dangling from the end of the derrick cable on Tillamook Rock. This was his last trip to the rock. The year: 1957.

When the light was discontinued September 1, 1957, the Coast Guard placed Tillamook Rock Lighted Whistle buoy TR tethered in 28 fathoms, about a half mile west of the rock. It displayed a 440 candlepower light flashing every five seconds, 16 feet above the water. After several months, despite some protests by commercial fishermen, that navigation aid was also eliminated.

Problems with Tillamook and its sinister reputation did not fade after its retirement. Put on the block by the General Services Administration, the winning bid of a mere $5,500 won the rock for the Academic Economic Coordinators of Las Vegas, a group of investors, most of whom had never seen the rock. Totally unacquainted with the problems of accessibility and supply for the abandoned crag, and amid rumors of their intentions of using it for atomic testing, they never did a thing with their investment and ended up selling it to General Electric executive George Hupman of New York. Hupman had some grandiose plans of turning the place into a summer retreat. The age of the helicopter had come, which presented the only safe way to get onto the rock. After long abandonment, the interior of the lighthouse was a total mess. All iron parts were red with rust, the furnishings were mildewed and the machinery in the fog house in shambles. Plaster was all soaked and peeling away. Everything was ruined. Nevertheless, Hupman assembled a small crew, including his wife, and went out for short visits in an attempt to clean it up. In time, they too threw up their hands in despair and sold it to a young man named Max Shillock Jr. of Portland for $27,000. Masquerading as a wealthy investor with his 1978 purchase of the rock, he had actually borrowed the money for the transaction from a Mrs. Joy Goolsby. Shillock's investment was to almost cost him his life. He and three companions attempted to reach the rock in a 12 foot motorboat. It capsized in the heavy seas drowning one of the party and nearly claiming the others. A Coast Guard helicopter spotted the men struggling in the breakers toward the mainland beach. Shillock suffered from shock and hypothermia, but along with the two others, survived the ordeal. Most of what he got for his efforts during the months he owned the rock was a considerable amount of publicity for the formidable plans he had for restoring the lighthouse. His dream, however, was soon to come to a quick end when Mrs. Goolsby sued him for lack of payment on the loan.

In the out-of-court settlement she in essence, became sole owner of the rock. But she had no plans so immediately placed the old lighthouse on the sales block. This time, the rock, due to all the publicity surrounding the place, fetched a cool $50,000. The purchaser, a group of investors from Portland who under the title, Eternity at Sea, would strip the lighthouse down to bare bones and convert it into the world's first lighthouse columbarium.

Mimi Morissette, an ambitious business woman, along with Joseph Haverbeke, Cathy Riley, Marshall Morissette and Richard Bartlett teamed up to bring the plan to fruition.

As sad as that seemed to many, it was probably one of the only uses for the rundown edifice. A work crew was flown to the rock to remove everything in the interior right down to the bare rock. They were to cement over all windows and place metal plates over the lantern panes. The entire structure was to be sealed like a crypt which in essence it was. An estimated $50,000 was expended on the

Original oil cans issued in 1881 for filling the fonts that fed the burners with wicks in the First Order lamp at Tillamook Rock Lighthouse.

conversion which included providing 100,000 niches for urns. The work was assisted by placing the lighthouse on the *National Register of Historic Places.*

When the century mark of the lighthouse arrived, Mimi spearheaded a big centennial celebration on the rock which many state dignitaries attended. Guests were flown out a few at a time from the Seaside-Cannon Beach areas in a small helicopter. It was a grand public relations gathering to both mark the historical occasion and to promote the columbarium.

Though the initial program presented every indication of a successful business venture, after four years of operation only seventeen urns with ashes and 100 promises had been secured. Still Mimi and her associate Rudi Milpacker, President of Eternity at Sea, remained hopeful. A study showed by the year 2000, fifty per cent of Americans would choose to be cremated instead of the old tradition of embalming and body burial, compared to seven percent when they purchased the lighthouse. Unfortunately, the plan didn't catch on.

Mimi, a successful real estate operator had good fortune in previous enterprises. At this writing she has hope for the columbarium. Purchase of the services include, weather permitting, a ride out to the rock in a small helicopter for a loved one to see an ash-filled urn placed in solitude inside the barren structure. Costs vary

Coast Guard standard 9 x 39-foot lighted, whistle buoy. After shut down of Tillamook Rock Lighthouse in 1957, 2TR was stationed about 1,000 feet northwest of Tillamook Rock. Buoy shown was replacing another that had been run down by a ship. The mission shown was by tender *Tupulo* out of Tongue Point Coast Guard Base at Astoria.

depending in what part of the lighthouse the urn is placed. Most costly is the sealed lantern room, the least expensive the derrick house.

The owners hire a crew occassionally to clean and repaint the exterior of the structure. Except for business trips to Tillamook Rock, the isle is abandoned as in pre-lighthouse years. The sea birds—mostly gulls—cormorants, murres and others have reclaimed the place. Seals and sea lions have now returned to the lower climes of the rock. Its a lonely, ghostly place today, the lighthouse sitting in solitude at the crest of a crusty, basaltic crag. Its heyday has ended in ignominy. The patter of human feet is noticeably missing. Its crown of lifesaving light is now as dark as a coal bin.

People along the shore are fascinated with its presence, and its castle-like appearance never fails to make it a topic of conversation.

Recently, an arrangement was made with the owners whereby the U.S. Fish and Wildlife Service would be overseers of the rock to retain its status as a bird and mammal preserve. And just in time, for some misguided person or persons had mysteriously gained access to the rock, torn off the metal door of the lighthouse and stolen three of the urns from inside the structure. Regrettably, not even the ashes of the dead could rest in peace.

Point Adams Lighthouse in the late 1800's. The keeper is on the gallery sighting ships off the Columbia River bar.

Chapter 12
Point Adams Lighthouse

Yes, there really was a lighthouse at Point Adams but it was discontinued then torn down so long ago there are few alive who will remember anything about it.

```
POINT ADAMS LIGHTHOUSE
Location:
46°11'32"N 123°58'37"W
Nearest town: Hammond
Built: 1875  Discontinued 1899
Type: Frame dwelling
      with square tower
Height above water: 99ft
Height above ground: 49ft
Light source: oil lamp
Beam: Fixed red
Optics: 4th Order
Power: (minimal, approx 1,000cp
             not stated in records)
Seen: 11¼ miles
Horn: Discontinued 1881

NOTE: Classic data is from Light List—Lights
and Fog Signals of the Pacific Coast, 1896.
```

Possibly one of the oddest details was that this colorful lighthouse was not on Point Adams. Point Adams juts into the Columbia River from its south bank at the town of Hammond. But the light was over one mile south and seemed to more face the open ocean to the west, than it faced the river to the north. But of course, its light could be seen in both directions.

In reality, Point Adams lighthouse stood watch over a graveyard of ships.* Hundreds have been lost at the mouth of the river even in modern times.

The entrance to the Columbia River has been the bane of mariners since the earliest times. Bruno Heceta, in 1776, didn't even realize he

---

*There are 234 identified ships that stranded, foundered, or burned between 1725 and 1961 in the vicinity of the mouth of the Columbia River, the area surveyed by James A. Gibbs from Tillamook Rock to Willapa Bay. *See: Pacific Graveyard. See* Bibliography.

was offshore from of a great river. He missed it but Captain Robert Gray entered the river and claimed it as American territory in 1792. When Captain Thorn, of the *Tonquin,* tried to enter in 1811, he was so thwarted by the rugged bar, he lost several seamen during his entrance.

Point Adams Light was truly a victim of progress. The extension of the south jetty in the 1890's throttled a need for this lighthouse from the river's side, but it continued to aid ships working their way up the coast although its neighbors, Tillamook Rock lighthouse, south of the river, and the light on Cape Disappointment on the north were directing most of the traffic.

Situated on a low sand ridge one mile south of Point Adams, the station building was a frame, square tower painted white, rising from a white dwelling. It had a black painted lantern and dome. From its base to the focal plane, it rose 49 feet, the light shining from an elevation of 99 feet above sea level. The optic was a Fourth Order lens of French manufacture. The oil lamp afforded a beam that was visible for 11¼ miles, but it was obscured by trees on Point Adams from the southeast.

The lighthouse was a standard design of the service, approved by the Light-House Board, and was duplicated at other locations where buildings of frame construction were established along the Pacific coast.

During its active years, Point Adams light was the neighbor of Fort Stevens Military Reservation, which was a Civil War harbor defense fort facing the river. It stood near where Battery Russell is presently located on the southwest 40 acres of the old fortress.

For more than a century militiamen, originally dressed in Union blues, stood watch at Fort Stevens. The early earthwork fort, named for General Isaac Stevens, was constructed during the Civil War and was equipped with smoothbore Rodman cannon which required 14 men to fire. There was also several Parrott "Rifles" used at the installation. In 1897, as part of a nation-wide program to upgrade coastal and harbor defenses, those of the Columbia River took on a new look with eight concrete gun emplacements. These were filled with rifled six-inch and ten-inch guns and twelve-inch mortars.

During World War II, these positions were manned by the Regular U. S. Army and with Oregon National Guard's Coast Artillery Corps. At the apex of war activities, about 2,500 men were stationed in the trilogy of the Columbia River Defenses: Fort Stevens, on the Oregon side of the river and Forts Canby and Columbia on the Washington side. Although these forts never shot at

Point Adams Lighthouse had a homey look and was the center of many local activities in its heyday. Blowing sand was often a detriment and kept the keeper's wife and her broom very busy.

an enemy, they were ready and able. On the night the Japanese Navy's long-range aircraft-carrying submarine *I-25* showed up and shot, with it's long-range—14cm/.45 calibre—deck gun, at Fort Stevens in the vicinity of Battery Russell in June 1942, the American Officer of the Day refused permission for the big guns to fire back. Thus, stated a noted Coast Artillery officer the next day, "We blew it for our Corps." Accordingly, within months the entire Army Coast Artillery Harbor Defense organization was quietly shut down and its manpower retrained as anti-aircraft gunners. When the war was over in 1945, the heavy guns and mortars of the Columbia River Defenses, as well as those in the Puget Sound Defenses, were removed and sold for scrap. The concrete gun emplacement at Battery Russell is now a part of Fort Stevens State Park. Also in the park is the Fort Stevens Military Museum which includes Batteries Mishler, Lewis and Pratt.

Direct access to the historical area, other than Battery Russell, is from the town of Hammond. Access to the gun battery that was shot at by the Japanese is through the state park.

Following the close of World War II, the Fort Stevens area was under the jurisdiction of the Army Corps of Engineers but the Corps relinquished most of it to the State Parks Division of the Oregon State Highway Department in 1976.

The Clatsop Indians had a rich, complex culture in the area long before written history. It was along the Clatsop shores that two castaways from shipwreck were swept up on the sands long before the discovery of the Columbia River. They were taken as slaves and dwelled among the Indians, one of which was Konapee, known as the "iron worker." He gained his freedom from the natives because of his "magic" (skill) for fashioning implements and weapons of iron that he salvaged from his wrecked* Spanish ship.

Originally, Point Adams light had a flashing characteristic but after completion of Tillamook Rock lighthouse, the optic showed a fixed red light. The station was sort of a dream facility for the keepers and their families. They had easy access to supply, much company

---

*The wreck was believed to have been Spanish although some historians claim it was a large Oriental junk.

and activities and it was not far from Astoria. Further, a fortress was nearby as were two villages, Hammond and Warrenton.

The initial keeper at Point Adams was H. C. Tracy. He, with his family, tended the light from 1875-1881. His replacement was Captain J. W. "Joel" Munson, one of the most enterprising, innovative and compassionate civil servants in the Lighthouse Service. He was also civic-minded. During his tenure, which lasted until the station was terminated by Uncle Sam in 1899, it was a center of many activities. Lots of visitors enjoyed tours of the lighthouse and the family frequently entertained in the spacious quarters. This was convenient as the dwelling and tower were a single unit.

Munson was an expert fiddler who played at nearly every local event when not on duty. No local square dance was complete without him. His wife, Clara, an excellent hostess, was as full of energy as her husband. In later years she became the mayor of Warrenton, plausibly the first female mayor west of the Rockies.

Joel Munson put in a third of a century of lighthouse service. He was born in New York in 1828 and came around the Horn to the Pacific Northwest as a young man. In 1859, he became involved in the fish and oyster business on Shoalwater (Willapa) Bay. In 1865 he was appointed head keeper of Cape Disappointment lighthouse, a post he held for 12 years. It was his concern for victims of shipwreck at the Columbia River entrance that prompted him to take action long before the U. S. Lifesaving Service was instituted in 1871.

He and his family had earlier homesteaded at a little village named Lexington on the west shore of Young's Bay, a landing where boats and wagons rendezvoused to exchange cargo and passengers. When the post at Cape Disappointment opened, Munson seized the opportunity to accept the appointment.

It was during his tenure there that the bark *Industry,* Captain I. Lewis, was wrecked on March 15, 1865 on the Columbia River bar with a loss of 17 lives. No lifesaving craft was available and that greatly disturbed Munson. On the beach he found a battered lifeboat fitted with air tanks. He was determined to rebuild it for rescue emergencies.

To garner money for repairs and lifesaving equipment, he arranged dances at Astoria and charged $2.50 per person. The local folk responded with enthusiasm. Of course he fiddled at each event. When the Lighthouse Service was advised of his activities, the district office gave him their blessings as long as it didn't interfere with the operation of the lighthouse. The little boat was put in excellent condition, and the Lighthouse Service provided temporary shelter.

Volunteers were solicited for duty if and when an emergency arose.

When the bark *W. B. Scranton* was driven up on the middle sands of the bar the following year (May 5, 1866), Munson's rescue craft put out to sea manned by two men from a government tug, two soldiers from Fort Canby and Munson. Initially, they rescued the Captain's wife and a woman passenger, then returned to the scene to aid in the rescue of the ship's master, Paul Corno and the remainder of the crew after it was determined the vessel would be a total loss. The *Scranton* had been en route to Portland from San Francisco and was carrying 810 tons of cargo. Valued at $25,000, the *Scranton* was insured for only $9,000. The lost cargo was worth $20,000. Ironically, Captain Corno was one of the seven survivors in the loss of the *Industry* the previous year.

Munson was considered a hero. In fact, his efforts were rewarded. It was only a few months later that the government agreed to establish an official U. S. Lifesaving Station in the lee of Cape Disappointment (Cape Hancock). Munson's famous craft was included as part of the station equipment and it was that lifeboat that rescued the crew of the bark *Architect* that stranded on Clatsop Spit, March 28, 1875. The bark became a total loss. After Munson resigned his position as principal keeper at Cape Disappointment, he built the river steamer *Magnet* at Astoria, which he owned and operated for three years. When offered the post of head keeper at Point Adams he decided to sell his river steamer and re-enter the Lighthouse Service. He arrived there in 1881 with his family and remained until its closure in 1899. Everybody for miles around knew and loved the "fiddling" lighthouse keeper.

For a time, Point Adams had a steam operated fog whistle but, fortunately for Munson, it was discontinued the year he took over the station. This greatly eased his responsibilities. The cancellation of the fog signal came about after constant complaints by navigators that it was inaudible above the roar of the breakers. During an 11 month period in fiscal year 1878-79, the noise maker operated a total of 516 hours with a consumption of 20,000 gallons of water. September was the foggiest month, the blaster sounding 107½ hours. A pressure of 72 pounds of steam consumed 130 gallons of water per hour. Many other Pacific Coast lighthouses logged a much higher ratio of fog than Point Adams.

It was perhaps expedient that the lighthouse be closed, but it must have been a lamentable episode when it came about. It had not only served as an aid to navigation but was also sort of a social center. In addition to the lengthened south jetty, which had a direct bearing on

The harbor defense guns of Battery Russell, Fort Stevens, were right next to abandoned Point Adams Lighthouse.

where ships would be positioned for inbound and outbound transit, the Columbia River Lightship had been placed off the river entrance in 1892. This lightship further negated the necessity of Point Adams lighthouse. Thus it came to pass on January 31, 1899, the lighthouse was blacked out forever.

Now vacant and with no eager hands to minister to its needs, it soon fell into disrepair and became a target for vandals. It took on the appearance of a haunted house and the traditional rumors were spread about weird noises emanating from its interior.

At the turn of the century it had been decided, as related, to build state-of-the-art harbor defense gun positions in the area. It turned out that right next door to the Point Adams lighthouse was the site for Battery Russell. Battery Russell would mount two 10-inch disappearing guns of the Buffington-Crozier design. The idea was unique. The guns would be fully loaded with gun crews at the ready but an enemy ship at sea could not see them. When the gun commander was ready to fire, a gun (or both of them) was "tripped" into position, that, raised on stout springs so the barrels pointed out over the top of the emplacement. As the gun was fired, the recoil threw the gun back down behind the parapet "disappearing" from view. These guns had a range of about nine miles. The 249th Coast Artillery Harbor Defense (HD) of the Oregon National Guard trained on and fired these guns every summer during the annual encampment for many years. These gunners, from the early days to the end of the program, could hit a towed target nine miles at sea "dead-on" often totally destroying the target which was a raft only 30 feet square.

(When the Japanese submarine episode occurred in World War II, spokesmen for the Army said the sub was out of range and the guns wouldn't hit it. "Not so" declared researcher Bert Webber who documented that the attacker was *within* range at the time of the firing and the submarine could have been knocked out of the water had a one-word order been given to the American gunners: *Fire!*)*

Soon after the guns were declared ready for duty in 1905, the Army made polite inquiries to the lighthouse people about their plans for dismantling the now unused and dilapidated Point Adams lighthouse. Finally, the Secretary of War declared the old ediface a menace to the security of Battery Russell. That was because, the Army reasoned, although their "disappearing" guns popped back out of sight on the instant of firing, the old lighthouse was close by and offered a target of sorts to a possible enemy. Thus the Army reasoned the light-house could become that target—too close to the gun battery for comfort.

In 1912, the order was received to demolish the lighthouse. The official reason, as published by the Secretary of War, was that the lighthouse was a fire hazard.

After the extinguishing of Point Adams light, a number of ships were wrecked at the river entrance. None was closer to the abandoned lighthouse than the bark *Peter Iredale,* beached October 25, 1906. To this day, part of the wreck remains on the beach and has become a popular tourist attraction. It is one of the best known visible wrecks around the country. How or why it has not been swallowed by the sands has remained a mystery. Other wrecks on the same beach vanished long ago, but somehow the *Iredale,* dying a slow and agonizing death, has remained as the tide ebbs and flows through its skeleton.

The *Peter Iredale,* in its heyday, was not unfamiliar to the keepers at Point Adams. She had carried cargoes of grain from the river on previous voyages. The ship was built at Maryport, England in 1890 with home port at Liverpool. On her final voyage she was inbound for Portland from Salina Cruz, Mexico under Captain Lawrence. The crew had been offered a bonus if they could cut five days off the estimated sailing time.

About 100 miles south of the Columbia River the 1,994 ton bark ran into dense fog. Despite the respectful suggestion by first officer John Clayton that the skipper should shorten sail to slow progress as

---

*See the chapter, "Panic At Fort Stevens" in *SILENT SIEGE-II: Japanese Attacks on North America in World War II. See* Bibliography. (See the updated 1997 edition.)

Popular tourist attraction, the *Peter Iredale* wreck
beckons thousands of viewers.

they approached land, Lawrence was certain of his dead reckoning.
On the evening of October 24, 28 days out from Salina Cruz it was
anticipated the fog would lift off the river entrance. Passing just west
of Tillamook Rock, which remained unseen, the ship clawed her way
in the murk. By morning, a gale was blowing and the visibility
remained at zero.

Suddenly, breakers were heard and an effort was made to come
about. Too little, too late. The vessel was driven up on the sands
amid white-crested rollers. She struck hard enough to snap the
mizzenmast, quickly followed by the fore and mainmasts resulting in
a jumble of rigging. Taking a list to port, the bark held fast in the
sand and the order to abandon was soon given. An attempt was made
to put a boat over the side but the nasty breakers prompted the crew to
wait for help to come.

Quick to respond was the Point Adams and Cape Disappointment
surfboats. They aided in bringing all hands safely to shore, Captain
Lawrence toting the ship's sextant, log and a demijohn of whiskey.
He lamented the loss of his command and in the hopes of salvage, he
and his first mate set up a temporary shelter on the beach to keep an
eye on the wreck while the remainder of the crew were housed at Fort
Stevens.

Periodic boardings of the wreck were made on the low tides and
during those efforts one man was drowned. A storm brought the
wreck a little higher on the beach and all hopes of refloating the big
sailing vessel soon dissipated.

A hearing over the loss ensued. In the interim, the *Iredale* became a pawn of the elements. The steel hull on iron frames defied the elements, allowing salvage of most of her deck gear. Until recent years, the bowsprit remained intact pointing upward in despair. Finally the rusted fittings gave way and it tumbled into the sea.

British vice counsel P. I. Cherry and the Board of Inquiry, after considerable deliberation, exonerated the captain and ship's officers from blame in the wreck. An apprentice crew member among the survivors of *Peter Iredale* was Claude Asquith who in later years distinguished himself as master of lighthouse tenders operating out of the Tongue Point, Oregon Lighthouse Repair Depot (later Coast Guard) facility.

Another big British bark, the *Cairnsmore,* was wrecked in 1883, very near where the *Iredale* later came ashore. But in her case, after several months, that ship was sucked down in the sands and failed to reappear.

Until 1912, the abandoned Point Adams lighthouse and the wrecked *Peter Iredale* were in view of each other, obstacles of tragedy on both land and sea.

Chapter 13
Desdemona Sands Lighthouse

Virtually forgotten in the mists of time is Desdemona Sands lighthouse which once stood proudly on piling in 12 feet of water on the westerly end of a shoal making off to the westward from Desdemona Sands inside the mouth of the Columbia River.

> **DESDEMONA SANDS LIGHTHOUSE**
>
> Location: **46°14'N 123°57'W**
> **Nearest town: Astoria**
> Built: **1902** Discontinued 1964
> Type: **White octagonal house on piles in Columbia River**
> Height above water: **48ft**
> Light source: **Incandescent oil vapor**
> Beam: **White**
> Optics: **4th Order**
> Power: **2,900cp**
> Seen: **12 miles**
> **Horn**
>
> NOTE: Classic data is from *Light List* 1934.
> U.S. Dept. of Commerce, Lighthouse Service
> and reflects details then in effect.

An interesting aid to navigation, it was a white, octagonal one-and-a-half story frame dwelling with gray-green trimmings rising from a rectangular platform on piling. From a bronze-colored, pyramidal roof, rose a gray-green cylindrical lantern which housed a Fourth Order Parisian manufactured fixed lens, displaying a white light. A small, one story projection for the fog signal was on the westerly side, a Daboll trumpet blasting for two seconds with alternate silent intervals of three and 23 seconds. A one story annex was attached to the easterly side of the dwelling.

Like a poor man's castle, the edifice rose 46 feet above the mouth of the river with its light visible for 12 miles at all points on the compass. Established in 1902, the lighthouse was at Astoria's front door and was passed by virtually every vessel entering the river, both large and small. It was the best marine view in the entire area and the keepers had a passing parade of ships at most any hour of the day.

Unique Desdemona Sands Lighthouse sat on a platform supported by pilings driven into the sand at the mouth of the Columbia River. When the Coast Guard took over the former U.S. Lighthouse Service in 1939, Desdemona Sands was later shut down in favor of an unattended lesser aid to navigation on the shoal.

Citizens of Hammond, Warrenton and Astoria were familiar with the mournful cry of the foghorn when the weather soured, and those who made their living from the sea placed heavy dependence on both the light and fog signal.

The lighthouse had a near-sister at Semiahmoo Harbor off Blaine, Washington at the Canadian border. That lighthouse was constructed in 1905 from the same plans.

Self-contained, Desdemona lighthouse had its own boat kept in davits on top of the platform. Rain water was captured in a cistern which supplied the needs of the station. And when staples ran low, or in an emergency, the boat could be lowered and rowed to shore. There were no lawns or gardens to maintain. The keepers were good friends of many of the seafarers which frequently passed the light, and it wasn't unusual when books and magazines were either tossed up on the platform or sent in with the right current in water-tight casks.

The main concern was the danger of fire. Oil had to be stored for the lamps and inasmuch as the facility was a frame structure and well away from any fire protection, caution had to be kept in mind. However, there was a narrow escape in 1916 when a keeper accidentally knocked over a container of alcohol which exploded and set the building on fire. As flames shot skyward, they were visible on both sides of the river. A flotilla of craft rushed to the scene but the alert keepers had rehearsed for just such a mishap and had the blaze pretty well under control by the time help arrived. Though seared and blistered, the lighthouse was saved from destruction.

The name Desdemona is confusing to some because it doesn't have the ring of traditional Oregon origin. Historically, the tricky shoals were named Chinook Sands. But the name Desdemona was derived from a wrecked ship of that name which became a victim of the shoal. It happened on New Years Day in 1857. For the bark *Desdemona* and her master, Captain Francis Williams, it was a most unfortunate start of a new year.

Before departure from San Francisco, the owner-agent, Thomas Smith, had promised Captain Williams a new Sunday suit if he could get his command to the Columbia River by New Years Day. Such a gift was not an uncommon prize for sailing ship masters when they made excellent passages. In William's case, he pressed on canvas coming up the coast and in an attempt to get inside the river, he elected to make it without a pilot.

His decision not only cost him the new suit but his ship as well. To his credit was a fast passage up the coast that had him waiting off the river at midnight. He wasn't unfamiliar with the vagaries of the Columbia's gateway and had waited to take his ship in until daybreak. The ship was a familiar sight on the river having been in the coasting trades since 1851. Built at Jonesboro, Maine in 1847, she was one of a great armada of vessels that had rounded Cape horn in the rush to California gold. The befuddled skipper, insisted the wreck was not his fault. He claimed the buoy marking the course into the river was not at its charted position.

The 331 ton vessel had made a successful crossing of the bar with a fair wind and flood tide but the missing buoy caused a navigation error and she not only struck hard on the sands but held fast.

At first the stranding of the *Desdemona* didn't appear fatal. She rested on an even keel for the first 24 hours. Offering assistance was the U. S. Revenue Cutter *Joe Lane,* but despite its best efforts in pulling the bark free, it was to no avail. The tall ship wouldn't budge from her sand cradle. All efforts were then turned to saving the cargo.

Captain Williams went ashore to gather volunteers from the Parker sawmill to assist in refloating the vessel. By the time he returned, the wreck had bilged and was beginning to break up. On January 3, the pilot boat came close enough to hail the salvagers of an impending storm. Hastily, a scow was brought to the scene to lighter off the recovered cargo. On the final trip, the lighter capsized in the heavy seas drowning George Cartland. The others were rescued but the operation came to a wet, sickening halt.

On January 6, Williams auctioned off the wreck and Moses Rogers was high bidder at only $215. He stripped her of everything possible and then abandoned the hull. The skeleton remained visible for a time but was soon sucked under the shifting sands, another victim in the graveyard of ships.

There were several other ships claimed by the shoal, but it was the *Desdemona* that had her name bequeathed to the obstruction. The shoal was always a concern, especially to sailing ship skippers. It seems strange that a lighthouse was not erected there until 1902. Be that as it may, the sentinel only saw four decades of service before being replaced by an unmanned minor navigation aid. The replacement was a small pyramidal shaped tower on the same platform, which in turn was replaced by a tiny white structure in 1955—finally a minor light on a dolphin. This was a kind of an evolution in reverse.

More efficient buoyage systems and radio contact lessened the role of the original Desdemona lighthouse. It was one of the first to go as the age of automation approached.

Eastward of Desdemona Sands, the mighty 4.1 mile Astoria trans-Columbia Bridge was completed in 1966. This was the last major link in coast Highway 101. It is the longest continuous truss span bridge in the world and has a place in the *Guinness Book of World Records*. The 1,232 foot span would have made the Desdemona Sands lighthouse appear like a tiny toy.

The bridge is just one great event in the evolving history of the lower Columbia River. As the dominant natural force in the Pacific Northwest, the great waterway, once referred to as the River of the West, has been the marine transportation hub from the sea to the valley, and to the inland empire, since Captain Robert Gray made the first crossing of the bar on May 11, 1792, completing the last great plum of American discovery. It was further the final goal of Lewis & Clark in their epic crossing of the continent by land and river in 1804-05. It was also at the mouth of the river where John Jacob Astor constructed his fur trading post in 1811, site of the present day Astoria which lays claim to being one of the oldest American settlements west of the Rockies. Following in the wake of the fur trade came forestry and commercial fishing and eventually the opening of a great portal of commerce and industry.

With the dangers at the river entrance the necessity for safeguarding maritime commerce gained impetus through the years.

The river entrance had gained a notorious reputation for claiming ships, their cargoes, and in some cases those who manned them. An estimated 2,000 vessels from small fishboats to large cargo ships have encountered trouble in the general vicinity, with dire results, and more than 1,500 have lost their lives. Multi-millions of dollars have been expended to safeguard the river entrance, probably more than at any other American continental river entrance.

The south jetty construction was begun in earnest in 1885 and rebuilt, repaired and lengthened through the years to its present six and one half mile length. Shortly after the south jetty was begun, the north jetty was constructed. The river, accumulating large quantities of sand and sediment at its mouth, built up a shallow area where the river and ocean meet in mortal combat. This makes it both hazardous and difficult to find a sufficiently deep channel for transit. Obviously the loss of ships was a serious impediment to the growth of waterborne commerce, thus the jetties were constructed by the Army Corps of Engineers under the direction of the Portland District Office.

Along with the jetties were lighthouses, lightships, maintenance dredging, buoy systems, lifesaving stations and an efficient pilotage system, all of which have played a vital role in the smooth flow of shipping on the Columbia River.

Some of the former navigation aids have been replaced or eliminated and Desdemona Sands lighthouse was just one of the facilities that served its purpose well during its time. Had the *National Register of Historic Places* been established a few decades back Desdemona lighthouse might still be standing today as a fine example of a period sentinel. Now, it is only found in books.

A news article appeared in the press in the summer of 1965 with the following information:

> Sixty-three year old Desdemona Sands Light was to be dimmed out and its fog signal quieted this week, according to the U. S. Coast Guard. Desdemona Light was mounted on a platform at the west end of Desdemona Sands in the Columbia River about five miles west of Astoria in 1902, and it was re-established at various intervals, the last installation in 1955. It served as a friendly beacon for ships and fishermen who plied the waters just inside the mouth of the river.

A series of red and black flashing buoys mounted with bells, whistles, and radar reflectors line the sides of the ship fairway between the river mouth and Astoria which apparently had made the former Desdemona light unnecessary. The Coast Guard announced that it would establish a new Desdemona Lower Sands lighted bell buoy No. 31 at the approximate location of the former beacon. But, it was undermined by the current and collapsed in 1964.

How fast the memory of a lighthouse disappears once it passes from the scene. The original Desdemona Sands lighthouse was completed in November of 1902 and its light was first shown on Christmas eve of the same year. It was a gleaming star to the people in Astoria. Total cost of the station was $24,000 in addition to the $11,000 proposed for the Fort Stevens light and fog signal made in 1896. Several months later, a windlass for hoisting small boats was installed at Desdemona. In 1905, scouring action at the river mouth demanded 2,105 tons of stone riprap to be placed around the outer row of piling. All that remains today is a few slanted piling and a heap of stone, inundated when the river is high.

In its later years of service, Desdemona Sands Lighthouse had its fixed light replaced by a Fourth Order revolving beacon which was a big improvement in the eyes of navigators.

Governor J. J. Geer of the State of Oregon officially turned over title to the watery acreage for the original lighthouse to the United States government October 11, 1901.

Chapter 14
Cape Disappointment Lighthouse

Though Cape Disappointment lighthouse is not located in Oregon State its history has always been synonymous with Oregon. The border between the two states is a line in the Columbia River. The lighthouse is the sentinel that has stood guard over the entrance to the Columbia River since 1856. When the land was first surveyed for a lighthouse on Cape Disappointment it was still Oregon Territory.

CAPE DISAPPOINTMENT LIGHTHOUSE
Location: 46°17'N 124°3'W
Nearest town: Ilwaco
Built: 1856
Type: White conical tower
Height above water: 220ft
Height above ground: 53ft
Light source: I electric
     incandescent bulb
Beam: White and Red
Optics: 4th Order
Power: 58,000cp white
     17,000cp red
Seen: 19 miles white
     21 miles red

NOTE: Classic data is from *Light List* 1934.
U.S. Dept. of Commerce, Lighthouse Service
and reflects details then in effect.

By the time the station was completed it had become Washington Territory, and not until 1889 did Washington become a state. But over and above those facts is that Cape Disappointment lighthouse was the very first primary navigation aid established in the Pacific Northwest. It has survived to the present day as an honored symbol of history.

Cape Disappointment (referred to by the Coast Guard as "Cape D") is described in the *Pacific Coast Pilot* as the rugged north point at the Columbia River entrance, the first major headland along the 20 miles of sand beach north from Tillamook Head. It comprises a group of rounding hills covering an area 2.5 miles long and a mile wide, divided by a narrow valley extending north northwest. The

Cape Disappointment Lighthouse has stood atop ageless headland since the lighthouse was completed in 1856. It is the first American lighthouse on the Pacific shores of Oregon and Washington.

seaward faces of the hills are precipitous cliffs with jagged, rocky points and small strips of sand beach. Cape Disappointment lighthouse is situated 220 feet above the water and is shown from a 53 foot white conical tower with a white horizontal band on top and bottom, and black horizontal band in the middle, on the south point of the cape. A radio beacon is at the station, and a U. S. Coast Guard station is on the lee, or east side of the cape, adjoining old Fort Canby, which has become a Washington State Park.

The prominent cape, which affords a magnificent panorama of the Columbia River bar, the Pacific Ocean and the northern Oregon coast, is claimed by geologists to be but 15,000 years old. Whether that claim is true or not, the cape offered the clue to the early explorers in finding the elusive River of the West. Some of the early chart markers standing offshore logged the cape as an island.

Bruno Heceta recorded in his log on August 17, 1775:

> The currents and the expanse of water made me believe it is the mouth of a large river or a passage to some other sea.

When he could find no entrance he named the cape San Rogue and neighboring North Head, San Frondoso.

John Meares, a British navigator and fur trader, sighted Heceta's San Rogue on July 6, 1788, and looked for shelter from adverse seas, but to no avail. He in turn named San Rogue, "Cape Disappointment" to show his feelings. He then wrote in his journal, "We can safely assert that no river San Rogue exists."

Captain George Vancouver, Britain's premier explorer and navigator, stood off the river for two days in 1792 and reiterated Meares findings. The renowned Captain James Cook, a few years earlier, had completely overlooked the location of such a river at that latitude. The honors went to the intrepid Yankee fur trader Captain Robert Gray, who crossed the Columbia River bar on May 11, 1792 and dropped his anchor off the present town of Chinook, Washington. Then he traded with the Indians and claimed the river and the surrounding lands for Uncle Sam. Thank you, Captain Gray!

Lewis and Clark solidified the claim on November 17, 1805, and camped for awhile at Chinook and later established Fort Clatsop on the south side of the river entrance. But England, which then ruled the seas, claimed ownership of Fort Astoria and Cape Disappointment during the War of 1812. The Treaty of Ghent however, provided that any land acquired by the British during that period would have to be returned to the United States.

On August 18, 1818, Captain James Biddle, master of the sloop USS *Ontario* arrived off the cape with a contingent of 150 officers and enlisted men and dispatched a shore party to erect a lead tablet and declare the cape as American territory. They landed in the lee of the cape where the present Coast Guard station is located. Less than two months later, in defiance of Biddle's claim, the frigate HMS *Blossom* put a similar party ashore in the same area and claimed the land for England.

The growing dispute raged on. Lt. Henry J. Warre and Merven Vavasour were sent by the British in 1849 to chart the lower Columbia and make recommendations for the placement of a gun battery on Cape Disappointment just in case the dispute would lead to war with America. During the survey they found James D. Saule, an American black man who had already laid claim to much of the land. He had often offered his services as a bar pilot, and though not successful at the trade, was generally believed to be the cook that had survived the wreck of the USS *Peacock* in July 1841 on what is now officially named "Peacock Spit."

Peter Skene Ogden, an official at Fort Vancouver, was ordered by his British superiors to set up a lookout and trading post on the cape. Ogden paid Saule for his homesteading claim only to find that the land actually belonged to two other Americans, William McDaniel and Newton Wheeler.

Ogden again paid for the land and erected a dwelling and storehouse. Hudson's Bay Company made minor usage of the buildings in 1850. The treaty of 1846 had given all the country south of the 49th parallel to the United States, but in those pioneer years there was considerable confusion over land ownership with Hudson's Bay Company, a Canadian-British enterprise being the largest influence in the territory. The "Grand Company" was headquartered at Fort Vancouver.

Credit the astute American, Lt. William P. McArthur for suggesting the cape as an ideal site for a lighthouse. That was in 1848. In his authorship of the *Pacific Coast Pilot* in 1850, he noted that

> ...one must pass close to Sand Island and fall into a range using as a guide three prominent cut off spruce trees growing at the cape's summit.

A ship would take a bearing on the trees from five miles offshore, then head for the southerly tip of the cape and thus sail through the deepest part of the river. Those directions were indeed a primitive aid to navigation.

On his 1848 survey, McArthur recommended that a lighthouse should be erected on the cape's southwest ridge and it was on his intelligence that Congress, in 1852, at the request of the Light-House Board, appropriated $53,000 for the erection of such a light station. The Columbia River bar had already gained a world-wide reputation for its sinister gateway as well as its great potential.

The bark *Oriole,* which brought the building materials for the lighthouse, ironically was wrecked directly below the cape, inbound from San Francisco, September 18, 1853. She also carried freight for the construction of other lights that were to have been built along the Pacific Coast. Everything was a total loss, the crew narrowly escaping with their lives.

The vessel had waited for eight days to cross the bar due to heavy seas breaking at the river entrance following a 22 day voyage up the coast. In command of Captain Lewis Lentz, the bark picked up a pilot, Captain Flavel, and with a southwest breeze the crossing got underway. Two hours later, the wind subsided and currents and tidal

226

Cape Disappointment Lighthouse shown in days before receiving a black band around its girth to distinguish it from nearby North Head Lighthouse.

action caused her to drag across the channel and grind up on the sandy bottom in 17 feet of water. The outgoing tide caused her to bump repeatedly on the shoals under the burden of her heavy cargo.

Stress caused the hull planking to pull free of the frames causing water to pour in. Suddenly, the rudder post was pushed up through the decking and the pumps could no longer handle the inflow. All the while the wind blew and the seas built with fury. Abandonment was the only alternative.

Boats were put over the side and chained together as darkness approached. In all, 32 men, including the ship's crew and several construction workers, were forced to spend a miserable night in the open boats, soaked to the skin, pitching and rolling as if their conveyances were corks.

Captain Lentz and Captain Flavel took charge of the boats all through the ordeal. Meanwhile the *Oriole* slipped off the reef, turned over on her beam ends, and sank with all the special cargo in more than six fathoms.

Come the break of dawn, weak cheers went up from the survivors as the pilot boat *California* hove in sight and rescued everyone.

Obviously, construction of the lighthouse suffered a major setback. Only preliminary work could get underway. Nearly two years would pass before the next shipload of building materials was forthcoming. Construction then got underway in earnest, but another delay was experienced when the tower had to be rebuilt when it was discovered its upper diameter was not sufficiently large to

227

accommodate the parapet and lantern house for a First Order lens and lighting apparatus. All the materials, including metal work and bricks, had to be hauled up from the landing in the lee side of the cape. Beasts of burden were utilized not only to build a crude road but to haul the heavy materials.

There was no small amount of excitement when the station was completed and the five-wick lamp illuminated on October 15, 1856. It cast a brilliant light through the prisms of the huge lens. The lamp, 18 inches across, consumed 170 gallons of oil a month and the keepers carried many heavy brass and copper oil containers up the circular staircase.

Many stories have circulated about the origin of the original lens used at the station. It is believed to have served in another lighthouse on the east coast before being sent to Cape Disappointment. Some claimed that it was one of the first of its type manufactured in Paris dating back to the 1820's, but that claim has always been open to speculation. What is known, is that the First Order beacon not only served Cape Disappointment, but was transferred for a time to North Head lighthouse on its completion in 1898. It saw duty in three and perhaps four lighthouses and is now on display at the Interpretive Center on Cape Disappointment. It is viewed with awe by scores of visitors each year.

In 1937, both Cape Disappointment and North Head lighthouses were electrified. The present optic at the former station is a Fourth Order Fresnel lens lit by a 1,000 watt quartz iodine light alternating flashing white and red, the range of the white flash 22 miles and the red, 18 miles.

When the station was first established, complete with spacious keepers dwelling, oil houses, and outbuildings, the keepers were not isolated. They shared their reservation with the men of strategic Fort Canby. For a period, big guns were placed along the fringe of the cape opposite the lighthouse. When they fired, it would shake the tower and often break the window glass in the facility. After numerous complaints and considerable damage, the armament was placed at locations farther away from the lighthouse.

For a brief time in its early history, the station had a large fog-bell, but when mariners claimed it inaudible against the roar of the sea, it was discontinued, last used at the Warrior Rock lighthouse on Sauvie Island, near St. Helens. After the turn of the century, there was a signal display station on the cape connected with Astoria by telephone, so that all approaching ships to the river could be reported.

Trouble erupted in 1896 that in a small way involved the

Soviet freighter **Vazlav Vorosky**, outbound for Vladivostok, went aground near Cape Disappointment Lighthouse April 3, 1941. Coast guard, in 52-foot *Triumph,* rescued crew. Ship broke up, sank.

lighthouse. A local "war" was threatened between Oregon commercial fishermen and fish trappers out of Ilwaco, Washington. Billed as the "Sand Island Fish War," the epicenter was Sand Island, a disputed bit of terra firma just inside the river's mouth. It got so serious that the National Guards of both states, along with the federal government, sent troops to the small acreage of sand.

How was the lighthouse involved? Some members of the Washington National Guard were visiting the station and purloining wood, coal and supplies which belonged to the attendants of the lighthouse. Complaints were made to the 13th District headquarters in Portland, and the U. S. Army, under General Otis, dispatched troops to put a stop to the pilfering. While there, the general put an end to the two-state battle involving the destruction of fishtraps by the Oregon fishermen and hostile retaliation by the Washington fishermen. The rhubarb came to a halt when it was determined the insular hunk of sand belonged neither to Oregon or Washington, but it was federal land in a federal navigable waterway.

Ever since the long-running dispute between England and the United States, 1812-1846, the cape had been considered a strategic military site. It was during the Civil War that the first battery of guns was positioned at Fort Canby. There was fear, by rumor, that the Confederate fighting ship *Shenandoah* would cross the Columbia River bar and steam all the way to Portland to destroy that city with its big guns. Such fears prompted the fortification of the cape's Fort Canby. The big guns near the lighthouse included two 300 pound

229

parrot 10-inch guns, five 200 pound 8-inch parrots and the most powerful of all, the affectionately named "Old Betsy," a 15-inch Rodman firing piece.

For a brief period in history, Fort Canby was known as Fort Cape Disappointment and the headland as Cape Hancock. Neither name survived. The later name officially applied in 1875, honored Modoc War hero General Canby, and of course, the name Disappointment was applied as we have been informed, by John Meares.

The military installation was shut down from 1887 until 1891, but when trouble occurred in Chile, followed by the Spanish American War, the fort was re-activated with new gun emplacements. There was also considerable activity at Forts Canby and Columbia and at Fort Stevens during both World Wars, especially after the shelling

Cape Disappointment U.S. Lifesaving crew in days of yore man their pulling boat going to aid of stricken vessel.

Oldest fog bell in the Pacific Northwest began service at Cape Disappointment Lighthouse in 1856 but was ineffective so was moved to Puget Sound. Then it was moved to Warrior Rock in the Columbia River in 1889 where it served until the light structure on which it stood was rammed by a barge in 1969. When the 1,500 pound bell was being salvaged it was dropped and cracked. Today this historic bell is exhibited in the Columbia County Museum, St. Helens.

of Fort Stevens by the Japanese in 1942.

Many gala events occurred at Fort Canby. In 1907-08 new buildings were constructed and a military wharf installed where river steamers docked with guests who came to hear the military band perform on special occasions. After World War II, the fort was used mainly by the National Guard, the caretaking chores left to a sergeant and two enlisted men until the bulk of the land was turned over to the Washington State Parks.

Though the fort has become a tourist attraction, the lighthouse has weathered time well and continues its vigil. The Coast Guard station below the cape is still an important installation not only involved with search and rescue operations, but also houses one of the only training schools for instruction in the rudiments of lifesaving and the use of specialized rescue equipment, with a fleet of motor lifeboats and patrol craft.

It is all a far cry from the day Joel Munson housed his first

Tuna seiner *Bettie M* wrecked below Cape Disappointment in 1976. The ship and cargo were a total loss.

lifeboat at the site of the present Coast Guard station. It was also the locale of the first U. S. Lifesaving Station, which for an early period, was under Captain Al Harris. The Coast Guard absorbed the facility into its operations in 1915, gradually replacing the old surfboats with self-righting motorized lifeboats and surf craft.

At this writing, a Fourth Order Fresnel is still in use at Cape Disappointment lighthouse. It was manufactured by Barbier & Bernard in 1896. The original First Oder fixed lens was a product of L. Sautter & Cie of Paris. It was manufactured, as mentioned, on an unknown date.

There appears some confusion as to who was the first principal keeper of Cape Disappointment lighthouse. The national archives do not contain that information, but the Pacific County census records indicate in its earliest pages that John Boyd may have been the initial keeper of the Pacific Northwest's first lighthouse. Undoubtedly the most revered keeper of the facility was Joel Munson.

Chapter 15
Columbia River Lightships

To the present generation, lightships are a virtual forgotten entity in the arena of aids to navigation. True, one can find some relics attached to museums and under the preservation of various societies, but where the coasts of the United States once had a large fleet of lightships all have been removed from active duty. Lightships were anchored where it was not feasible to build a lighthouse. They were expensive to maintain as they had to be constantly supplied, and each carried crews, more than double the number it took to man isolated lighthouses. Money, however, was not a factor when the safeguarding of commerce was involved. Those stout vessels of yesteryear were always placed at dangerous, exposed maritime crossroads or well offshore where they received the full fury of storms and rough seas.

```
COLUMBIA RIVER LIGHTSHIP

Location:  46°11'N  124°11'W
    Anchored in 210 feet off
    entrance to river 5.3 miles sw off
    end of s jetty on Main Channel
    Range Line. Established: 1892
    Discontinued 1979

Type:  Ship, red hull
Height above water:  67ft
Light:  1 electric incandescent
Beam:  White
Optics:  375mm drum
Power:  13,000cp
Seen:  14 miles
Horn
Radio beacon

NOTE: Classic data is from Light List 1934.
U.S. Dept. of Commerce, Lighthouse Service
and reflects details then in effect.
```

It was a lonely, tedious and demanding job for those who manned the lightships. As late as 1961, the Coast Guard was operating 27 lightships. There were not too many tears shed when the advent of modern electronic aids to navigation and automation spelled their end.

The first lightship placed on the U. S. West Coast was the ur-

Left: Ready for launching into Baker Bay after lengthy salvage operation. *Lower:* The wrecked *No. 50* hard aground before overland trek.

Columbia River *Lightship No. 50* slipped her moorage at sea during a storm and was driven on to the beach near McKenzie Head on Cape Disappointment. *No. 50's* rescue was not by the usual method but house movers jacked her up and hauled her overland for half mile then launched her into Baker Bay.

gently needed *Columbia River Lightship No. 50,* on station on April 9, 1892. And the last to be withdrawn was the *Columbia River Lightship No. 604,* on November 2, 1979.

Let us go back to the beginning to look at the lightship pioneer.

The government awarded a contract to the Union Iron Works (later Bethlehem Steel's shipbuilding division) of San Francisco for the vessel's construction. The keel was laid for *No. 50* on August 19, 1891 and she was launched into San Francisco Bay March 26, 1892. The finished product measured 123 feet overall, 112 feet between perpendiculars, with a breadth of 29.6 feet and a draft of 13.6 feet.

Her displacement was 425 tons and gross, 250 tons. Built as solid as a wooden-hulled craft could be, the hull was sheathed in 1½ inch thick white oak covered with hair felt. This and coppered tar was fitted between the sheathing and planking. The sheathing was secured to the planking with four-inch composition spikes. This decking was 3½ x 3½ inch thick pine secured with 9/16 inch diameter iron bolts. The deck houses were all built of wood and the anchor windlass was driven by a two cylinder steam engine.

The companionway in the forward end of the main house led down to the crew's quarters on the berth deck. The after companionway on the main deck led to the officers' quarters. Four flush scuttles in the main deck led to the coal bunkers.

For generating steam, two natural-draft Scotch boilers were employed for general heating, the fog signal and for the windlass. This early lightship could have been called a "special equipment barge" as there was no engine for propulsion. The vessel was rigged as a kind of two-masted schooner but sail was only to be used in emergencies.

The *No. 50* carried two smaller craft. One was a 26 foot officers gig. The other was a whaleboat of the same length.

For handling the optics, described as "fountain lights," a cluster of oil lamps about the topmasts, a chain halyard and hand winch hoisting gear was used to raise them to proper position each nightfall. During the day, the lamps were stowed in hinged top houses. The day shapes at the masthead were two net-covered frames fixed 90 degrees apart. Short topmasts contained lightning rods.

On completion at the yard (the same yard where the famous battleship *Oregon* of Spanish American War fame was built) the $80,000 *No. 50* was towed up the coast by the San Francisco tug *Fearless*.

Of composite construction, wooden planking over steel frames, the lightship proved to be a rugged vessel when anchored securely to her post in 210 feet of water off the entrance to the Columbia River. This position was about 8½ miles southwest from Cape Disappointment. Tethered with three anchors, a mooring anchor of 5,000 pounds and two others of 2,500 and 1,800 pounds, *No. 50* was designed to be a permanent fixture to be moved only if dry-docking or general repair was essential.

The maritime industry received the lightship with jubilation. For the first seven years of service, she performed admirably with her crew of eight. Ships entering and departing the Columbia came to depend on her presence, especially in foggy weather when the 12-inch steam foghorn blasted at regular intervals. The *No. 50* not only was an aid to navigation but also a place of refuge for survivors from shipwreck.

All that changed on November 28, 1899 when the lightship was in the path of a raging storm. The sea was running high. At 6:30 P.

M., her anchor cables parted. Frantically, the crew was ordered to make sail to keep the vessel away from the inshore perils. Before long, the howling winds ripped the canvas to ribbons and the lightship was now at the mercy of the elements. By morning, the lighthouse tender *Manzanita,* plus the tugs *Wallula* and *Escort* had steam up and were rushing to the aid of *No. 50.* All three were able to get lines aboard the wallowing vessel but the strain was so great they all parted. The *Escort* stood by until early evening watching helplessly as the vessel drifted into the breakers that drove her up on the beach near McKenzie Head, between North Head and Cape Disappointment.

Fortunately, one final line between the tug and the lightship had remained until after the vessel was clear of a rock outcrop that could have ripped out her bottom planks. Also fortunately, she grounded on a small parcel of sandy beach and was soon turned, laying broadside to the breakers. To all intents and purposes her career appeared over. Not so! As if she had a soul, the vessel had a will to live.

Lifesaving stations at Disappointment and Point Adams were alerted to the crisis and personnel hastened to the scene with beach apparatus. These crews were assisted by Army troops from Fort Canby's Battery M, Third Artillery, as well as local civilian volunteers. Trees had been downed by the continuing storm and though debris was everywhere, the lifesavers had a Lyle gun in position by 7:30 in the morning in the hope of shooting a line to the wreck. The first shot fell short but the second carried across the lightship's deck. Unfortunately the gear became fouled. It was not until 11:20 that the first survivor was brought ashore via the breeches buoy. Captain Joseph H. Harriman and his crew of seven were all removed in good order. Most had suffered minor injury or bruises from their frightening but exciting experience. The worst injury was to Anton Enberg, who had some of his ribs broken when the spokes of the ship's wheel struck him.

Seemingly forlorn, but certainly not forgotten, the wreck was a target for the watery onslaught all through December. These were broadsides that would have destroyed other wooden-hulled ships. When it was apparent *No. 50* was not going to go the pieces, the tugs *Wallula* and *Escort* returned in January. These tugs, working together, made further attempts to tow *No. 50* back into the water. But every effort proved a failure despite the fact that a beach mortar had been placed on one of the tugs, able to fire a line 2,500 yards.

Frustrated, the Lighthouse District in Portland called for bids to salvage the lightship. Captain Robert McIntosh, a contractor, got the nod on January 9. But he immediately ran into trouble after setting cables, buoys and mushroom anchors. The adverse weather continued with one storm after another breaking the moorings and inflicting considerable damage. By March, McIntosh succeeded in moving the vessel 40 feet toward the sea and briefly she was afloat. But no tug was nearby at the time, thus the incoming tide and breakers shoved her higher onto the sand than she had been before.

Again in April, McIntosh tried on a flood tide, by attaching a steel cable extending from a buoy in deep water to the lightship so it could be kedged off the sand. As progress was being made, the cable snapped. By the time it could be restored, the tide advantage was lost. The tug *Wallula* retrieved the offshore anchor with a small derrick and moved it closer to shore for another try, but without success.

By mid-June, Commander W. P. Day, of the 13th Lighthouse District, canceled McIntosh's contract and called for new bids. Most of the proposals favored pulling the vessel back to sea, though three desired to attempt to drag the ship over a narrow neck of land to the calm waters of Baker's Bay inside the mouth of the river. Bids were opened in the Washington D. C., Light-House Board headquarters. Though McIntosh was again low bidder, Wolff & Zwicker Iron Works of Portland was awarded the job.

As seafarers mourned the loss of the lightship from its permanent station, Wolff & Zwicker set about the salvage work by placing a large crew of men and equipment at the wreck scene. But the weather was still adverse to getting the work done. On August 13, with anchors placed, lines run out, cables set, buoys, a barge and a tug in position, it was discovered a large sand bar had built up on the seaward side of *No.50*. It would have to be scoured away. On application, the contract was extended until October 25. In the interim, pumps were brought in to wash the obstruction away but with inadequate tides, Wolff & Zwicker, despite all of its equipment, was unable to salvage the vessel.

Almost ready to throw in the towel, Commander Day decided to call for bids one more time. This time, he specified the overland method. Opened in Portland, January 19, 1901, the proposals carried price tags from $14,650 to $25,000. Much to the amazement of the interested parties, the Portland house-moving firm of Andrew Allen and J. H. Roberts got the green light on a bid of $17,500.

The decision raised many eyebrows—a housemover salvaging a shipwreck? Had Day taken leave of his senses? The route called for a long, slow haul overland through sand, gravel, and forest, then over a rocky hill. Was this folly? The firm claimed they would do the job in 35 working days. Amazing!

Be that as it may, the firm meant business and initially placed an electric light plant on *No. 50* so work could proceed around the clock. Next, railroad ties were stacked with other blocking material in a framework underneath, so the lightship could be lifted by jack screws just as when moving a house. Then a wooden cradle would be fashioned to hold her steady. Teams of horses would be used to assist in the pull.

Work began on February 22, with a crew of 40 men and $12,000 worth of equipment. Heavy swells retarded immediate progress but in March, laborers were able to get several cables under the lightship and secure four jack screws in place. By April 3, the contractors had raised the vessel several feet above the beach and the cradle around the hull was under construction.

Time ran out however, and with a penalty clause of $100 a day, the operation was in jeopardy. The government liked what they had been watching. With likelihood of success, the penalties were waived.

By April 12, the unique land voyage began over the hill and through the woods on rollers. So fascinating was the undertaking, the Astoria newspaper played up the salvage effort to such a degree as to bring scores of spectators rushing to the area to watch the progress. A riverboat, charging a dollar per passenger, was making special excursions from Astoria for the sightseers. Business was brisk.

Battered but not defeated after a year and a half of punishment, *No. 50* had lost her keel, sternpost and rudder. Part of the starboard bilge keel was also gone as was some copper sheathing.

On April 21, the vessel was only 250 feet from Baker's Bay when Roberts reported an additional contract had been awarded to his firm to repair the ship's keel. A lack of carpenters, however, held up the work for an additional two weeks. In the meantime, a launching ramp was readied and new keel parts were finally in place by May 15.

On June 2, 1901, at 11:45 P. M., on a high tide, *No. 50* was successfully launched into Baker's Bay and taken in tow by the awaiting steamer *Callender*. When *No. 50* arrived in Astoria, on the morning of June 4, the vessel was greeted by scores of small craft and crowds of viewers along the waterfront. It was as if the lightship had been resurrected from the dead. Amid whistle salutes and celebration, the lady of the sea was alive once again.

The lightship was towed to Portland for drydocking and repairs then returned to the Tongue Point base on August 12. There she took on a supply of coal and staples preparatory to going back to her post. Three days later, she was returned to duty with a crew that was proud to be aboard.

The rest of her active service went smoothly except for a minor stranding on a sand bar in 1905, and an incident when the entire crew tendered their resignations because of unpalatable food being doled out by the ship's cook.

Her vigil came to an end after the new, self-propelled steel lightship *No. 88,* steamed around from the east coast in an armada of lighthouse service vessels in 1908-09. The antiquated *No. 50* was sold by the government and commenced a new phase of her career, but not before a period of idleness.

In 1914, old *No. 50* was sold for a mere $2,600 to a Mexican firm and operated as a freighter under the name *San Cosme.* Coming back under the Stars and Stripes in 1920, she became a unit of the Red Salmon Canning Company and was re-christened *Margaret.* The end came in 1935 when a tired old *No. 50,* her lightship days virtually forgotten, was junked at Antioch, California not far from her birthplace 43 years earlier.

Lightship *No. 88* was indeed a remarkable departure from her predecessor. She was built in Camden, New Jersey, launched in 1907, and had a gross tonnage of 683 and a net of 246 tons. Measuring nearly 113 feet between perpendiculars, she was 125 feet overall with a breadth of 29 feet and a draft of 14.9 feet. Her steam propulsion plant put out 325 horsepower. Accommodations were available for five officers and 11 crewmen.

The ship was destined to put in several years as the guardian of the entrance to the Columbia River. In fact, except for occasional drydockings and resupply when temporarily replaced by a relief lightship, she was on duty from 1909 until 1939. Her journals were full of dramatic entries of great storms, high seas and tragic shipwrecks, but always her vigil was kept with impunity.

On January 4, 1913, when the Point Adams surfboat rescued three survivors of the ill-fated tanker *Rosecrans,* which was pounding to pieces on dreaded Peacock Spit with the loss of 33 lives, the seas were so rough that the trio of survivors had to be housed aboard the lightship along with the crew of the surfboat. While trying to secure the rescue craft alongside, it broke loose and drifted away bearing the body of a dead crewman, a victim of the wreck. That was just one of many incidents when the lightship was able to assist shipwreck victims.

Through it all, the lightship displayed an occulting white light every ten seconds with a 375mm lens. It was later fitted with a radio beacon and radio communications equipment. By 1930, there were still about 55 lightships and relief lightships operating along the coasts of America, including those on the Great Lakes. Today, the number of active lightships is absolutely zero. There were also a near equal number of lighthouse tenders but by 1930 that number had been greatly reduced under Coast Guard jurisdiction. Those remaining were referred to as buoy tenders or cutters.

One of the most devastating storms weathered by the crew aboard *No. 88* occurred in the winter of 1914. It is best told by the words of Captain Nielson's official report:

> On January 2, 1914, at 5 a.m. it was blowing a very strong gale from the southeast and very unusual large seas running. In order to hold the vessel on station I found it necessary to steam strongly ahead from 5 a.m. to 4 p.m. during the first part of the gale. At 9:30 a.m. a large sea boarded on the starboard bow carrying away a 1½ inch pipe framework for the forward awning, also smashed starboard door, bent radiator pipes, dislocated steering compass from its foundation, bent the shaft in the spindle of the wheel, tore the bridge binnacle from the deck, tore off forward starboard ventilator and galley smokestack. Tore off the deck one of the coal bunker plates and carried some overboard, tore off the deck bolt for after main smokestack guy, broke stud on forward leaf of engine room skylight flooding engine room; smashed forward window in after lantern house; iron stantion of the after wheel grating carried away, also one of the gratings. Seaman H. K. Hansen, being on the wheelhouse at the time had a close call having been carried with the wreckage of the wheelhouse along the deck and just managed to grasp the railing to keep from going overboard. He escaped with a few minor cuts from flying glass. Luckily, none was badly hurt. We have made such temporary repairs as are practicable. The vessel was laboring heavily and shipped seas over during the time. The damage is such as we cannot wait until the vessel comes in for annual repairs.

Such storms, along with the long hours of constant blasting of the fog signal when the weather thickened, made life in a lightship similar at times to being inside of a drum in a Fourth of July parade. It took a special breed of men to prevail.

On February 2, 1924, the lighthouse tender *Rose* rendered valuable assistance to the oil tanker *W. S. Porter* which suffered a

Columbia River Lightship *No. 88* on station off entrance to river after steaming around Horn from builder in Quincy, Massachusetts in 1908. She was reassigned to Umatilla Reef as *No. 513* when Coast Guard took over the Lighthouse Service in 1939. After active duty, she was assigned as *Relief* lightship before being sold as surplus to Columbia River Maritime Museum. In later years she was sold to Canadians and converted into a sailing vessel.

broken steering gear and was lying broadside to the bar between Clatsop and Peacock spits, at buoy 3. Due to the efforts of the tender, the tanker was saved from going onto the spit which could have resulted in a similar tragedy suffered when the tanker *Rosecrans* went down a decade earlier. In 1917, the commercial fishboat *Naselle* went to the aid of the fishing vessel *Leonora* which had swamped at the river entrance. After rescuing her crew and taking the wreck in tow, the seas became so cantankerous that the rescue craft was unable to get across the bar and in turn had to seek out refuge on *No. 88*. With difficulty, all of the fishermen were taken aboard and given succor, while the two fishing vessels were secured alongside. It was several hours before the guests were able to leave the lightship.

The Columbia River Lightship was not to be omitted from the dramatic saga of the attack on Fort Stevens by Japanese Navy Imperial submarine *I-25* in June of 1942. The lightship was blacked out, except for the small anchor light. Testimony by late skipper Meiji Tagami of *I-25*, to researcher Bert Webber, brought fourth Tagami's statement that because of the blackout, he had sailed right past the lightship and did not see her. On board the lightship, a Coast Guardsman later told Webber, "Hell, if we had been attacked, as we were unarmed our only defense would have been to throw lumps of coal at them."

Relief was on the Columbia River Lightship's station the night in June 1942 when the Japanese Navy's submarine *I-25* passed a short distance away, the Japanese skipper saying later he was unaware of the lightship. *Relief* was blacked out except for its small anchor light. Now, half-a-century later, *Relief* is permanently exhibited on Seattle's Lake Union, owned by Northwest Seaport.

When the Coast Guard took over the Lighthouse Service in 1939, *No. 88* was shifted to Umatilla Reef and reclassified as *No. 513*. The newer *Umatilla No. 93* took over guardianship of the Columbia River remaining on duty until *No. 604* arrived from the builder's yard in 1951.

During World War II, the old *No. 88* was requisitioned as a military recognition ship, but *No. 93* remained on station. Ater the war, *No. 88* returned to Umatilla Reef and later served in a relief capacity.

The replacement for *No. 93* was a splendid version of a modern latter day lightship. She was built in 1950 by the Rice Brothers yard in East Boothbay, Maine. Measuring 128 feet in length, with a 30 foot beam and an 11 foot draft, she was propelled by a 550 horsepower Atlas Imperial Diesel engine. Her ground tackle included a 7,500 pound mushroom anchor with 150 fathoms of two-inch anchor chain.

The crew consisted of a warrant officer as commander backed by

Old fog bell from *Lightship No. 88* was removed when the ship was sold to private interests. The bell is now part of a display in the Columbia River Maritime Museum in Astoria.

a crew of 15 enlisted men. The navigation aid, with a fifteen mile range, was displayed from the 57 foot forward mast. The diaphone fog horn had a range of five miles and the radio beacon had a range of 100 miles.

On April 11, 1892, when the first *Columbia River Lightship No. 50* was placed at the river entrance, her position was five miles off the river. No. 604 was located 5.3 statute miles southwest of the end of the south jetty and nine statute miles south southwest of Cape Disappointment lighthouse.

As floating aids to navigation, the positions of lightships on nautical charts were represented by the anchor position since the lightship was subject to movement around the anchor by wind, current and tides.

Ships approaching the Columbia River would cut speed and wait near the lightship for a bar pilot to board for the crossing of the bar. In severe weather, bar-bound commercial vessels would anchor near the lightship and sometimes wait for days even weeks at anchor amid 20 and 30 foot swells. In addition to her traditional duties, the *604* also provided weather information on a daily basis and oceanographic information for institutions of higher learning. While on station, the crew served on a rotation with six weeks aboard ship and three weeks

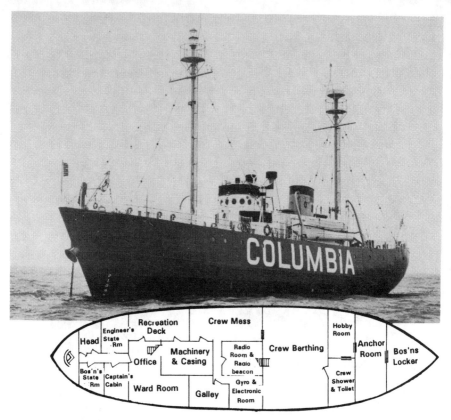

Galley labels within diagram:

Head / Engineer's State Rm / Recreation Deck / Crew Mess / Hobby Room / Anchor Room / Office / Machinery & Casing / Radio Room & Radio beacon / Crew Berthing / Bos'ns Locker / Bos'n's State Rm / Captain's Cabin / Ward Room / Galley / Gyro & Electronic Room / Crew Shower & Toilet

Lightship WAL-604 was the last lightship on the Columbia River Lightship station. It was removed by the Coast Guard in favor of automation with a sophisticated self-contained buoy. The lightship is now part of the Columbia River Maritime Museum.

off. Supplies and transfer was made by motor lifeboats from the Cape Disappointment station or with a buoy tender out of Tongue Point.

The *No. 604* served until November 1979 when the Coast Guard replaced her with an unmanned, automated super navigational LNB buoy. The LNB is 40 feet in diameter and 42 feet in height. Its strobe light is visible for ten miles and is additionally equipped with a fog signal, radar reflector, and transmits radio signals around the clock. For a fraction of the cost of maintaining a lightship, the buoy performs flawlessly and is the ultimate in automation for navigation aids.

The old *No. 88*, later *No. 513*, after a stint as a relief lightship, was decommissioned in 1960. The Columbia River Maritime Museum of Astoria purchased her for $20,000 from a Seattle ship breaking firm and she was installed as a floating exhibit in 1963. When maintenance and repairs grew excessive, the museum sold the vessel in 1980 to Pierre Pype of Cathlamet for conversion into a floating restaurant. When that plan failed to materialize, the vessel was purchased in 1982 by Skipper's Charters Ltd., Victoria B. C. Rebuilt and converted into an auxiliary brig with a new name, *Belle Blonde,* she became a sail-training vessel under owner Captain Claude Lacerte.

Columbia River Lightship No. 604, replaced the *88* at the Maritime Museum in 1980. She was acquired from the State of Oregon through the Federal Surplus Program to become a floating exhibit. Visitors now walk her decks getting a feel of what lightship life must have been like.

Kept in excellent condition, her steel decks and aluminum superstructure are much easier to maintain than those of her predecessor. Her main engine and all machinery are kept in operating condition, allowing for occasional short cruises to other river ports. The museum itself, founded by the late Rolf Klep, is not only a highlight in the historic city of Astoria, but is one of the finest of its kind in the country. It is a mecca for lovers of ships and the sea.

Many lamented the days when the West coast's last lightship was removed from active duty. No longer did she display the circle of reflecting lights from the masthead, her aid to navigation producing 15,000 candlepower. Nor did the diaphone foghorn any longer blast its warnings. As far as the Coast Guard was concerned, the discontinuance of the lightship greatly reduced its responsibilities which had included the constant risk of the lightship being accidentally rammed in foggy weather. It did happen on a few occasions that cargo ships sideswiped the Columbia River Lightship but fortunately, none of the floating lighthouses were sunk as was the occasion on other coasts.

The lightship crews also worked in conjunction with the Columbia River bar pilots. On one occasion, her crew was called to use the lightship's two boats to take the bar pilots out to bring in several submarines headed for the Portland Rose Festival. This was because the pilots didn't have any boats adequate to handle the job.

The Columbia River Bar Pilots Association is a group of skilled master mariners who perform an exacting and sometimes dangerous job in escorting commercial ships in and out over the Columbia River bar. Their smoothly operating services are unequaled. Now, however, instead of rendezvousing with the lightship, the super buoy is somewhat of a seamark off the river as it constantly transmits its call letters.

Many time-warn activities and occupations have faded from the scene in this advanced age of technology. Though much progress has

245

been made, the personal touch has been eliminated by automation and electronic evolution. Without the human element on hand it is never quite the same.

Lighted Navigational Horn Buoy (LNB) "CR" that replaced the Pacific Coast's last lightship, WAL-604, in November 1979, has itself been retired from service. It is now on exhibit at the Columbia River Maritime Museum in Astoria. Its retirement was based on the danger of servicing the conveyance in rough seas because boarding it was difficult at best., "CR" was replaced by a smaller utilitarian buoy. The retired LNB is 40 feet in diameter and 42 feet in height. Its strobe light was visible for 10 miles. She joins the Columbia River Lightship WAL-604 as a museum piece. Original cost was $435,000 and was the latest idea for such service. Now its light, fog signal, radio signal and radar reflector no longer operate. The last LNB in service on the West Coast operated well off shore from San Francisco's Golden Gate.

Chapter 16
The Lighthouse Tender *Shubrick*

In order to maintain and supply west coast lighthouses and minor aids to navigation in the early years, it fell, for the most part, to lighthouse tenders. These were seagoing vessels that often ventured into dangerous waters where others would never go. In the beginning, there was an acute shortage of that type of vessel. In fact, for two and a half decades, the entire burden for service along the Pacific Coast was the obligation of the *Shubrick.*

USS *Shubrick*
Armed, Steam, Lighthouse Tender
Length: 140 feet
Beam: 22 feet
Displacement: 305 tons
Power Plant: Single expansion steam engine with 3 coal-burning furnaces.
Boiler: 12-foot x ll-feet diameter
Speed under steam: 10 knots
Equipped for sails
Constructed: 1856-1857
Place: Philadelphia Navy Yard
Description: Black hull, white ribbon waist, red paddle wheels in white boxes, black bowsprit and rigging, copper sheathing.
Armament: 3 Dahlgren guns: One 24-pounder on Forecastle. Two 12-pounders at stern posts. Equipped with special catapult for throwing scalding water from boiler onto deck intruders

---

The isolated lighthouses were totally dependent on supply from the sea and that made things difficult when only a single ship was covering 1,500 miles of coastline.

Her story dates back to 1856-57. The *Shubrick* was built at the Philadelphia Navy Yard. Completed on November 25, 1857, the staunch wooden-hulled vessel was the first steam-powered lighthouse tender built from the keel up to the orders of the U. S. Light-House Board. (The first lighthouse tender was the schooner *Rush*).

Named for Commodore W. B. Shubrick USN, who at the time was president of the Light-House Board, the ship was destined for a

USS _Shubrick_

colorful and adventurous career. She could have qualified as a fighting ship because of her construction with a hull of live oak and white oak. She did for a time serve as an armed revenue cutter. Measuring 140 feet long with a 22 foot beam, she displaced 305 tons. One could identify her from a distance by her black hull, white ribbon and waist, red paddle wheels, white paddle boxes, black bowsprit and rigging, and copper sheathing.

Boasting a single expansion steam engine and three furnaces which fed a 12 foot boiler 11 feet in diameter, she was rated at 284 horsepower. The _Shubrick_ carried an auxiliary sail rig with fore and mainmast, typical of a brigantine. For her time, she was considered fast at ten knots under steam and had been known to hit 12 knots when spreading her canvas with a favorable wind.

So as not to be tampered with by hostile Indians on her west coast assignment, the _Shubrick_ mounted a 24 pound Dahlgren cannon on the forecastle and two Dahlgren 12 pounders at the sternposts. Further, she had an ingenious apparatus for throwing scalding water from the boiler onto unwanted intruders who might to try to capture the vessel.

On December 23, 1857, the _Shubrick,_ Captain F. A. Harris, having completed her trials with flying colors, departed for San Francisco via the Straits of Magellan. Aboard was Commander J. DeCamp who was to become the first official inspector for the 12th Lighthouse District. The arduous voyage demanded stops at St. Thomas, Barbados, Permanbuco, Montevideo, and Rio de Janeiro for fuel and supply. Out of Rio, Yellow Fever broke out and eight of the crew became ill. The assistant engineer succumbed to the disease causing the ship's Chief Engineer, T. J. Winship, to be a man short. There was great fear for a time that the entire crew might become ill.

Adverse weather and heavy seas were the menu of the day. In the Straits, the ship ran out of coal necessitating the chopping up of furniture and wood paneling to feed the furnaces. Additional stops were made at Valparaiso and Panama Bay before arriving at San Francisco under both steam and sail. The *Shubrick* came into port on May 27, 1858. It had been a five month trip. A mild welcome was accorded, but the *Shubrick* certainly did not look like a new ship when she passed through the Golden Gate.

After repairs and resupply, the vessel was immediately underway and for the next three years serviced aids to navigation all along the Pacific Coast.

In 1859, she set the first buoys on the Columbia River marking the channel from the bar to Astoria. Then followed an epic voyage that to recent times has astounded navigators. In command of Captain Frank West, who had relieved Captain Harris, the vessel was navigated up the Columbia River past Fort Vancouver and well above the present day site of Bonneville Dam to a place called Fort Cascades. To achieve her goal the *Shubrick* skirted rapids, barriers, obstructions and debris. The river in those days was not the placid Columbia River of today thus the feat was nothing short of remarkable.

On the return trip down river, Captain West shot the rapids the steamer going at such a breakneck speed that guest Army officers, badly frightened and distressed, leaned over the side and "fed the fish"—an old sailors term for seasickness.

With the decades of the 1860's, the *Shubrick* had placed iron buoys on the major harbors and bar entrances in Washington, Oregon and California waters. Shorage of funds, probably due to the Civil War, and a reluctance to establish new aids to navigation gave the vessel a slight reprieve. But she was always on call. Her presence in many cases with the blasting of her guns, had proven a deterrent to unfriendly Indians who were bent on destruction of property on lighthouse reservations.

During the Civil War, the Treasury Department annexed the vessel on a temporary assignment as a U. S. Revenue Marine Cutter. Captain William Pease USRM, replaced Captain West as skipper. Under new orders, the *Shubrick* steamed along the Pacific Coast enforcing laws and Customs practices. For three years she was considered the strong arm of the law first out of San Francisco and then out of Port Townsend on upper Puget Sound.

249

Like a cat with nine lives, the *Shubrick* changed duty again and entered the third segment of her career as a U. S. Naval vessel. She was ordered to San Francisco for an overhaul and provisions. There she took aboard Colonel Charles Bulkeley of the Russian American Telegraph Company and became the flagship of a six unit fleet to make a survey for laying a cable across the Bering Strait. On April 1, along with the steam tug *Wright*, bark *Golden Gate* and three smaller vessels, the *Shubrick* arrived off New Archangel (Sitka) and traded 21 gun salutes. This was the capitol city of Russian Alaska. Colonel Bulkeley and the *Shubrick's* commanding officer, Captain C. M. Scammon, along with other American officers, went ashore to pay respects to Prince Matsutoff, governor of the territory.

In the interim, three crewmen left the ship without orders, celebrated too much at a local grog house, and were accordingly slapped in irons by an irate Captain Scammon after he returned to his ship.

Unfortunately, the laying of the cable was delayed for several years but it was the survey of the Bering Strait that proved invaluable when the project was finally completed after America purchased Alaska in 1867.

After return to San Francisco, the *Shubrick* began the fourth chapter of her colorful chronicle when the Secretary of the Treasury on December 24, 1866 transferred her back to the Lighthouse Service after a thorough drydocking and overhaul.

It was while employed with carrying building materials for the construction of Cape Mendocino lighthouse in California, that the sidewheeler ran into trouble. On September 8, 1867, in heavy fog, she ran afoul of a rocky underwater obstruction near Point Arena 30 miles south of Mendocino. Damage was major and the shipmaster considered her a total loss and ordered the crew to abandon. But the more optimistic chief engineer, who elected to remain aboard, determined to save the vessel despite its punctured hull.

Gallantly, he went about his task and succeeded in persuading volunteers to assist in his efforts which some labled as foolhardy. He off-loaded the boiler, machinery, cannon and stores to lighten the burden on the broken hull. Raising her on skids in a remarkable salvage effort, which suddenly got the attention of government officials, the vessel was slowly moved 500 yards along the barrier to a smooth, sandy beach. There it was discovered that a huge boulder had lodged itself in the port bow so tightly that gunpowder had to be used for its removal. The result was a hole eight feet by seven feet. It was probably that boulder, acting as a plug, that had kept the vessel from going to the bottom.

So skeptical was the Light-House Board over Chief Engineer T. J. Winship's salvage effort, that funds had already been requested for the construction of a replacement vessel. The Board members underestimated the uncanny abilities and determination of their engineer. He had nursed the *Shubrick's* engine a decade earlier, when coming around from the east coast on her maiden voyage, and had been with the ship for the better part of a decade. He knew her better than any other man and treated the ship with the respect of a specialized surgeon trying to save the life of an important person. Not only was he victorious in patching and getting the ship afloat, but with her machinery reinstalled at the site, he steamed back to San Francisco to undergo a complete refit at a whopping price of $162,399. This was three times her original cost.

Phase number five began with a new lease on life. With her same dependability, the *Shubrick* was back attending the needs of navigation aids along the entire Pacific Coast. The work became so demanding that a second tender was urgently needed. But it would not be until 1879 that the companion ship became a reality. This was the screw steamer *Manzanita,* built by the H. A. Ramsey Shipyard of Baltimore.

The *Manzanita* arrived in San Francisco the following year and took over the 12th District duties. The *Shubrick* was transferred to the 13th District headquarters in Portland, and later voyaged as far as Alaskan waters establishing the first 22 iron buoys in the Inside Passage.

Strenuous demands on the *Shubrick* began to show in the early 1880's as much of the muscle had gone out of her steam plant. The hull also began to show signs of age. The Light-House Board, on advise from the district office, determined that she could no longer properly tow a first class whistling buoy into position, thus forcing the placing of lighter second class buoys. That was somewhat an overstatement for that grand old lady of the sea, but the Board was convinced the ship was no longer able to perform properly. A request for funds was made for a replacement.

The innovative steel-hulled tender *Madrono* was launched in Camden, New Jersey in 1885. This was the third such vessel to be assigned to the Pacific Coast. She arrived in San Francisco the next year and relieved tender *Manzanita,* which in turn was shifted to the Pacific Northwest to replace the *Shubrick.*

Phase six came when the service decommissioned the veteran tender on March 20, 1886. At a public auction she was sold for $3,200. The new owner purposely ran her up on a sand bar in San

Traditional lighthouse tenders which frequently supplied
Tillamook Rock in early times. The stalwart *Columbine* (top)
and (lower) the venerable second *Manzanita*.

Francisco Bay where he proceeded to strip everything of value. He sold the furnishings, rigging, armamant, engine and boiler. Then without remorse, he torched the hull to recover all her yield of copper and brass. That was death by cremation, and the *Shubrick's* chapter in maritime history came to an end.

Down through the years there were many lighthouse tenders that performed yoeman service on the Pacific Coast. After the Coast Guard took over, several modern buoy tenders were constructed and their services are still required on virtually every waterway, though automated lighthouses per say, no longer have to be supplied by sea.

Working in dangerous waters, the old lighthouse tenders were always facing danger. Like the *Shubrick,* they occasionally suffered serious damage or loss. The first *Manzanita,* for instance, ran afoul of Warrior Rock off Sauvie Island in the Columbia River in the fall of 1905. Cradled on the barrier, she eventually slipped off and sank in the river. The crew had to abandon with haste with only the clothing on their backs. Broken steam pipes and a hissing boiler added to the concern, but all escaped safely.

USCGC *Iris,* 180-foot long buoy tender, performed yoeman service in Pacific Northwest waters in servicing buoys. She has long operated out of the Tongue Point Depot east of Astoria.

The Light-House Board abandoned the wreck on advise from the Portland office. There were demands from the survivors for payment of possessions and property lost in the mishap. That payment had to wait for seven years, the total reimbursement for all personnel coming to $1,642.

Because the wreck was a hazard to river navigation (only the *Manzanita's* mast protruded from the water), Kern & Kern of Portland won salvage rights and succeeded in raising the wreck. She was rebuilt as the steam tug *Daniel Kern,* named after the head of the firm, and continued in active service until 1936 when it was burned for scrap, north of Seattle. The tug had served as a unit of the Bellingham Tug & Barge Company.

A new tender was built shortly after the Warrior Rock incident, and given the name of her predecessor. Over time, many staunch lighthouse and buoy tenders served Pacific Northwest waters. Their adventures could fill another book. Oldtimers still recall the *Columbine, Heather, Hemlock, Rose, Lupine, Cedar, Fern, Sequoia, Kukui, Armeria, Madrono, Fir, Bluebell, Iris,* and others.

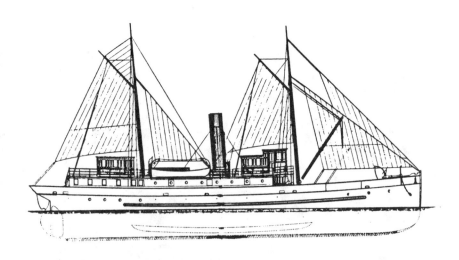

Outboard profile drawing of U.S. Lighthouse tender *Columbine*.

Epilogue

We, in our present age of high-tech innovations, find it hard to believe that evolution has progressed so rapidly in the field of electronics. It seems inconceivable that it was as recently as 1879 that Thomas Edison produced the first commercially practical incandescent electric light. He was also responsible, in 1881-1882, for developing the initial central electric power plant in the world. It was his inventions that would completely change the living standards of people around the world and bring about remarkable changes in the illumination of aids to navigation. Despite the use of electricity, inaccessibility to lighthouses made them among the last facilities to be so blest. There were some West Coast lighthouses still using oil lamps until the decade of the 1940's.

Until Edison's generation, oil lamps still provided the lighting for homes, factories and lighthouses. Perhaps the first big breakthrough in more efficient oil lamps is credited to Swiss scientist Aime Argand who invented an oil lamp that produced a smokeless flame in 1782. He designed a circular wick along with a tapered glass chimney that provided for a current of air up the center and outside the wick at the same time. His creation did much to erase the smut that nightly blackened Fresnel prisms and lantern panes, which often gave keepers of the lights fits, creating considerably more labor.

Constant improvements were made on his invention utilizing as many as ten wicks formed into a concentric pattern to maximize illumination. Early fuels were whale oil, rapeseed and vegetable oils along with mineral oil. But after 1860, kerosene (coal oil) became the most widely used. For over a century Argand lamps were the standard. Such illumination was a great improvement from ancient times when open brazier fires in grates fed by wood or coal were the mariners guideposts. To climb to the top of such towers demanded herculean labor on behalf of those entrusted with keeping the open fires burning brightly. Failure to do so often brought about severe punishment.

In 1901, another great advance in the field of pharology was made when Arthur Kitson developed vaporized oil burning lamps. David Hood took it one step farther. He made it practical to utilize kerosene, vaporized under pressure mixed with air, and burned to heat an incandescent mantle. Incandescent ("IOV") lamps were six times more powerful than the oil wick lamps. By 1910, the U. S. Lighthouse Service had thoroughly tested and was in the process of refitting the lamps in American lighthouses with IOV lamps. It not only afforded a cleaner light but gave a much greater candlepower per unit of oil.

In that same decade, Gustav Dalen, of Sweden, pioneered the application of acetylene gas lamps that proved invaluable for unattended lights. The light produced was equal to that of oil and could be readily controlled. For the first time, unattended lights were feasible—the forerunner of automation. Additional advances were made which included ingenious mechanisms and burners to operate the pressure of gas itself. Shortly after, came the automatic change of burners, the sun switch (sensor) for turning gas lights on and off automatically, plus mechanical linkage to control gas valves.

The Lighthouse Service adopted the gas principal for unattended lights beginning about 1915, with Alaska one of the prime areas where the use of unattended lights, especially in isolated areas, proved invaluable.

The evolution of electric filament lamps in lighthouse lenses in the United States was first begun in the 1920's. The ultimate result was ten times greater than that of the vaporized oil lamp. At this writing, the Coast Guard is utilizing, in their Oregon lighthouses, General Electric Quartzline Precision 120 volt, 1,000 watt lights. These are 9½ inches high and 2½ inches in diameter supported by Carlisle & Finch two-place lamp changers. Each sentinel also has a smaller 250mm standby lamp usually mounted on the lantern gallery or catwalk.

*   *   *

The day of the traditional lighthouse keeper is gone because the lights along the shore are all automated. Computer systems alert Coast Guard bases when a repair is needed at lighthouses, and qualified crews are dispatched to meet the need. In some cases, private firms are hired to perform maintenance.

The somewhat secondary role of the lighthouse is obvious today, due to radar, direction finders, fathometers, radio ship-to-shore apparatus, radio beacons, Racon Loran and Echo long distance navigation systems. Though the traditional lights and foghorns are still in use at lighthouses and on navigation buoys, their importance has been reduced compared with yesteryears. Even greater electronic innovations are still in the offing. Only the good Lord knows what

the future holds

Though fading from the American scene for their original intent, public input and sentimentality for the old sentinels has given them a new impetus. Some have been dismantled while others have become museums. All are tourist attractions and more than a few keep shining as active aids to navigation. If they ever pass from the seascape, there will be no replacements. A light on a utility pole or an aero marine type beacon atop a building, can perform the same service.

Winds rise and clouds cream the shores yet the lighthouse stands. Huge claws of brine batter basaltic cliffs and headlands weaving an intricate pattern of power, hissing and growling like sea monsters yet the lighthouse stands. Nature throws down its gauntlet of destruction and evil magic, still through it all a golden shaft of light spears the murk. The lighthouse stands.

May the warm, friendly glow of the lighthouse beacon live on.

Finis

About the Author

James A. "Jim" Gibbs is one of the fortunate fellows to be born and reared in the Pacific Northwest where his heritage was to enjoy refreshing ocean-borne air to breath, and salt water and ocean-going ships within sight. A native of Seattle, he graduated from Queen Anne High School which stands high atop Queen Anne Hill where one can easily look out a classroom window and watch the marine commerce on Elliott Bay. He attended the University of Washington then joined the Coast Guard for World War II service. He was in the Coast Guard Rockaway and Pacific City (Oregon) Beach Patrol detachments that had been formed specifically to guard against Japanese invasion along the northwest coast. He went to sea duty on USCGC *Nemaha* WPC-148, an Active class patrol cutter, then he did lighthouse duty on famed Tillamook Rock off the Oregon Coast. He spent four and a half years in the Coast Guard.

Jim Gibbs established the Skunk Bay Lighthouse, a private aid, on Puget Sound in 1967. He was employed, mostly as editor, for 20 years of the *Marine Digest*, a Seattle maritime trade weekly.

He lived in Seattle and in Bellevue and on Maui then established Cleft of the Rock Lighthouse on the north spur of Cape Perpetua on the Oregon Coast. That was in 1976. Cleft of the Rock is the only privately-owned working lighthouse on the Oregon Coast.

Jim Gibbs is the author of 17 earlier books about lighthouses and ships and shipwrecks as well as a number of magazine articles. He is the former President of the Puget Sound Maritime Historical Society, Seattle. He is a deacon in Yachats Baptist Church.

He and his wife, Cherie, enjoy their life at Cape Perpetua. They have one grown daughter, Debbie, who, with her husband, Ray Pedrick, are near-neighbors also on the cape.

*　　　　*　　　　*

Bert Webber is a research photojournalist, editor and publisher. He has written and published a number of books on a wide variety of subjects primarily about Oregon and the Oregon Trail.

For lists of books by Gibbs or by Webber, consult *Books in Print* which will be found in most public libraries and book stores.

Illustration Credits

259

Bibliography

Adamson, H. C. *Keepers of the Lights.* Greenberg. 1955.

Armstrong, Chester H. *History of the Oregon State Parks 1917-1963.* Oregon State Printer, 1964.

Beaver, Patrick. *A History of Lighthouses.* Citidel. 1973.

The Coast Guardsman's Manual. USCG. U.S. Dept. of Transportation. 4th Ed. 1964.

Davidson, George. *Pacific Coast Pilot,* U.S. Coast & Geodetic Survey. 1889.

Ehlers, Chad and Jim Gibbs. *Sentinels of Solitude.* Graphic Arts. 1981.

Floherty, John, *Sentries of the Sea.* Lippencott. 1942.

Gibbs, James A. *Pacific Graveyard.* Binford & Mort. 1964.

_____, *Sentinels of the North Pacific.* Binford & Mort. 1955

_____. *Shipwrecks of the Pacific Coast.* Binford & Mort. 1957.

_____. *Tillamook Light.* Binford & Mort. 1953.

_____. *West Coast Lighthouses.* Superior. 1974.

_____. *Lighthouses of the Pacific.* Schiffer. 1986.

Graham, Donald. *Keepers of the Lights.* Harbour. Madeira Pk. B.C. 1985.

_____. *Lights of the Inside Passage.* Harbour. Madeira Pk. B.C. 1986.

Guthorn, Peter J. *United States Coast Charts.* Schiffer. 1984.

Hebert, Gerard A. *Lighthouses of the Oregon Coast.* U.S. Coast Guard Coos Bay Station, Oregon. 1987.

Holland, Francis Ross Jr. *America's Lighthouses.* Steven Green Press. 1972.

_____.*The Old Point Loma Lighthouse.* Cabrillo Hist. Soc. San Diego. 1978

Howes, James M. *The Old Yaquina Bay Lighthouse.* Lincoln County Hist. Soc. Newport, Ore. 1968

Instructions to Lighthouse Keepers. U.S. Lighthouse Service. 1902.

Lester, Reginald M. *The Observer's Book of Weather.* Warne (London). 1955.

Light List, Pacific Coast (United States). U.S. Dept. of Commerce, Lighthouse Service. 1896-1920

Light List, Pacific Coast (United States). U.S. Dept. of Commerce, Lighthouse Service. 1934.

Light List, Pacific Coast and Pacific Islands. Vol. III. U. S. Dept. of Transportation. 1950-1991.

Marshall, Don. *Oregon Shipwrecks.* Binford & Mort. 1984.

Massey, Raymond F. Jr. *Lighthouses and Other Aids to Navigation in Alaska.* U.S. Coast Guard, Juneau. n.d.

Pacific Coast Pilot. U.S. Dept. of Commerce & Labor. 1909.

Peterson, Emil and Alfred Powers. *A Century f Coos and Curry Counties.* Coos-Curry Pioneer & Hist. Assn. Binford & Mort. 1952

Putnam, George R. *Lighthouses & Lightships.* Houghton Mifflin. 1917.

Report of the Light-House Board to the Secretary of the Treasury. U.S. Gov't Print Office. 1881.

Rue, Walter. *Weather of the Pacific Coast.* Writing Works. 1978.

Shanks, Ralph Jr. And Jeanette Shanks. *Lighthouses and Lifeboats on the Redwood Coast.* Costano. 1978.

Stevenson, Alan D. *The World's Lighthouses Before 1820.* Oxford. 1959.

Talbot, Frederick. *Lightships and Lighthouses.* Lippencott. 1913.

United States Coast Pilot, Pacific Coast... U.S. Dept. of Commerce. 18th Ed. 1982.

Webber, Bert. *SILENT SIEGE-II: Japanese Attacks on North America in World War II, Ships Sunk, Air Raids, Bombs Dropped, People Killed.* Webb Research Group. 1988. [This book was substantially updated as *Silent Siege III* in 1997. The earlier title *Silent Siege II* is out-of-print.]

_____. *Panic! At Fort Stevens.* Webb Research Group. 1995.

Webber, Bert & Margie. *Battery Point Light[house] and the Tidal Wave of 1964 Crescent City, Calif. Includes St. George Reef Light[house].* Webb Research Group. 1991. [Expanded 2000]

_____. *BAYOCEAN: The Oregon Town That Fell Into the Sea.* Webb Research Group. 1989. [Expanded 1999.]

_____. *LAKEPORT: Ghost Town of the South Oregon Coast.* Webb Research Group. 1990.

_____. *Terrible Tilly: Tillimook Rock Lighthouse, an Oregon Documentary; the Biography of a Lighthouse.* Webb Research Group. 1998.

Index

Page numbers in *italic* are illustrations
Miscellaneous data about each lighthouse in not indexed when it appears
within the chapter for that lighthouse except photographs are indexed.
See: Table of Contents on page v.

LH = lighthouse

Addendum
Pelican Bay Lighthouse

Bill Cady has lived in and around lighthouses since birth so when he perceived the idea that a lighthouse would be useful to mariners in locating the vicinity of the entrance to Southern Oregon's Chetco River, he decided to build one. Then he obtained Coast Guard approval for its use as a working lighthouse.

PELICAN BAY LIGHTHOUSE
Location: 42°02'N 124°15' 45"W
Nearest town: Harbor
Built: 1997
Type: White octagon tower
    attached to residence
Height above water: 141ft
Height above ground: 35 feet
Light source: 110v electric -
    incandescent
Beam: Clear (white) 1.5 sec on;
    2.5 sec off for three
    sequences then 20 sec off
Optics: FA-250 acrylic Fresnel
Power: 2,483cp
Seen: 18 miles

NOTE: Data from spec sheet Automatic Power Inc.,
Coast Guard form CG-2554 and Bill Cady, owner

Cady's love for lighthouses was inherited. His father, Malcolm Cady, entered the U. S. Lighthouse Service in 1903 and he was a lightkeeper at six California locations: Point Loma at San Diego Trinidad Head, Cape Mendocino, also Point Arena, Humboldt Bay and Point Reyes. Bill was born at Ferndale, California. He was quoted in the Medford, Oregon *Mail Tribune,* "I've always wanted to have my own lighthouse" he declared, and at age 75, his dream came true. His light was switched on at 11:02 p.m. July 4th, 1999 just as the annual Brookings-Harbor Fourth of July fireworks display ended.

Starting with a two bedroom house built in 1950 that he and his wife, JoAnn, owned in Harbor, a suburb of Brookings, about seven miles north of the Oregon-California border, Cady worked with Paul Viale, a local contractor, to develop a lighthouse using his house as its base.

But the location, on Oceanview Drive, proved not to be a good one. The couple purchased property on Short Way, on a bluff, that allowed for an unobstructed view seaward. Although the lighthouse was completed on Oceanview Drive, in 1990, in 1997, the couple moved their three-story tall lighthouse addition to its present location.

The move was a major project as the lighthouse was too tall to pass under overhead electric and telephone lines so the utilities cooperated in providing work crews. The workmen hoisted the wires so movers could slowly roll the tall lighthouse, temporarily on wheels, under them without damage to the lines or to the lighthouse.

As vehicles speed along the street in front of the lighthouse, it is usual that the people in the cars pass without noticing the lighthouse which is on the high bluff above the road - 141 feet above mean sea level.

The light shines seaward 18 miles but the back portion of the light, that segment that would blind neighbors, is blacked out. The apparatus was constructed by Automatic Power, Inc., of Houston, Texas. The fixture holds four special lamps of CC-8 filament design and operates on 12 volts, stepped down from ordinary household current. The fixture's extra bulbs are rotated into use position automatically if the light goes out. As the Pelican Bay Lighthouse is now on official navigation charts, should the lighthouse be out of service for any reason, Cady must notify the Coast Guard promptly.

This lighthouse is the only functioning seacoast lighthouse between Cape Blanco, Oregon and Battery Point at Crescent City, California.

Pelican Bay Lighthouse is one of only two private aids to navigation on the Oregon coast. The other is Cleft of the Rock Lighthouse on the north side of Cape Perpetua near Yachats. This is owned and maintained by Jim Gibbs, a former Coast Guardsman who, among other duties, served at Tillamook Rock Lighthouse during World War II. *Both of these lighthouses are private residences open to the public only by special invitation.* Pelican Bay Lighthouse above Harbor's Best Western Motel, and visible from most places in the Harbor boat basin.